Hetta and William

Also by Jacob Empson

Human Brainwaves
Sleep and Dreaming

Translated into Chinese
Sleep and Dreaming

Hetta and William

A Memoir of a Bohemian Marriage

JACOB EMPSON

authorHOUSE®

AuthorHouse™
1663 Liberty Drive
Bloomington, IN 47403
www.authorhouse.com
Phone: 1-800-839-8640

Published by AuthorHouse   11/14/2012

ISBN: 978-1-4772-4597-2 (sc)
ISBN: 978-1-4772-4601-6 (e)

Contents

Acknowledgments

I would like to thank many people who have helped me in this endeavour. It was John Haffenden, my father's biographer, who first encouraged me to write an account of my life with my parents, and I am grateful to him for that, if only for the experience of the past two years in exploring my own past and theirs. Frances Wilson was the leader of a 'Guardian Masterclass' in memoir-writing which I attended in 2012, and she was not only encouraging and inspiring during that weekend but took the time to read and comment on my work, even coming to my house on one occasion in North Yorkshire.

Others have shared memories, and provided photographs and other documents, and were supportive of this venture. In particular, my brother Simon has been a great help. He read a very early draft of some chapters, and was suitably critical as well as positive. He also helped in a number of ways in providing more detail to some of my accounts, as well as new memories of his own. My cousin Ronelle provided information about my mother's South African family, and early life, as well as the studio portrait of her taken in 1938. Corinna MacNeice went to great trouble to dig out our childhood newspapers from her barn in the depths of a New Mexico winter, and then to scan them and send them to me. She also contributed by correcting and amplifying my accounts of our holidays together. Mirabel Ward provided at least one photograph from our time together. Shastri Boothe was enthusiastically supportive, and I am grateful to her for the use of Walter's collection of letters which are now stored with Hetta's in the Sheffield University Library. Blake Crozier shared her memories of our disastrous boat trip to Walton on the Naze on board the sailing barge-yacht *Platanna*. My first wife, Janet, also provided photographs, and put me right on one or two solecisms.

Jacob Empson

Preface

Our time in China, from 1947 to 1952, had a profound influence on both Mogador and myself, as our early development was shaped by our relationships with Chinese servants and our experience of going to nursery school. We were pretty well immersed in Chinese culture. However, precise memories of those early years are rather patchy, for me, partly at least because I was mainly speaking Chinese as a small boy, a language which I largely forgot after our return to England. The recall of events in a forgotten language is obviously going to be difficult. My memories of this period are scattered, although sometimes very vivid, and they have of course 'benefited' from being repeatedly rehearsed throughout my life. However, there are fortunately plenty of surviving letters and other documentary evidence which I have used in addition to my own recollection, in constructing this account. In particular, there is a lengthy correspondence between my mother Hetta and Walter Brown, who had been sent to Shansi University to teach English language. They wrote almost every week, and even sent each other telegrams. The result was a continuing commentary on our lives in China which has made it possible to put my own memories into a proper sequence, as well as bringing in additional material.

It was only after Hetta's death that it became clear how much she had managed to save and hang on to, in boxes under her k'ang and in drawers. My brother Mogador did a preliminary sorting of the letters into categories according to their senders (and also recipients, as she had a habit of keeping carbons.) We then took them all, with a range of other documents and books, to the University of Hull to be stored in the Brynmor Jones Library archive. Although the collection was eventually moved to the Sheffield University Library, Hull kept photocopies, which are now stored in the Hull History Centre.

In 2001 I made a trip to the United States to visit Walter at his farm in Michigan, and to pick up his collection of letters from Ma, with the idea of uniting both sides of the correspondence between them. I set off for Detroit from Humberside Airport, taking an empty briefcase for the letters as hand luggage. An official decided that my briefcase had to be put in the hold, as he said it was too big to go in the overhead locker in the tiny plane that was taking us to Schipol Airport, Amsterdam for the connection to the U.S. (In fact the plane was half-empty and I could have put it on a spare seat, if not my knees.) On arrival in Detroit, the briefcase had been lost in transit. I had arranged to rent a car, which I picked up at the airport. It turned out to be an enormous brand new Buick, with all sorts of electronic refinements. It really did have only two miles on the clock. What a responsibility! What with the long flight and the hassle about the briefcase I was already feeling harassed. Once on the road, and lost, with gigantic trucks coming up from behind, I was feeling more and more frightened. By the time I got to the farm I had resolved not to drive again until it was time to go back to the airport.

Walter was in residence in his studio—a large room in an ante-bellum barn behind the farmhouse. He had lived on his own, with a succession of tenants in the house, since his partner Joseph had died over ten years before. (Before that Joseph had been the main bread-winner, working at the Chevrolet factory in Detroit.) The house was now let to a young man, Geoff, and his girl-friend. The arrangement seemed to be that they were running errands for Walter, and looking after him in return for their keep. (Walter's eyesight had been steadily deteriorating for years, with macular degeneration. He also had a heart condition, and had recently been discharged from hospital after by-pass surgery.) Geoff was delighted with the Buick, and immediately took charge of it, taking us to the shops in it, and so on. I did not have to drive it again.

Despite his ailments Walter was in good spirits—his usual affable self—although he was more or less confined to the house and barn, unless taken anywhere in the car. He was pleased with his arrangements in the studio, which was a partitioned-off section of a much larger barn. His Franklin stove was now gas-fuelled, so didn't have to be filled with coal, and everything was more or less to hand. There was a small kitchen area, with a sink, and his bed on the floor (with a mattress next to it for visitors such as myself). There were bookshelves and a chest of drawers, and a huge television set. Geoff had helped him tune the TV to a large number of stations, including Canadian and CNN, so Walter felt that he had a 'window on the world', which he could watch if he got really close to the screen, lying on his bed. His favourite channel showed the British sitcom *Are You Being Served* back-to-back all afternoon. Walter would be smiling and laughing all the way through, shouting out, 'Did you hear that?!' and so on, even though he must have seen each episode many times before. There was no evidence that he had lost his marbles—he was simply determined to be very easily pleased.

There was a big day during my visit when the almoner-cum-social worker came from the Veterans Administration hospital where Walter had been treated. Geoff and partner had to make themselves scarce, and Walter was in the house to receive the visitor, pretending he was living there. I hid in the barn. His total bill for surgery and after-care came to over $60,000, but, with his status as an honourably discharged veteran (and, presumably, being a respectable home-owner but with no income or savings) this was reduced to less than $10, to cover the cost of phone calls he had made. Walter wrote a cheque and retired, with a sigh of relief, to his studio.

The letters that I had come to collect were in a box in the back of the barn, and it turned out that they were all saturated with water—unknown to Walter, the roof in that part of the building was leaking. I spent two days separating the sheets, and spreading them out all over the place in the house to let them dry, even resorting to a blow heater to speed up the process. While this was going on somebody from the airport arrived at the house with my empty briefcase, which had turned up. To compensate for the trouble caused by losing my luggage, the airline also provided a voucher for me to travel anywhere else in the United States.

I took advantage of their generosity by going to a travel agents in Northville, the nearest village, and booking a flight to Albuquerque, to visit Corinna MacNeice at her home in Santa Fe. There we drank sparkling wine bought at the Red Indian garage down her street, reminisced about old times, and laughed ourselves silly. Eventually it was time for me to return to Yorkshire.

Corinna and me in the cold, dry sunshine at her ranch in
New Mexico, November 2001.

On my return to England these letters joined the others in the
Brynmor Jones Library at Hull University, and for a few years
they were totally neglected. It was ten years after this trip that I
started working on this history in earnest, using the Walter-Hetta
correspondence to inform my writing about our time in China from
1947-1952, largely relying on the photocopies in the Hull History
Centre, being more convenient. So far as later periods are concerned,
I have been better able to rely on my memory, but also have been
hugely helped by John Haffenden's biography of my father[i]. This
has allowed me easily to check dates and the sequencing of events
in which to spin my own narrative. I have in fact contacted him
to resolve a difference between my recollection and his account,
of the incident involving a poet wetting their bed at the London
Hilton, and the bill for a new mattress being sent to my father via
the U.S. Embassy. I recalled it was Allen Ginsberg, while John had

it as John Berryman. John's advice was that a memoir is essentially a fiction, so I should stick to my version. In fact I have done my best to temper my recollections with hard evidence where I can. My younger brother Simon looked at some early drafts, reminded me of additional stories and details, and was generally helpful. Corinna has also been extremely kind in sorting out when and where we spent our vacations with her and her family, and sending me scans of the holiday newspapers which we produced together. She also provided some photographs. So far as the memoir being a fiction is concerned, many of the stories are collective ones—part of a family myth—so I am not solely responsible for any inaccuracies.

I was most disappointed not to be able to speak to Meifang Blofeld about the period we spent together when I was twelve years old and was left in her care. Sadly she died in 2011, before I could speak to her, but not before she had received a letter from me and had talked about that time with her daughter Susan and son-in-law Andrew. They talked to me about her impressions of the time at her funeral, and gave me some photographs of Meifang looking particularly lovely.

Any memoir is automatically suspect—for being self-serving, selective, or even grossly inaccurate. My account of family life during my early years is certainly one of reconstruction, on my part, from my own memories, from family traditions, and from written sources. Few of us can remember much of what happened to us before our third birthday. However, when we have a conversation with a young person of three years old they seem to be able to remember fairly well what had happened to them in the recent past. These memories are almost all destined to be forgotten—victims of 'childhood amnesia', as the process is called by psychologists. We are left with a few little scenarios, as well as a general impression of life. The scenarios that are remembered have had the advantage of being recalled and related many times over the years. By the time that we are in our sixties, and recalling events in our threes and fours, these memories of our early life are at the mercy of many processes of confabulation—the reconstruction of accounts of our lives from incomplete fragmentary memories.

'False memory' is also a well established phenomenon—the recall of particular memories which turn out, on objective analysis, to have been totally erroneous. It seems that the rehearsal of stories of early life which are obviously false, to begin with, can, with time, persuade us into accepting them as 'real' memories. A famous example of this was provided by the distinguished developmental psychologist Piaget, who recalled being abducted by kidnappers, and then rescued by his nurse. This lady confessed in her old age to having lied about the whole incident, and that no kidnapping had taken place. She had invented the whole story to reflect glory on herself. The young Piaget had accepted her story, and had constructed his own account of it as a memory. I do not confess to any memory of being kidnapped, but the general rule applies—that early memories are suspect.

These psychological challenges to truthful recall of events of one's early life are an inevitable difficulty for any autobiography. The recollections which follow, in the first couple of chapters, are almost certainly contaminated by such distortions, but they are all memories which I have lived with all my life. They are supported by John Haffenden's biography of my father and by readings of contemporary accounts such as mother's correspondence. My mother, in particular, rarely spoke about her early life in any detail. Fortunately she kept a large number of letters, going back many years, which were a great help, together, of course, with my father's papers. Where I have included conversations, these have been more or less verbatim from these sources, with a context constructed to support a narrative. John's interviews with my mother which informed his brief biography of her in Chapter 1 of the second volume of his biography of my father, *William Empson: Against the Christians*, also provided more material.

My parents were both extraordinary people, and my father turned out to be a giant of literature. This is the story of their marriage, and of my experiences of living with them.

Chapter 1

Hetta and William

Hetta and William met in August 1941 when they were both students at what they called the 'Liars School'—a two-week training course for new personnel ('Talks Assistants') at the BBC Foreign Service. William ('Bill' at this time in his life) was to broadcast to the Far East, and Hetta to South Africa. In an article in *The Listener* many years later William was to play down this jocular if not schoolboy title for the course, explaining that it 'had only dealt with lies in passing, and only under the form of warning us against the methods of the enemy. I chiefly remember two young disc jockeys who put on a very saucy turn with two gramophones and two copies of a record by Churchill; the familiar voice was made to leave out all the negatives, ending with "we will (hic) surrender."'[ii] All the same, it was a course specifically intended for those who were going to be working in the Foreign Service, broadcasting the British message to foreigners, sometimes in their own language.

The twenty-odd recruits on the course (including E.A. Blair—George Orwell—and the actor Marius Goring) were treated to the screening of a propaganda film called "Freedom Ferry, no. 15

Missions to Seamen", which took place at the *Monseigneur Cinema* at Marble Arch. As a merchant ship was seen to wallow through the sea, broadside to the camera, Empson cried out, "What about the Plimsoll line?" This criticism of the ship's overloading, and of the consequent uselessness of the film as propaganda, attracted the attention of my mother, who thought, 'That's my man!' before following him out of the cinema with the books and papers that he had dropped as he left.[iii]

Thus began what was to be a very improbable alliance. Their journeys in life up to this point could not have been more different. Hetta was a South African, born in 1917 in the Orange Free State into a 'boer' (Afrikaaner) family. The Orange Free State had been colonized by successive waves of emigrants from the Cape Province who wanted to escape British Rule. They were of Dutch, French Huguenot and German descent, and first arrived in 1824, and then later on the 'Great Trek' in 1836 to 1838, which gave these farming communities their name—'boer' from 'Trekboer'. The re-establishment of British Imperial authority over these rebellious farmers, and others in the Transvaal, during the Boer wars of 1881 and 1899-1902 left the Afrikaaners with a permanent, and perhaps justifiable, sense of grievance against the British. This curious combination of victimhood and of master-race superiority over the blacks gave them a unique and sometimes toxic ideology.

Their religion was the Dutch Reformed Church—a bleak Calvinist doctrine of simple living, strict adherence to the scriptures, and predestination. When Hetta went swimming in the river on a Sunday her father beat her and called her a 'whore of Babylon'.

In later life she would talk about her parents with little affection, particularly her father, who liked to call himself 'the general'. There was some respect for his strength, and his boasted ability to 'throw a steer'—to throw it to the ground by grabbing it by its horns. Otherwise she felt alienated, despising his ostentatious displays, such as the trucks laden with dead game after a hunt. She rarely spoke about her mother, if at all. There were three older brothers, Jurgen, Hendrik and Jacobus, and a younger sister, Lilla.

In her own words, in a draft of an account of her early years,

> A magical world it was, to get out of bed at four-thirty in the morning and catch the dawning on the veldt; all alone with the fairy tumble-weeds and the gigantic sun; red at first before it became golden. Everything was still, and immense, I felt it all belonged to me. I was six. Later there was a kaffir, a servant, who came with me and showed me how to mould the clay in the dongas into oxen. He could make a whole span of oxen very quickly. Wide horns, big shoulders, narrow flanks, he showed me how.
>
> Then one day one was not allowed. The tyrant, my father. No running around before daybreak. Off to school, and back at the break, home at once, and off to bed after the evening meal. Prayers before meals; all on your knees, and the servants in the doorways—even if they didn't understand a word of High-Dutch (a garbled version), the silly heathens, sons of Ham.
>
> Not a silly man, I suppose. He did what he did according to his beliefs. But I never did like him, though like the rest of us five children, I was in awe of him and helped him off with his boots, when every afternoon he used to yell for us, confusing the names, or maybe not; calling each name in turn, to unlace those high-laced, black, and rather deliciously-smelly boots. Often one fell

back with a thud after pulling them off. He yelled with laughter then.

Mostly he was away from home, buying cattle in South-West Africa, and sending cryptic telegrams to my mother, like 'Everything in the garden lovely, home next week'.

It was not uncommon for young white children in South Africa to spend a good deal of time with African children, as well as African grownups. (They were of course usually being looked after by African nannies, in any case). Then, as Hetta says, once they went to school they were expected to forget their friendships with black people and to move into the white world. She grew into a gangly (5'11" tall) teenager who attended a bi-lingual school, where she distinguished herself athletically—particularly in swimming and rowing. From there she went to Bloemfontein University. This conventional academic progression was interrupted by a series of four deaths in the family, in swift succession. Her eldest brother died of food poisoning. Then both her parents died of pneumonia. She left university at the age of eighteen without graduating, and went home to Kroonstad to live with her brother Hendrik. Finally, Hendrik too was struck down with typhoid while away on a trip in the Cape, and died. Strangely, during his illness she suffered from what may have been a sympathetic fever, taken to hospital, diagnosed with typhoid, and, the first she heard of his condition was that he was dead. Her own symptoms all disappeared as soon as she heard this news.

Hetta left home and went to live in Cape Town, becoming an apprentice sculptor with Ivan Mitford-Barberton, a graduate of London's Royal College of Art. In his biography of William Empson, John Haffenden wrote, 'She lived with a community of artists below the Malay quarter, on the slopes of Table Mountain. A seminal 'hippy', she was to be long remembered for the fact that even in the 1930s she wore a kaftan and walked barefoot'. She was to remain associated with his studio for a couple of years, but also took some time out to travel to Germany and study in art school in Munich. It was when she returned from Germany that she became politically active, working as the publicity manager for a left-wing newspaper. Finally, during a six-month period in Johannesburg she became recruited into the Communist Party. The Communist Party of South Africa (CPSA) had made great efforts during the 1920s to establish itself as the party for the black majority, as part of its 'Native Republic' campaign, bringing its black membership to over 90% of the two thousand odd members. Their aim was black majority rule, and the return of the country to its native inhabitants. By the mid 1930s the CPSA responded to the rise of fascism in Europe, and the events in Spain, with a policy to include progressive whites as part of a united front against the right, and Hetta's recruitment was part of this drive. At that time the Party was typically being run by immigrants from Lithuania—almost all Jewish. They gave Hetta the task of agitating for trade union membership for black workers in the clothing industry, and then of travelling around South Africa raising funds for the Party.

The Party, and, in particular, the middle-aged Jewish intellectuals who took her in to their midst, replaced the family which she had virtually lost, and from the remnants of which she felt completely alienated. Although she still loved Lilla and Kootie (Jacobus), they were well adjusted to the status quo, living as conventional Afrikaaners in a different world from the one that Hetta was aspiring to. Despite her rebellion against it, in a curious way the authoritarian nature of the Party simply replaced that of patriarchal Afrikaaner society. The twin pillars of Stalinism—'democratic centralism' and 'party unity', effectively meant that members took the political analysis from the top as gospel, and did what they were told. However unlikely it may seem, the rebel who had just re-invented herself as a bohemian in mixed-race Cape Town readily took to this mixture of authoritarianism and security. She was to remain a Party member for the next twenty years.

While in Cape Town she fell in love with a fellow artist and socialist, Rene Graetz, a German national whose family lived in Switzerland. Trained as a printer, he had arrived in South Africa in 1929, and was now dedicating himself to sculpture. She and Graetz were living together in a flat with a studio, working on their art, and political agitation. Despairing at the provincialism and inertia of South African society, they formed a plan to leave the country for good, and to live in England. There was a problem in that they had no money for tickets, until they hit upon the wheeze of making use of Graetz's practical accomplishments by printing ties and scarves—with appropriate Afrikaaner images to commemorate the centenary of the Great Trek of 1838. This was a success, although a limited one, which provided them with enough money to repay a loan from Hetta's brother Kootie, and to pay for their passage to Dunkirk. They visited Paris, then Switzerland to pay their respects to Graetz's relations before heading for England. They had every intention of getting married and having children.

Hetta Crouse, 1938

Before she left Cape Town forever, she went and had her photograph taken professionally, and gave a couple of prints each, including the one above, to Lilla and Kootie.

Arriving in England in June, 1939, she and Graetz were broke again. He was treated as a potential enemy alien, not only ineligible to find work but liable for internment if war broke out. They had left a few hundred of their scarves and ties in the hands of an agent, but never received a penny from him. Graetz was indeed interned during 1940, and was sent, first to the Isle of Man, and then to Canada, to spend the war as an enemy alien. Hetta wrote many letters pleading his case, but he was one of many socialists, Jews, and other anti-Nazis who were interned despite their undeniable credentials.

After the war he was to return to Germany, and to resume his career, becoming a successful sculptor in East Berlin.

From her letters to her friends in South Africa she sounds very much the outsider in London, although having a knack of gaining entrée. After working for a week as a model at the Slade School of Art, which then closed for the summer vacation, she was invited to pose for Vanessa Bell and her Bloomsbury Group.

Writing to her friend Frieda in Cape Town, she says,

'I feel very well today. I earned 7/6 for three hours posing for Vanessa Bell, the sister, I think of Clive Bell. I am treated justly and civilly enough but am kept in my place—as a model should be, no doubt.

Heighho! What does it matter?—let them paint their laborious pictures, these English artists; I half-close my eyes and dream as I stand.

I made a poem whilst I was posing but I think it was a little bitter—one should not get too intense—

When I was a model . . .
wraith-like and brittle
lady-like wraiths
hovering primly over their daubs
and I stand
rooted
swaying
slumbrous
strong
reflecting bitterly
feline flexing
strong

while they dibble-dabble primly
brittle and thin . . . these English ladies.

The next day, writing to Mrs Kibel, one of the Johannesburg communists, she says,

> 'I did some "char-ing", and then graduated to the status
> of model for emasculated English artists who measure
> you with a ruler to make sure they get the proportions
> right—with all their -isms they are more academic than the
> Royal Academy itself, hidebound, zealous, gutless little
> revolutionaries with no balls, to speak of—only now do
> they accept what the French artists discarded twenty years
> ago and bolster it up with their labels, constructivism,
> abstractivism, and surrealism, determined at all events to
> shock,—they are such a puritan race, the English.'

She was certainly not going to be impressed by the Bloomsbury Group's established status and aristocratic background!

Her membership of the Party meant that early in the war she was unable to directly engage in anti-fascist work because the Soviet Union was in an alliance with Germany. She even wrote to her brother Kootie in South Africa pleading with him not to enlist, as this war was going to be same as the last one, and would only benefit the capitalists. These scruples would not prevent her working as an artist, however, and from the start of her time in England she was trying to get involved in camouflage—an activity which had attracted many artists at the time, combining, as it did, a practical application with the opportunity to express oneself artistically—in particular, to develop ideas of surrealism in art. Surrealism and war do have an intellectual affinity and she was determined to explore this.

On 10th July 1939 she wrote to Research and Experimental Dept., (Camouflage) A.R.P.

> Dear Sir,
>
> I am a South African art student, and as I have had some experience of painting in all materials and especially in decorative Art, I wish to offer my voluntary service in your Department of Camouflage work.

This was the first of a number of applications to the Camouflage Research Department, but despite her persistence they went unheeded. Eventually, she was to become an ambulance driver. She and her friend Mabel Sharpe enlisted in the Auxiliary Ambulance Service, and they were to work together, based at the Starcross Street depot behind Euston Station. The experience was gruelling and traumatic, including six months of the Blitz on London, between September 1940 and May 1941. Neither of them had what we would call paramedical training. Mabel had been a successful painter, who had exhibited in the Paris Salon, and Hetta had driven since she was 14. Neither of them knew London very well. Such were their qualifications. On one of their missions Hetta held a man's hand in the back of the ambulance all the way to the hospital, only to find out that he'd been dead all the time. They worked a tough schedule, including twelve and sixteen hour night shifts. As the Blitz started there was a rule that they should not be out during raids, although this was soon rescinded so they had to drive through them. She described her experience in her letters to friends in South Africa, but never mentioned feeling afraid. Rather, she reported feeling a permanent sense of humiliation. Presumably this was to do with being unable to do anything about the continuous bombing—no possibility of fighting back, which would have been her natural reaction.

In a letter to her friend Mrs Kibel, in October, 1940, she wrote:

> For a month now life has consisted of cowering at home at night in a basement, with gunfire and high explosive bombs overhead, rocking the very foundations; and at the Station, sitting in a brick shelter in the garage, waiting for the telephone to ring for the next Ambulance out, and hoping that the worst of the bombing will have died down when one's turn comes to go out during the raid—and yet wishing that one could go out immediately, even envying those who go before,—anything to make this warfare seem less impersonal and detached, divorced from what once were the realities—anything to release one even temporarily from this humiliation which has been thrust upon one.
>
> Although when not out in it I do not feel any paralysing fear, rather an exhilarating excitement, and then comes the despair, perhaps days afterwards—with the continuous raids the feeling futility grows . . . [But] I feel I cannot just leave, one's life becomes inextricably bound up with the events, almost incomprehensibly so. Travelling by underground at night, the platforms lined two deep with women, men, young and old, children too, lying or sitting with their bundles of blankets even food for the long night, and just staring mutely or helplessly sleeping close-packed, one knows one cannot escape merely because one happens to be able to leave the

country. And then, in the early light of morning, long lines, dim forms, emerge tiredly from the undergrounds, wearily—and they go to work, whilst from early in the afternoon children, sent to keep the places in the long queue for the next night in the underground, stand or rest with the family's bundles on the sidewalks. What depths of humiliation—we are just creatures—sub-human, and without dignity. So one stays.

By the spring of 1941 she had taken a job driving a delivery van, which paid a good deal more than the Ambulance service, was living in Camden Town, and had started to get to know some of the artists living in London. The painter Rupert Shepherd had a South African wife with whom she became close, and she became friends with Feliks Topolski, Oskar Kokoschka, and Leslie Hurry. Perhaps these connections helped her to find a room in a house on Downshire Hill belonging to Freddie Uhlman, where she met the Marxist, collagist, and illustrator John Heartfield among the other tenants. At left-wing political meetings she described how they would be joined by an African who would stand at the back who rarely spoke, and held a spear. The point he was making was that European politics were all very well, but only of marginal significance to Africans still living in Europe's colonies. It was Jomo Kenyatta, the author of *Facing Mount Kenya*, and later to become Kenya's first president. He had been living with Dina Stock in West Sussex, working on a farm but travelling to London once a week to pursue his anthropological studies with Bronislaw Malinowski. Now he was concentrating on his political work for the Kikuyu tribe, whom he was representing in England.

After the German attack on Russia on 22nd June 1941, and the declaration of war between Germany and the Soviet Union, Hetta became free to join the war effort, and she applied to the BBC to make use of her Afrikaans language (and German, which she had learned at school and become fluent in during her year in Munich) in broadcasting to South Africa. Having qualified from the 'Liars School' she took up a post in Foreign Broadcasting, which did not only involve broadcasting news—she also had her own weekly program, which purported to be the diary of a hard-pressed housewife in Germany, called Suki Trottle. Suki would for instance report all the difficulties of wartime shortages in Germany and the effects of the bombing. It was aimed at German-speaking South Africans (a sizeable minority) who may have had lingering sympathies with, if not loyalties towards their fatherland and the Third Reich. At any rate, it gave Hetta the opportunity to be creative, and she would talk about Suki Trottle many years later with some affection.

The wife of the poet G.S. Fraser, Paddy, recalled her as being

> Large-boned, half-way between a powerful Greek goddess and one of the large cats, tigerish, I suppose is the word, something fierce, even frightening at times, combined with a lithe strength. But this is too feline an image, too smooth; Hetta had a tremendous directness, a brutal frankness, a don't-give-a-damn attitude, which was surprising and refreshing: it was this, I believe, that attracted William from their earliest meeting . . . She was so much herself, so totally unconventional. Once she raised me in her arms and threw me like a doll up to the ceiling. I was terrified.[iv]

William's journey up to the incident at the *Monseigneur Cinema* where he had loudly commented on the Plimsoll Line could not have been more different. He came from a conventional English land-owning family in Yorkshire—members of the squirearchy. A brilliant student, he had gained scholarships to Winchester College at the age of 13, and then to Magdalene College, Cambridge, in 1924. He was reading mathematics, but also involved in literary magazines and writing poetry. Under the strange university regulations of the time he was allowed to complete a degree in mathematics (getting a highly rated 2:1) and then allowed to switch to the English Tripos, under the tutelage of I.A. Richards. After only one year of supervised study in English he gained a first class degree, with 'special distinction'. This led to the award of the 'Charles Kingsley Bye-Fellowship' at Magdelene College for 1929-1930.

In a tragic-comic turn of events, soon after his move within the college to the superior rooms appropriate to a junior fellow, he was denounced by his bedmaker, Mrs Tingey, to the College authorities. She reported that he was in the habit of having a woman in his rooms until late in the evening, and also, that she had discovered "various birth control mechanisms" among his belongings while helping him move rooms. The Governing Body of Magdalene College promptly deprived him of his fellowship (and in fact attempted to remove his name altogether from college records).

Lorna Sage was to comment, after the publication of Volume 1 of John Haffenden's biography in 2005, that the Cambridge dons of the time were likely to have viewed homosexual activity with complete indulgence, while being genuinely shocked by a fellow having sex with a woman (and of course possession of condoms was absolute proof of heterosexuality at the time.) Unlike Oxford, Cambridge University had continued to impose a medieval rule that dons should not marry, which was only rescinded in the early 1920s. Many of the dons in William's day were thus still unmarried, whether by choice or necessity, and with little experience of relationships with women.

This dismissal from Magdalene College was a very serious, if not disastrous setback for an academic career in the U.K., but did not prevent the publication of his *Seven Types of Ambiguity* a year later in 1930, or another work of criticism, *Some Types of Pastoral*, in 1935. By the early 1940s he would, to some extent, have overcome his academic disgrace, and, despite not having an academic position, become a well-established name in poetry and criticism. But that was ten years ahead.

On leaving Cambridge that disastrous summer he went home to Yokefleet Hall, where he was 'hanging about' (as his mother put it), putting the final touches to *Seven Types of Ambiguity*. After a few months he moved to London, and found a small flat in Marchmont Street, where he stayed for a couple of years. It was then, as even now, a thriving little community of shops and flats in the midst of a bleak landscape of tenements. He had a small income from the Yokefleet Hall estate, but it was not enough to live on, and unreliable. As his brother Arthur, who had inherited the farms explained, 'Generally speaking, however, the family situation about money is a little murky; no doubt it will buck up again but I should certainly not forgo any chance of earning an honest penny if I were you.'

His mentor in Cambridge, I.A. Richards, had been trying, without success, to find him a post in China, where he had taught himself. Then, out of the blue, there came the opportunity to step in to replace the poet and social historian Peter Quennell, who had suddenly left his post at Tokyo University. So, in 1931 he took the boat-train to the Continent, and then the Trans-Siberian Railway, to travel to Vladivostock and thence to Japan, to work as professor of English Language and Literature at the University of Literature and Science (Tokyo Bunrika Daigaku), for a three-year appointment. This was a teacher training college, in all but name, and of low prestige. He was however also giving lectures at the Tokyo Imperial University—Japan's premier institution of learning. These three years in Japan were important for him. He was taken seriously as a poet and a scholar, by both students and colleagues. He also found love. Finally, he had the opportunity to travel in Korea and China, as well as Japan, in his ongoing investigation into Buddhist sculpture. On his way back to England, travelling by sea, he was able to break the journey and visit even more temples and other sites with Buddhist sculptures and frescoes in Burma, Ceylon and India.

Back in London, he again found another flat in Marchmont Street in Bloomsbury. He was enjoying the literary life centred on 'Fitzrovia', but was very short of money, and was resorting to tutoring and book reviewing to supplement his small income from Yokefleet. He seriously considered applying for a position at the University of Singapore, and actually applied for one at the Egyption University in Cairo. While the party life in London was enjoyable, he felt that he was wasting his time. However, in 1937 he was to leave Marchmont Street again, giving instructions to the removals firm Carter Paterson to go to his flat and collect all his belongings into crates to be sent to Peking. He again travelled on the Trans-Siberian Railway, this time to China, finally to take up a three-year appointment at the National Peking University, a leading Chinese university, fulfilling his ambition to follow in I.A. Richard's footsteps.

This appointment was derailed by the Japanese occupation of Peking: when he arrived he was to find that the university had closed. The Northern Chinese universities were now to retreat and to combine and reconvene in Changsha, in South China, as the 'Temporary University'. By coincidence a conference on Basic English was arranged to take place in Changsha that month, and William flew from Peking to Changsha to take part, 'bumping' another passenger off the plane to gain a seat. (Despite his distracted, preoccupied appearance, he seemed to have acquired some worldly accomplishments). He joined Ivor and Dorothea Richards at the conference, and then afterwards, for a while. Taken in charge by a junior government minister, they meandered, with about another dozen displaced foreigners, in a convoy of cars and trucks which had to halt whenever Dorothea wanted to climb another sacred mountain, before finally being deposited at the Vietnamese border. The junior minister's priority had been, presumably, not so much as to take them anywhere in particular, but to keep these foreign VIPs safe, and to give them the opportunity to leave the country.

William then had to make his own way back to join the Temporary University, where he was to stay for two years. There was a shortage of books, among other things, as the university library had been left behind. He was famous for using his memory to inform his lectures—although, as he would modestly say in later life, many Shakespearean actors would know almost the entire works by heart, so his accomplishment was by no means unique. The teaching of 'Basic English' was an important part of his work, which was a novel method, invented by his Cambridge tutor I.A. Richards, allowing foreigners to learn English using a limited vocabulary. In a letter to his mother in June 1939 William reported that at a final summer school in 1939, devoted to Basic English, a

Chinese colleague proposed to recruit a class of children with no knowledge of English, and demonstrate that after six weeks they 'know absolutely everything'.

In his book *China Evergreen* Victor Purcell (one of the other foreigners in the meandering convoy) was to describe William Empson as being

> 'slender and of somewhat avian appearance, partly due I think to his hawk nose and the unblinking, rather bead-like eyes behind his spectacles. His face was of an aristocratic mould with a fine forehead and sensitive lips . . . . He was usually in a state of abstraction.'[v]

This state of abstraction was a life-long trait. If he was not preoccupied with something literary then he would be intensely working on a mathematical puzzle. As Purcell noted,

> 'during the time we were in China he would, when there was nothing else to do, work on a problem on a scrap of paper. It was always the same problem. I saw the diagram of it on at least two hundred different bits of paper, accompanied in some cases with a page and a half of algebraic signs, but I never ascertained exactly what the problem was. It had something to do with proving that a certain circle touches a triangle at nine points—which sounds nonsense so I must have got it wrong. (Empson) said that he could prove it easily enough by algebra, but that there ought to be a simple geometrical proof if he could only find it. He was not aware whether anyone else had ever found it, so he could not say whether he was

searching for the lost tribes of Israel or, on the other hand, for another planet. In any case he found it a never failing source of consolation.'[vi]

During his time with the Temporary University, based in the town of Mengtzu, he was in the habit of going for long solitary walks, against all available advice, which was that the countryside was ridden with bandits. On one of these, coming back from visiting some abandoned tin mines in the dark, and suffering from cramp, he was indeed set upon—as he wrote to his brother Arthur,

'three suddenly converged, with daggers, I assure you, flashing in the moonlight. Maybe if I had been more frightened or more angry the cramp might have solved itself, but as it was I had to go on rubbing my left calf. Two men held me with what seemed scientific efficiency while a third went through the pockets. Scientific efficiency however interfered with rubbing the left leg and threatened to bring on cramp in the right leg; I had to object, and a compromise was reached. The wristwatch was taken without comment, the very small amount of money carried was a matter of course; the spectacles were taken, and I stopped rubbing my legs to represent the absurd injustice of this step—there was a fateful pause, and they were put back on my nose. Then the important thing happened; the searcher found the cigarettes and the matches. All three gasped with pleasure. I think it says a good deal for the local police that the boys couldn't slip into the town and buy cigarettes. After a pause one sinister figure came back and asked if I wanted help up

to the gate; he was sorry he couldn't take me in. I assured
him I would be all right in a minute or two, so he melted
back again.'

Having returned to England at the outbreak of war, William got a
job in a secret 'Monitoring Unit' based at Wood Norton, near Evesham
in deepest Worcestershire. The unit was set up to provide a daily
summary of the contents of foreign broadcasts for the civil service
and intelligence organizations. (Military transmissions received in
Morse code were dealt with by a different group on the same site,
who passed their work on to Bletchley Park for decoding and further
analyses.) He was joined there by Gwenda David, amongst others,
who was to become a lifelong family friend. They worked twelve
hour shifts, from 2pm to 2am, for four days a week, and were put up
in digs in the town. William famously rode his bicycle to work while
reading a book, and was in the habit of writing poetry during office
hours, even giving some of his efforts to Gwenda (who unfortunately
subsequently lost them.) While important and demanding work, it
was also grindingly dull, requiring the daily reduction of pages and
pages of poorly translated transcripts of foreign broadcasts (provided
by the listeners fluent in the relevant languages) into a few hundred
words of understandable English. An opportunity to escape from this
daily chore, and to return to London, came when in February 1941
R.A. Butler, then in the Foreign Office, pressed for the recruitment
of individuals within the BBC who could broadcast to the Far East.
When this suggestion was eventually implemented later that year,
William applied. It was on his induction training course for this new
role that he met Hetta, who had applied for broadcasting in Afrikaans
to Southern Africa.

They were married on 3ʳᵈ December, 1941, in St Stephens Church in Hampstead. The witnesses were William's brother Arthur who travelled down from the family estate at Yokefleet Hall in Yorkshire, and Mabel Sharpe, who had worked with Hetta in the Ambulance Service. Her ex-husband was the vicar who married them. William's sister Molly also attended (his other brother, Charles, was serving abroad in the Diplomatic Service). The wedding party was held down the road at their flat at 160A Haverstock Hill, where two of their guests, Dylan and Caitlin Thomas, ended up fighting under the table. While Gwenda David did not get to the wedding (still working at the Monitoring Unit in Worcestershire) she was well aware of developments, and was to comment,

> We were amazed. Who was this woman who had won William, when we understood that he was not interested in women or marriage? She must be someone very special. She was. She was beautiful, had a very quick wit and a very sharp tongue; you couldn't play games with her; she was an arrogant woman who laughed easily and got angry easily.

As the last of the wedding guests were leaving, William got up to go as well, saying 'Well, I'll be going along, my dear', going back to his digs, either having forgotten that he had got married, or, possibly, simply to pick up some of his belongings. Despite this inauspicious beginning to conjugal life a son was born on 9ᵗʰ November the following year. He was given three names, one to commemorate each of his parents' nationalities, and one to commemorate a contemporary war-time action. Born on the day of the U.S. landings in North Africa, at Mogador in Morocco, which were a politically significant event, even if militarily unremarkable, his third name was Mogador. There was little or no resistance to the Americans. His second name was Hendrik, after his uncle in South Africa, and his first, William, after his father. In due time their second son's names were to be Jacobus Arthur Calais, after another South African uncle, his father's brother in Yorkshire (and his grandfather), and the French port which was the scene of a bitter battle on the day of his birth—part of the Allied attempts to secure usable ports to support their invasion of Europe, and the Germans' determination to prevent them achieving this.

During 1941 and 1942 Hetta and William were not only both in full-time employment but fully committed to their war work. In addition, Hetta would have had her Party meetings to attend. After Mogador's birth she took a few months of 'maternity leave', during which she had only one broadcast a week, and worked from home the rest of the time. When she took up full-time work again in March 1943 Mog was then placed in a crèche. A colleague at the BBC, George Ivan Smith, was to recall,

> 'Near midnight at another time I was duty director and
> had to telephone his Hampstead home. 'William, where
> is your baby?' He consulted wife, Hetta. I reported that
> the police had telephoned me. The infant had not been
> collected from the crèche.'

There were some lighter moments. The commissionaire who acted as receptionist at Bush House was notorious for his fierce rudeness. He was called Arthur. One evening, when they were sat in The George after work, the Irish poet Louis MacNeice, also employed at the BBC, joined them and said, "Have you heard what Arthur did last week?"

'No,' they said, 'go on and tell us.'

'Well, this tall distinguished man presented himself at the door, and said,

"I have come to make a broadcast."

'You can't. You've got to have an appointment,' says Arthur.

"I have been invited to make a broadcast."

'All right, what's your name?'

"I am the king of Norway".

Arthur went to his telephone, dialled a number, and then looked up and said,

'The king of where, did you say?'

You couldn't make it up!

By the time Jacob was born the war was in a different phase: while during 1941 and 1942 it must have seemed a distinct possibility that there would be a German victory, it had now become clear, with the Soviet Red Army defeating the Germans at Stalingrad and Kursk, the Americans winning battles in the Pacific, and the invasion of Europe, that they were not going to win. The desperate times were not quite over, but Hetta and William were no longer working as Stakhanovites, and had settled into a sort of domesticity. Hetta took the time to make a terracotta head of Jacob, as a newborn baby.

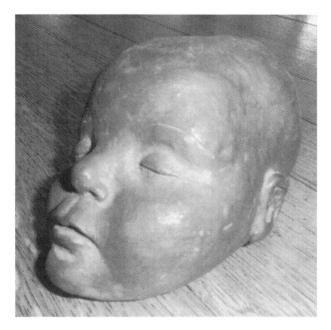

Terracotta head of Jacob as newborn

For a while, Mog and Jacob had various carers (including an eccentric Russian aristocrat who had filled her tiny flat with books). They lived in a basement flat, 160A Haverstock Hill, in Hampstead. However, after the death of William's mother in 1946 they were able to buy the lease on a large property—Studio House, 1 Hampstead Hill Gardens. They were there for only a few months before the planned trip to China—a stipulation of William's on proposing marriage was that she should be prepared to go to China, so this was just a trip postponed by the war. The large grand rooms on the ground floor of the house were then let to the Hampstead Artists Council. (This was an organization set up after the war by a group of artists, including Henry Moore, to promote the arts and provide educational facilities for artists.) Some other tenants took rooms in the rest of the house, including John Wright (and old friend of Hetta's from South Africa), and his partner Zoe with their puppet theatre in the basement, and

Pat Miles and Iqbal Singh in the rooms upstairs. John was left in charge of the house.

Studio House as it is today

Chapter 2

Early Days in China

William had been working on a short book of art history before they left for China. It was to be called *The Face of the Buddha*, and was based on his observations of Buddhist sculpture during his terms teaching in Japan (1933-1935) and China (1937-1939). He had been impressed by the Buddhist sculptures shown in the China Exhibition in London in 1932, and when he went to Japan the following year he made a point of visiting temples to see more of them. This became an ongoing pre-occupation, if not an obsession, during his time in both Japan and later in China, and he had spent almost all his vacations travelling to ever more remote locations to see more of these sculptures, and to collect postcards of them where possible. His final work on the book was done on the basis of his recollections and on the 100 or so postcards which he had kept, as well as being informed by the major books on the subject, such as Coomaraswami's *Art in India and Indonesia*. Now finished, he had left the manuscript and photographs with his friend John Davenport to take around to editors and publishers, to see if it could be published.

They left England in February 1947, travelling by ocean liner from Southampton to Hong Kong. On the boat Hetta set about teaching herself Mandarin, and had learned 100 characters by the time they arrived. They had to stay in Hong Kong until there was a boat taking passengers to Tienstin, the port nearest to Peking in the north, and this took a month. Hetta was having lessons in Chinese three times a week from a Major in the Nationalist army, whose father was a professor at Hong Kong University. However, she was unable to practise her Mandarin, as nobody in Hong Kong could speak it—they all spoke Cantonese. They took some day trips on buses into the hills, and to the beaches, but, with a four-year-old and a two-year-old to carry when they were tired, there wasn't much walking done.

By the middle of May they were finally on board a steamer travelling first to Shanghai, then Tienstin. It was frustratingly slow, with fog most of the way keeping the speed down to about five knots. The navigator told Hetta over dinner that he calculated the ship's position by the stars, and by dead reckoning using a compass and dividers—the same instruments as used in Nelson's time, he proudly informed her. However, the weather was making things difficult for him, with the continuous cloud cover. At night the fishing junks were dodging about trying to avoid the steamer, and the fishermen were shouting out to tell them where they were. It seemed a chaotic situation.

There were 150 Chinese deck-passengers, separated from the 20-odd westerners by an iron grill. In addition, there were eight uniformed and armed anti-pirate guards ('APGs') standing watch day and night. They were there to prevent any attempt to take over the ship—the usual practise was for the pirates to pose as passengers, and then, at a given moment, to reveal their weapons, and to force the captain to land at a port of their choice and unload the cargo. However, her friendly navigator reassured Hetta, things had improved, as the chief pirate had been given an important job by the shipping company, Butterfield and Swine. He was now working for them in Hong Kong, so all should be well. What with the APGs and the generous employment of the chief pirate in Hong Kong, their boat eventually arrived in Tientsin without incident, and they loaded their trunks onto a train for Peking.

The University (officially, Pei Jing Da Xue, or Pei-Ta for short, by which it is known to this day) had provided accommodation for their new Professor of English Literature in a compound near the campus, at 11 Dong Gau Fan. Dong Gau Fan was a *hutung*, a narrow lane. Their accommodation was in a compound which was a larger entity belonging to the University, with multiple residences with courtyards, and a grand entrance on to a main street with a gate keeper in his gatehouse. Their set of two courtyards had its own entrance onto the *hutung*, so had its own address. There was nowhere for William to have a study to do his work, and for the first few months he went to the British Embassy compound to work on his book, where they provided him with a room. Eventually the university was to provide more space by allocating them another adjacent courtyard. There he was to have his own study and bedroom, and even access through another door into the rest of the compound.

In 1947 China was entering perhaps the most unstable period in its long history, culminating in the establishment of the Peoples Republic of China in 1949. These events were rooted in China's history over the previous century. For the reader unfamiliar with it, a brief account of the history of China over this period will be useful.

The Manchu dynasty had ruled China for over three hundred years. Unlike the Japanese, with their Meiji Restoration, in China there was no government-led attempt to incorporate Western technology and industrialization in an acceptably oriental way during the nineteenth century. Development was piecemeal, and China was unable to engage effectively with the modern world, let alone join it. The Western powers fought one another, and the Chinese, for trading concessions.

At the beginning of the twentieth century the Manchu dynasty was without an emperor, and was ruled by the strong-minded Dowager Empress. At her death the infant Pu Yi came to the throne. (His story became the subject of the movie *The Last Emperor*.) Government by regents who were more often than not in dispute with one another was the final straw for the old regime. Their corrupt and ineffectual rule provided the pretext for civil war, with revolutionary movements calling for the overthrow of feudalism and of the imperial government. In 1911 all China south of the Yangste River was in the hands of the rebels, and in 1912 Sun Yat-sen was to be briefly the President of the new Chinese Republic. He was the leader of an organization devoted to the re-distribution of land amongst the peasantry, and the abolition of feudalism and serfdom. The new republic was not prepared to embrace these reforms, however, and Sun Yat-sen and his Kuomintang Party were not to rule China for long. He died in 1925, his final letter being to the Communist Party of the Soviet Union, expressing solidarity with their revolution, and the hope that China would follow in their footsteps under the leadership of the Kuomintang Party.

Only two years later the Kuomintang Party, under the new leadership of Chiang Kai-shek, was to abandon its progressive policies and to shift to become a right-wing nationalist party, emulating the Spanish and German fascists. The Kuomintang then turned on their former comrades in the Communist Party of China in a series of massacres. A new Kuomintang nationalist government was formed, and twenty years of conflict was to follow. Japan invaded China in 1931, and was not to leave until 1945. Initially, the Kuomintang chose to continue the civil war against the communists, and make concessions to the Japanese, allowing them to occupy large areas of China, even providing them with quisling Chinese armies to keep the communists at bay. By 1934 the Communist Party and its army was at its lowest ebb, and undertook the legendary retreat from Kiansi and Fukien provinces, through eleven provinces, to their northwestern base in Shaanxi. This 'long march', which began with 100,000 soldiers in the Red Army, ended a year later with a force of 30,000. (Estimates of these figures vary, but there was undoubtedly a very great loss of life during this retreat.) In Shaanxi the survivors of the long march were joined by a much larger communist force, so that the Red Army, or Peoples Liberation Army as it became known, was reinforced to its previous strength.

The start of hostilities between the Allied powers and Japan after the attack on Pearl Harbour changed everything. In *Revolution in China*, C.P. Fitzgerald says, 'From 1941 to the Japanese surrender in September 1945, there were really two wars in China. The Kuomintang positional war, mainly passive defence, in the south, and the Communist guerrilla war in the north and north-east. These two forces maintained to each other an attitude of suspicious and armed neutrality . . . . The civil war, if not in actual operation, was manifestly merely in cold storage; Japanese invasion alone restrained the two parties from open warfare, and even that menace was not always sufficient'.[vii] After the sudden Japanese capitulation in 1945 following the nuclear attacks on Hiroshima and Nagasaki the civil war was to resume, although not as quickly as might be expected, since both sides in China were completely taken by surprise by this turn of events. They had both anticipated a longer war in Japan followed by an American invasion to defeat the Japanese and expel them from China.

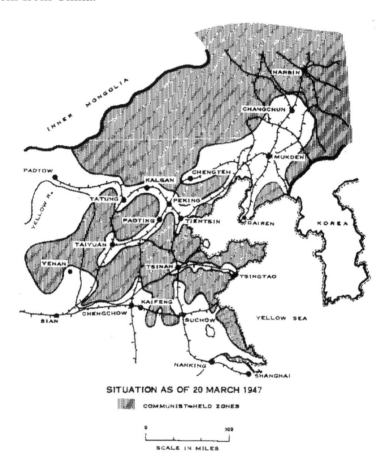

SITUATION AS OF 20 MARCH 1947

COMMUNIST-HELD ZONES

SCALE IN MILES

Map showing extent of Communist control in the
North China countryside in 1947

By the mid-1940s the Communists had built up their own infrastructures in the countryside, although they remained relatively weak in the cities. They were particularly strong in the north of the country, with the Kuomintang retaining control of much of the countryside in the south, as well as the big cities. The map (above) comes from Lionel Max Chassin's *The Communist Conquest of China*[viii], showing the degree of communist domination of the countryside in North China in March, 1947. The main cities remained under Nationalist (Kuomintang) control, but were almost completely surrounded by Communist zones. When the Empson family arrived in China the situation was relatively stable, with the two sides in a state of hostile confrontation, but not actually fighting.

The first thing that William and Hetta did was to take the opportunity to travel to Yun-Kang, taking the boys with them, to see the statues that William had first discovered ten years before, and which played an important part in his book, *The Face of the Buddha*, which he had left with John Davenport. They are sited in Datong, Shanxi province, labelled 'Tatung' in the map above, about two hundred miles West of Peking. They travelled by train, and stayed overnight. As they stood in front of their first statue of Buddha, William started to explain the curious snail-like curls representing the Buddha's hair,

'The Buddha naturally wore his hair when a prince and shaved it off on becoming a monk, and worshippers want to think of him as both. (On the same principle his earlobes are pierced and pulled down by the weight of jewels, but he has taken them out.) Compromise was achieved by a legend that when in meditation he failed to observe that the shadow of the sacred bo-tree had moved away from him and he would have got sunstroke if a number of devout snails had not climbed onto his head. (The leaves of the sacred tree still tremble at the memory of the struggle they witnessed.)'

'Don't you think,' he said, as they stood in front of one of the colossal statues, 'that it has an expression of ironical politeness and philosophical superiority?'

"It's certainly a different convention than the Christian one—the simpering Madonnas and the suffering Jesuses," agreed Hetta.

'Yes, very different—but in other ways too I think one is haunted by parallels to the medievals in this early Buddhist work. These Yun-Kang buddhas and the virgin of Chartres, for instance, make a real parallel in their use of the half-shut eye. They are not using it to be "mystical" (in the sense of withdrawn from the world) not yet sly (in any way that would make them insincere); the point is that they are keeping a certain reserve of social force. They can remain conventional and yet act independently of the conventions; they remain modest though they are decisive.'

'There seems to be a feeling that the last achievement of the mystic is something that a really well brought up girl knows already. It may seem very unlikely that Chinese monks should feel this, and yet China not long after was to take the mysterious step of turning the Bodhisattva of Mercy into an upperclass woman.'

All this was lost on Mog (as Mogador had very quickly become known) and Jacob, as they followed their parents about—Mog, almost five, asking for ice creams, while Jacob had not yet started to speak. Fortunately North China was enjoying a warm, mild autumn, with plenty of sunshine, so the trip was not as arduous for the boys as it might have been. They had lunch in a café on the site (it had been a place of pilgrimage, if not a tourist attraction, for hundreds of years) and then went back to look at some of the smaller (life-size) statues.

It was then that William started talking to Hetta about his special theory about some of the faces being asymmetrical. He said, 'The Chinese did want him human, and it's here at Yun-Kang that they fell upon this convention—the easiest way to make a statue lively is to make the two sides of the head different.'

'Look at this one, it's just what I'm talking about!' continued William, 'on the right the eye and mouth slant, and this gives the sardonic quality; in fact the thing approaches the standard European head of Satan. It requires to be balanced by the left, which has the mystical and all but childish eternity of traditional Buddhism.'

Many of the statues had been decapitated, with the heads sold off to wealthy collectors—mainly Americans. William had travelled home, in 1939, by way of the U.S., and when he was in Boston had suggested his theory about the asymmetry to an authority at the Museum of Fine Art. They had said that, yes, of course they were asymmetrical. In fact, they did not advertise the fact as it was one way in which they identified fakes.

Statues at Yun-Kang (courtesy of Wikipedia)

Head from the Yun-Kang caves, 5th or 6th Century
(postcard dating from 1937, from
The Face of the Buddha)

On their return to Peking there was still no letter from John Davenport about what had happened to the manuscript of *The Face of the Buddha*. William was to write to him repeatedly over the next few years, asking if he had found a publisher for it. In fact, John's guilty conscience did not allow him to write, as he thought he had lost it—that he'd left it in a taxi when drunk. What had really happened was that he had delivered it to Tambimuttu, a Ceylonese editor of poetry, working in London. (Tambimuttu was one of the regulars at the Fitzroy Tavern who coined the term 'Fitzrovia' for the literary clique who regularly gathered there.) Afterwards John had

37

continued on his way, in a day of heroic drinking, and completely forgot what had happened to the manuscript. In a series of mischances Tambimuttu passed it on to Edward Marsh, an eminent but quite elderly patron of the arts, as he was going abroad. Before he could find an appropriate editor for it, Marsh was taken ill. He died in 1953, and the manuscript, together with the illustrations, lay in a box of papers neglected for the next fifty years. They eventually turned up in the British Library, to be identified by John Haffenden in 2005. Over the years William would often talk about *The Face of the Buddha*, and of his theory that some of the Buddhas had asymmetrical faces as part of a convention, to represent the two sides of their godlike characters. There was never any question of attempting to rewrite it, as of course all the illustrations were now lost.

A month after their trip to Yun-Kang a full-blown civil war had resumed, and there was no cessation of hostilities until the Communist victory in 1949. Hetta had arranged to be accredited as a foreign correspondent for *The Observer* newspaper before leaving for China, relying on her experience in the BBC as a broadcaster as her credential. She sent periodic reports to *The Observer*, some of which were published, and in 1948 she was to join an investigative expedition into Inner Mongolia. This was to attend a Mongol festival commemorating Genghis Kahn, due to be held at Edjin Horo. It was normally an annual event, but Japanese invasion, and civil war, had prevented it being held for a number of years. She went with three other Western journalists, Adrian Conway-Evans, Jim Burke, and John Warner. By then the rail link between Peking and Tatung was broken by the civil war, and they would have to fly to Kweisui (due West of Peking), and then travel North by train to Baotou ('Paotow' on the map), and then Inner Mongolia by road.

Having arrived in Kweisui by plane, and then proceeded by train to Bautou, they were welcomed by the China Relief Agency (CRA) who had to inform them that the festival had now been cancelled. As an alternative they were sent off in a CRA weapons carrier to visit a Mongol temple and llamasarie in the mountains forty miles to the north. The monks welcomed them and killed a sheep and boiled it, after which their guests were to hack at it with sharp knives. Hetta's experience in dealing with game carcasses in South Africa proved very useful here, and she was able to cut out the best pieces for her companions. Their hosts were insistent that they should enjoy the fatty flesh of the tail.

As a woman, Hetta was not allowed to sleep in the monastery with the men. Rather, she had to spend the night with the CRA drivers, drinking Pai Gar (rice wine) in the garrison. (This might seem an odd twist on scruples, if not on gallantry. However, it was unthinkable for a woman to sleep in the monastery, but leaving her to share a k'ang with the drivers was perfectly all right, as it seemed that the Mongols did not regard Western women as sexual objects). In the morning she was able to get out on her own for a little walk, and saw the Mongol women, in their heavy coral and silver headdresses (from which they were never parted, and which, presumably, made them the desirable sexual objects that western women like Hetta were not) making their way to the well.

They were resigning themselves to making their way back to Peking when they were approached by a Mongol affiliated to a warlord organization, the 'Ottok Banner'. He offered to take them by truck to Nalin Nor, through the desert of the Ordos. This sounded like an adventurous alternative to simply going home. The four of them therefore joined him and set off in two trucks, which kept breaking down, and the journey took a lot longer than they had anticipated. Nalin Nor itself was a disappointment, what with the dreadful weather preventing them even going out of doors much. The trip was very memorable, however. Hetta described seeing many groups of refugees, some of them stranded, not allowed to travel in case they were communist sympathisers, and relying on the rather erratic charity of the Mongols. There was also an encounter with the Ottok warlord himself who was most hospitable (providing another boiled sheep). There was even more challenging food, varied landscapes—some with herds of antelope, and more opportunities to smoke opium. By now Hetta and Adrian Conway-Evans seem to have struck up a relationship, perhaps based more on a shared interest in opium than politics.

The expedition was, in the event, rather aimless, and although demanding and potentially dangerous, it was also tedious. When a lone wolf was spotted the men in the party took turns to take pot shots at it with a rifle. What was supposed to be a ten-day trip turned out to take well over a month. Hetta kept a diary, but also wrote a more formal account of the adventure to her Party comrades in London, which, to her disgust, was published as a 'note' accompanying the woodcuts she had been collecting over the previous year. They appeared in a book entitled, *Contemporary Chinese Woodcuts*. As she wrote to David Kidd in 1951:

> From the New Statesman we saw that a book of woodcuts describing through their art the revolutionary struggles of the Chinese peoples, with "notes on China by Hetta Empson" has been published at 12/6 a go. The bastards. Those are the pictures and booklets I sweated and toiled at more than a year ago and sent off in all good faith, but does anyone even so much as send me a copy?'

There was a small but interesting expatriate community in Peking. Long-term residents included the American Bob Winter, who taught at Tsinghua University, and the New Zealander Rewi Alley, a communist who had founded the Chinese Industrial Cooperative. Both of them were to spend the rest of their lives in China.

Another long-term expat was the Canadian David Crooke, a life-time communist who recalled Hetta in his memoirs:

> At the end of April 1949 a British gunboat, the Amethyst, became embroiled in the P.L.A.'s crossing of the Yangzi River to take Nanjing. The incident reportedly caused 252 Chinese casualties and on April 30 Mao Ze-dong issued a blistering statement condemning British imperialism for intruding into Chinese inland waterways and militarily intervening in China's civil war.
>
> Shortly after this there was a knock on our door and in came Hetta Empson, a South African-born sculptress (she was herself a statuesque figure), then teaching English at a Beiping university. Being married to the English poet and literary critic William Empson, Hetta was a British subject and she and one or two other local left of centre Britishers, including her husband, were circulating a petition. It was to protest to the Attlee government, by way of the British Embassy, against Britain's intervention in the Chinese civil war. We were overwhelmed by the entry of this Junoesque personage with her male entourage, all the more so as we rather fancied ourselves as the sole

41

representatives of British anti-imperialism in China. We happily signed the petition and were soon occasional visitors at the Empson's. There we argued about literature and knocked back Chinese white spirit which flowed freely in their home.[ix]

These three were significant people to their parents, but had little importance to Jacob or Mog.

There were others who did become significant family friends—for instance the German, Hundhausen, who was a translator and publisher. Hundhausen lived outside the city, on an island on a lake. There was his solitary house, with an orchard of fruit trees which had been vandalised years before by the Japanese invaders. To visit him you had to brave the water in a very leaky dinghy, with the risk of being attacked by leaches. Once in his house, leaches were removed by being burned with lighted cigarettes. The house was stacked high with books, which even went up the stairs. Whenever they visited, Mog and Jacob had the task of going upstairs to fetch down Hundhausen's pipe—a massive carved thing about three feet long, which he could not light by himself as his arms were too short to reach the bowl. Then they could fill it with tobacco and light it for him, to his loud satisfaction. He maintained that it was only when they visited him that he could smoke his favourite pipe. More often, he would make the trip into Peking to call on the Empson family for lunch on a Sunday. He had a translation and publishing business, but it was not clear what had brought him to Peking in the first place, or what kept him there.

David Kidd and Walter Alison Brown were much more intimate friends, who became part of the household. They were two young Americans who taught English language at Tsinghua University, just outside Peking's city walls. David was slightly the younger of the two, and had come to China on an exchange studentship from the University of Michigan in 1946. He was strikingly handsome, with a mane of blond hair. One of his English language students was the director of the Summer Palace in the Forbidden City. David made sure to cultivate him, and brought him around to 11 Dong Gau Fan to meet William, Hetta, and Walter. Lubricated with bai gar, and succumbing to the attention of his glamorous teacher, he promised to find an apartment in the Summer Palace for David, in lieu of fees for his language course. It turned out that many if not most of the useable apartments and villas had been occupied, if not spoken for. The grandest was reserved for Chiang Kai-shek himself. The apartment that the Director managed to allocate to David was, he claimed, formerly a favourite of the Dowager Empress. It was restored and the gardens replanted. David liked to claim that this was all for his benefit. It was actually opened to the public, so this was not quite true. However, he did have a special claim on the place, and could stay the night there if he wanted to.

In March 1948 William and Hetta joined John Blofeld, Adrian Conway Evans, Walter and David Kidd for a night there. They took some photographs, which showed it as having a certain grandeur, but hardly any furniture. There was obviously no heating. They slept on the floor, and heard ghosts all through the night, having drunk a lot of the Director's bai gar mixed with vodka during the evening. In the morning they had breakfast at the restaurant by the marble boat, starting with beer and ending up with canned pineapples, probably because of the vagaries of what was available, rather than by choice. The marble boat in the Summer Palace was famous for having been built in 1893 on the orders of the Dowager Empress, and its construction consuming the entire budget for the Chinese Navy for that year.

David Kidd, William, Walter, Hetta and John Blofeld at dawn in the Forbidden City apartment.
Adrian Conway-Evans took the picture.

Dowager Empress Cixi's marble boat in the Forbidden City

David's knack of gaining entrée to unlikely places was to continue, with his introduction into the household of an aristocratic family. He was now to marry a daughter of the house. The Yu family had suffered under the Nationalist government, and were to suffer even more under the communists. Under the Nationalists they had lost their estates—liberated by the communists, with the land re-distributed to the peasants. They had then given up their savings (in gold bullion) in exchange for paper Nationalist money. This was in response to a government appeal for patriotic citizens to support the currency and hand in their gold. The currency swiftly became worthless, so, having been robbed by the communists, they were now robbed by the KMT. They were now without rents from their estates, or their savings in gold, and their mansion with 101 rooms was their surviving asset. This would be turned into a hospital by the Communists once they gained control of Beijing, and the elaborate gardens flattened. Aimee Yu almost certainly married David in order to escape from this catastrophe. Hetta was to say that David had almost certainly married her for her frocks.

David Kidd returned to America with his wife in 1950. They were to separate, and Aimee to pursue a career as an academic physicist, while he was to specialize in Oriental antiques, and after a few years in the U.S. to return to the East and live in Japan. David kept in touch with Walter, and with Hetta, over the years, and occasionally visited the Empson family in London. In later life he was obviously exclusively gay, with a long-term Japanese partner who helped him in his antiques and educational ventures. Curiously, given the similarity in their looks, he came to meet the pop star and actor David Bowie, possibly as a customer for his Japanese antiques, and they became good friends.

Walter was a year older, and had served in the U.S. Army in Burma as a muleteer, before returning home in 1947, and then arriving in Peking in 1948. It was always said that he and David had been to high school together, and had vowed to meet up in Peking when they were 21. Walter's time in the U.S. Army was also the subject of legends, which emerged gradually over the years, some of which Jacob only heard when he was an adult and visiting him in Michigan. The mules that he looked after were extremely valuable, carrying essential provisions for the U.S. forces. They were so precious that when they were wounded they received the blood plasma supplied by the Mothers of America for the boys at the front. In fact, as he confessed to Jacob's younger brother Simon, they even gave them transfusions to combat fatigue—one shot of the Mothers of America elixir, and they would be on their feet and ready to go. The only time he killed anyone was a guilty secret: when they were spending the night on a narrow mountain ledge, and a mule was competing with him for space to lie down, Walter lost patience and kicked it hard. He then had to pretend that it had fallen to its death by turning over in its sleep. These stories had an uncanny resonance with Sam Fuller's movie *Merrill's Marauders,* set in the Burma campaign, where the sergeant actually carries a mule on his back, because it was so precious and heroic. Walter's war service was to stand him in good stead towards the end of his life, when he received free health care in Detroit's Veteran Administration Hospital as a decorated veteran (with two bronze stars, awarded to soldiers who stayed at their posts when under fire.)

Walter was to become Hetta's first long-term lover during her marriage, and he spent much of his time with the family, although late in 1948 he was re-deployed to work in Shansi University, a hundred miles or more south-west of Peking, to teach English language (in particular, using Basic English). Presumably David's degree from Michigan University qualified him to stay and teach at the more prestigious Tsinghua University outside Peking, while Walter, with only his high school diploma, had to go to a provincial college as a teaching assistant. He and Hetta then kept up a regular correspondence during term-times for the next two years, much of which has survived to this day.

Other Westerners in Peking included C.P. Fitzgerald ('Pat', or 'Possum' to his family) who was in charge of the British Council in Peking in 1948-1949. An anthropologist and historian of China, he was to become an eminent professor at Australia National University, and his daughter Mirabel and Jacob would renew their acquaintance again years later. John Blofeld was an English scholar of Buddhism who had been studying and teaching in China for a few years, and who was to stay in Peking until 1949. Max Bickerton was a New Zealander, communist and homosexual, who was a regular visitor to their home. He was later to live in their house in Hampstead until his death.

It was not until they went to China that Hetta discovered the enduring nature of William's sexuality. As she told Jacob many years later, 'he wanted to go there for the boys'. (It is difficult to believe that nobody had told her what he was like, as many friends, such as the publisher Gwenda David, were astonished at his decision to marry. Perhaps she thought that she had seduced him into permanent heterosexuality.) Jacob's impression over the years was that his interest in sex was probably very intermittent—but evidently complicated. In any case, at his suggestion Walter became part of their household, and would normally be sleeping with Hetta in the Ke T'ing, and William would be in his own room in a separate courtyard. ('Ke T'ing, or, literally 'guest room' would be the main living room of a house, where guests might be received, but would also be furnished with a 'kang' or large, heated platform where the whole family might sleep.)

Summer 1948 by the gate to their third courtyard

Mog and Jacob were a bit ambivalent about this turn of events. On the one hand, Walter was good fun, and they missed him when he left Peking to go and teach in Shansi. On the other, it was obviously an irregular arrangement. Mog, in particular, rebelled against Hetta's infidelity, on one occasion getting up in the night to go and beat his fists on the glazed door into the *ke t'ing*, where she was sleeping with Walter, breaking the glass and cutting his hand.

Jacob, as he eventually learned to speak, referred to himself as 'ickle Jacob'—a name which stuck.

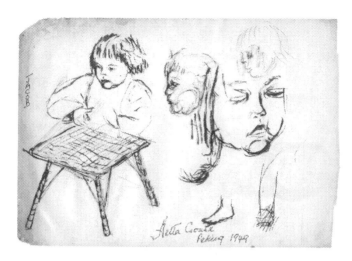

Hetta's sketches of Jacob in 1949

Servants were an issue for Hetta, when she first arrived in China. Having rebelled against a culture of servitude in South Africa, she was used to doing her own cooking and cleaning in England. The idea of employing servants went against all her Communist principles. The fact was, though, that it was impractical for a foreigner to go shopping for food (or anything else) without such a good command of the language as to be able to bargain a reasonable price, particularly in a period of hyper-inflation. In addition, it was expected of foreigners to provide employment, and refusing to do so would simply be depriving some people of jobs. She gave in very soon, and to begin with they had a cook (Lao Yu) and an amah, an elderly lady tottering about on bound feet, to look after Jacob and Mog.

Not long after these servants had been taken on Hetta came screaming out of the wash house where she had seen a snake making its way over the lip of the 'lotus jar', a large pottery receptacle which served as bath and washbasin, and had a hole in the bottom. She insisted on the university authorities (their landlords) being alerted to this intrusion by a dangerous reptile. Eventually a distinguished looking gentleman in traditional Chinese dress came to investigate. He found the animal's mode of entry to the room, through its hole in the wall, and established its species as being harmless. He arranged for the hole to be filled in to prevent its return to the wash house. Hetta and William were embarrassed to discover that they had not been sent a pest controller or rat catcher, but the Professor of Zoology himself to deal with this problem.

Wherever they went a crowd would gather. They would surround them, at a safe distance (just beyond arms length) and simply watch in silence. Nothing would prevail on them to go away—they presumably had nothing better to do, and they were a novelty to be beheld in great seriousness. Talking to them, or attempting to look them in the eye, had no effect whatsoever. Walter developed a way of dealing with these watchers, which he said always worked, which was to look at their shoes. The shame of having their footwear observed made them melt away.

A different aspect of the Chinese was their treatment of people in adversity. Possibly because of the recent history of China—of foreign invasion and then civil war, lasting well over twenty years, the public seemed completely inured to suffering. Beggars did not do well, even with ghastly disfigurements. Their personal experience of this came when Jacob was out on a cycling expedition with Hetta. He was seated behind her, and his foot became caught between the wheel and the strut holding the seat up, so that the rotating spokes were stripping the skin off his ankle. His screams made her stop. They were seated on the pavement, with Hetta hysterically trying to sort out his foot, and appealing to passersby for help. Instead of gathering around to stare, in their usual way, not one even looked at them. There is a convention, perhaps apocryphal, that Chinese culture requires an offer of help to be unconditional—that is, anyone who had stopped and offered assistance would have been morally obliged to do more than simply arranging for a taxi home for us, but perhaps even pay medical bills, and who knows what else.

Another instance of 'ickle' Jacob's accident-proneness was his falling into the canal. These canals were virtually sewers, and dumping grounds for all sorts of rubbish—not bathing sites in any sense. But Hetta dived in without hesitation to rescue him from drowning in the cloacal mire. Was he testing his mother's devotion? The story of this incident was recounted so many times that the truth became submerged in embellishment, but it definitely became part of the Empson household canon of anecdotes.

During this time there was a change of cook. Lao Yu had a number of problems with the authorities. He was facing conscription into the army, had some obscure personal problems, and finally went berserk, banging his head on the rockery until he was taken away. (In fact he went to work for David Kidd, outside the city near Tsinghua University, where he felt that he was beyond the reach of any Peking authorities who might be looking for him.)

Guan Shi Fu was the replacement for Lao Yu. He was a man of considerable presence, and was to become much more than a mere cook. By repute, he had been employed in the German Embassy, and was trained in the traditional French culinary repertoire. It was a permanent disappointment to him that he was hardly ever allowed to demonstrate his accomplishments in European cuisine, and was almost always required to produce Chinese meals. As time went by Mog and Ickle Jacob spent much of their time in his kitchen, learning bawdy songs and obscene swear words with which to hold their own with the other children in the compound. He liked to show off his skills, too, for instance making noodles the traditional way by juggling a piece of dough between his two hands so that it first divided into half a dozen thick strands, then more, and finally he was waving his hands with hundreds of thin noodles bouncing between them, ready to be plunged into the boiling broth. He would also demonstrate how to kill and pluck a chicken, and he even allowed Ickle Jacob to watch him beheading a turtle.

Most of all, though, Guan Shi Fu used his personal presence and authority to instil what was right and proper in his young charges. As John Haffenden described in his biography of William, he was 'a Manchu and ultra-conservative: he would always speak of the free-spirited Hetta with awed admiration—from of old, he had heard of Manchu ladies who carried on like Hetta'ˣ. A curious combination of discipline, high moral rectitude and unlikely songs and anecdotes, he became the final authority for us boys on issues extending well beyond the kitchen, not only on matters Chinese but much more.

The weather in Peking ranged from the baking hot in the summer to being bitterly cold in winter, and the springtime was characterised by a high wind from the West, carrying sand from as far away as the Gobi Desert. At the same time as the sandy wind, there would be camels appearing in the streets, carrying salt and other goods from the West—it seemed as though the wind had blown them into town. In the winter there were hot sweet potatoes on sale in the street to keep you warm, although their feet would get so cold that when they got home they had to put them in tepid water to warm them up. In summer there was sugar cane, sold in lengths of a foot, which you could chew as you walked along.

Jacob and friend Yu Wei

In 1948 William had a trip to the U.S., to a summer school at Kenyon College, in Ohio. The Chinese currency had been under severe pressure, and inflation was raging. It was a true story in their canon that Pa took three rickshaws, piled high with notes, to the airport to pay for his ticket to San Francisco, but there still wasn't enough, and he had to get another rickshaw's worth from the bank to make up the shortfall. In fact, John Haffenden's careful research has shown that only one large bag of bank-notes was involved, although upon counting at the airport there was indeed a shortfall (presumably with changes in exchange rates during the rickshaw trip, and the counting process), and more notes did have to be obtained.

The university had resorted to paying its staff in kind (giving out heads of tea, and bags of rice) in addition to paying wages which had become virtually worthless through inflation. William was able to send U.S. dollars home from Ohio, and was also spared having to pay any U.S. income tax on his salary from Kenyon College on account of his high travelling expenses, and family commitments. He met Walter and David Kidd's mothers, who gave him parcels to take back for their sons. He also bought *Alice in Wonderland*, *Alice Through the Looking Glass*, and a selection of Beatrice Potter books to bring back to Peking for his boys. While in America he was offered jobs by Ohio State University, and Iowa University, as well as being offered $500 by a literary magazine to republish three chapters from his book, so felt quite pleased with himself in his letters to Hetta. He had the $500 in cash which he proposed to sew into the shoulder pads of his jacket, which would 'stand a search by a lowminded customs official'. Unfortunately this was not to be—what was left of the $500 was stolen from him when his dawdling boat reached Manila.

The civil war finally came to Peking itself with the Communist Eighth Route Army of the PLA (People's Liberation Army) surrounding the city and enforcing a siege. C.P. Fitzgerald wrote that Fu Tso-yi (the Kuomintang general defending Peking)

'retired into the walled city of Peking, an oblong enclosure measuring fourteen miles, and in this medieval fortress prepared, in the twentieth century, to stand a siege against an army provided with heavy artillery. His garrison numbered about seventy thousand men, the civil population exceeded two millions. In all the records of modern warfare no other such improbable operation as the siege of Peking has occurred to enliven the task of the historian. Yet for six weeks, from 13 December 1948, to 22 January 1949, this strange siege continued'.[xi]

This was an exciting time for the household, and of course they had their hopes for a Communist victory. It was therefore with mixed feelings that Jacob submitted to being played with, thrown in the air, and entertained by Nationalist troops in the *hutung*. The city was absolutely full of these KMT troops, who were there to shelter from the communists more than to act as a credible defence of Peking. As the weeks passed it became clear that their cat *Mao* was missing, until Walter spotted his pelt stretched out to dry outside the gatekeeper's lodge of their compound. Although they did not suffer severe food shortages (with the university supplementing salaries in the form of heads of tea and rice) it was clear that some of their neighbours were very much more vulnerable, and were suffering near-starvation. Cat meat is not a favourite of Chinese cuisine, but of course when circumstances dictate almost any sort of meat can be accommodated—and completely without shame.

The Communist armies were quite close to the city, and had occupied Tsinghua University, just outside the city boundaries. Hetta decided to go over to the communist-held territory, in her capacity as an international journalist representing *The Observer* in London. This would also allow her to take provisions—bedclothes and flour—for colleagues teaching at Tsinghua who may have been stranded there. One of William's students was the son of the Garrison Commander, and he provided her and Walter with a car with an official badge on the windscreen. There was no problem in leaving the city by the Western Gate, where the main road was full of soldiers on lorries, horse-drawn carts and on horseback, making their way in the opposite direction, into the city. Once out of the city their driver removed the official badge and sat on it, in case they met Communist troops. At the Tsinghua campus they found that lights were blazing, and the students were relaxing by skating on the Lotus

Pond. (In Peking itself there had been no electricity or mains water for two weeks.) Classes had been resumed in the university, and there was an air of normality, although the vice-chancellor had in fact disappeared. Colleagues in the English Department she spoke to told her that he had absconded to Nanking with all the university's money, so now there was nothing with which to pay their salaries. Otherwise, they were coping well, and the Eighth Route Army had left the university strictly alone after restoring the electricity and mains water supplies. There were even notices on the gates into the campus forbidding the soldiers to enter.

Although all was now peaceable, there had been a bombing raid by the KMT in the last days before their withdrawal from the area. In an amateurish attempt to bomb the campus, which would have been farcical if it were not so dangerous, a small transport plane had circled for an hour and a half before the door opened and some bombs were pushed out. Fortunately there were no casualties. Hetta and Walter were offered the hospitality of dormitory beds, but, more importantly for her, the first hot bath she had had in two weeks. They stayed the night before returning home the next day, which was not so easy. All would have been well at the check point, with their official car, if she had not been recognized by a couple of Chinese who had been detained, and were not being allowed to pass into the city. They were professors at Tsinghua, who were trying to get home to their families in the city. They asked Hetta to help, as they'd been kept there for three hours already. When she collected letters from her friends to take to their families, the soldiers became more unfriendly, and she and Walter were kept in the guardhouse, sitting with a lieutenant and a group of soldiers. They said that they had to find out whether she and Walter were Communist infiltrators. This involved smoking her cigarettes, asking silly questions, and even giving Walter a machine gun to see if he knew how to work it, while their identity cards were being checked. After two hours of this, Hetta suggested to the lieutenant that the man checking the identity cards might be illiterate, which was why he could come to no decision about them. This seemed to hit the right note, as they were then sent through the gate with their cards, to be checked over by the state police in the city.

William, not to be outdone, remembered that he was scheduled to give a lecture on *Macbeth* at Tsinghua University on 31st December, and, using this as a pretext, braved the lines to go there. He was immensely impressed by what he called the beautiful evangelistic feelings of the communist troops who captured him. They let him proceed to Tsinghua, where, in fact, the boys did not want to be lectured to. He did not go the following week, but it had been a very elegant New Year for him.

As an accredited journalist with *The Observer*, Hetta was sending them regular despatches, including telegrams, many of which were published, although payments for them were rather erratic. On 11th July 1949 she wrote to Mr Tomlinson, her editor at The Observer,

> Dear Mr Tomlinson,
>
> I am informed by my bank (Midland Bank, Belsize Park) that you have paid in some £18 to my account after I had sent five news stories to you, most of considerable length. I paid for the cabling costs of the first two. What I have heard from private letters leads me to believe that all were published. I am surprised to have had no statement from you, and would be glad to hear why no further payment has been made. You informed me that full rates had been agreed upon.

> You understand that the Military Government,
> under which we are still living, does not allow any
> correspondents' activities, but the establishment of a civil
> Government in a few months and the whole position may
> then be changed.[xii]

The fact that she was sending regular despatches despite the government ban on foreign correspondent activity meant, of course, that she was putting herself at risk of arrest if found out. Her motivation here must have been political—to make sure that events in China were brought to the attention of the progressive readers of *The Observer*.

C.P. Fitzgerald's *Revolution in China* describes how General Lin Piao, leading the Eighth Route Army besieging Peking, was most concerned to take the city without significant loss of life, and with minimal damage to historic buildings. When he first arrived outside Peking the plan had been to storm the walls after an artillery bombardment. As he had occupied the two universities of TsingHua and Yenching, ten miles outside the city, he took the opportunity to consult the leading architect and archaeologist in China, Professor Liang Ssu-ch'eng, on whether the walls in question were of historical or archaeological significance. Professor Liang told him that the proposed point of attack included a wall almost unique in being a surviving piece of Ming military architecture, and suggested an alternative site, which was then adopted as the preferred point of attack, should that become necessary. There cannot have been many military campaigns planned with so scrupulous a regard for archaeology and architecture.

There had always been shit carts in Peking, carrying the 'night soil' out of the city gates to fertilize fields in the country. They were extraordinarily smelly, although, curiously, if you got close enough to one then the smell seemed to disappear (presumably the ammonia, by then, completely overwhelmed the sense of smell). Apparently the city had been provided with wonderful drains, in antiquity, and there was even a Minister of Drains. Every year there was an inspection of the drains, when the Minister was carried through them in his litter (after they had been thoroughly cleaned). At the end of the tour there was a banquet, the Minister applied his seal to confirm that the drains were in good order, and the Department of Drains was given their annual all clear. One year, an enterprising manager in the Department came up with the idea of having a banquet before the inspection. The Minister could be relied upon to be too drunk to notice that he had not been carried through the drains to the final banquet, where he applied his seal without realising that he had been duped. The drains did not have to be cleaned. This practice became a tradition, so that by the time of the liberation of Peking, in 1949, the drains had been completely blocked for many years, and the city was now relying on the shit carts. (There was also an economic reason for the continuation of this practice, in that the contents of the carts had a commercial value, being used as fertilizer on the fields outside the city.)

During the siege of Peking the shit-carts were of course not allowed to leave the city, and, it being winter, there was no risk to public health as all their contents were frozen. One of the considerations that the Nationalist commander of Peking (Fu Tso-yi) had to take into account, in the event of the siege being prolonged into the spring and summer, was that there would certainly be widespread cholera. The Garrison Commander's son (the same who had lent Hetta the official car for her trip through the lines to Tsinghua University) had overheard talk of a plan to execute all foreigners rather than let them witness the consequences of holding out. According to Fitzgerald[xiii], Fu's reluctance to give in was related to his personal feelings about the Communist general facing him, Lin Piao. He felt that Lin had gone back on his word, and he had been deceived. Lin Piao was guilty of treachery in coming and besieging him. The reality of the situation was that the nearest Nationalist troops were over five hundred miles away (apart from those besieged in Tientsin), so there was no realistic outcome except defeat. Mao Tse-tung and Chu Teh (another famous general and Long March veteran) solved the problem by relieving Lin Piao of his duties in Peking, and sending him to supervise the taking of Tientsin, on the coast. They appointed another general, Nie Jung-chen, to negotiate with Fu. 'Face' was thus saved, and Peking was surrendered on the 22nd January, and all the foreigners survived.

One day, shortly after the end of the siege, and the 'liberation' of Peking by the Eighth Route Army, Ickle Jacob was on his own in the middle courtyard when there was a hammering on the door into the *hutung*. This was imposing structure, a *ch-lan men*, or, literally 'barrier-gate. It had a high stone threshold, and the heavy door was lacquered crimson, with brass fittings. He went and opened it. Standing in front of him was an officer of the PLA, and behind him, as far as he could see, were PLA soldiers in neat formation. The officer looked down at him and said, 'Let us in. We are billeted here.' Despite his approval of the PLA he could see that they could not possibly put all these people up, so he did the only thing possible. He slammed the door in his face, and ran off to find Guan Shi Fu. It was obviously a problem which would be beyond his parents. Guan Shi Fu duly came and sorted out where the soldiers were really supposed to be staying.

The civil war was by no means over, although the north of the country was entirely under Communist control with a government installed in Peking. Normal life continued in the North as the civil war proceeded in the South, and William was able to go to the United States during the summer, as planned, to his summer school at Kenyon College. Despite the fact that there were still Nationalist forces holding out in the south of the country, and Chiang Kai Shek had yet to make his retreat to Formosa, by Ickle Jacob's fifth birthday (30th September 1949) the Communist government was celebrating victory of the new republic, with Peking as the capital, with an Inauguration Day parade. Hetta and William both went with David Kidd to join the crowds in Tien An Men square and watch the spectacle, which was both military and civilian, and went on for hours. The Department of Geography from Peita had pledged to dance all night.

Chapter 3

China: From Liberation to Tilbury

E ven after the siege was over, and the establishment of the Peoples Republic, travel was not permitted. Nobody could leave the city without a permit. Hetta even had a recurring dream of flying with her friend Irene Vincent, over the city walls—a Freudian wish-fulfilment if there ever was one. At long last there was a dispensation on travel for a trip to the Great Wall by Peking University students and staff. This required a good deal of forward planning and applications, organized by Max Bickerton. The anticipation only increased their excitement about the trip, and, not surprisingly, when the big day came it was one that was partly a disaster.

At the station there were students marching in columns of four going up the platform. Jacob was running. All of a sudden he was on the ground, having collided with one of the iron columns holding up the roof, and was lying there bleeding. The impact had knocked him out for a moment, and he was confused, unable to remember what he was doing there or who he was with. Nobody took any notice of him, but kept up their progress marching along the platform. At last somebody he recognized broke through the ranks and came to his rescue. Reunited with his mother, a bandage was found, and the trip continued.

At The Great Wall he was given a donkey to ride, on account of his having fallen over. There was a big bandage around his head which kept falling down over his eyes, and having his hands holding onto the saddle made it difficult to push it back up. Now and then the wound would be re-opened, and blood would be coming down over his eyes, again obscuring his view of the Wall. He felt sick.

At the clinic where he eventually had stitches put in the medics were interrogating Hetta, questioning her account of the accident having only just happened, and obviously aware that Ickle Jacob's cut on the head had been neglected all day. 'Examine your ideology, comrade' was something that was said in reproach for this neglectful mother. Jacob smiled to himself as his mother was being criticised. Quite right, too!

A few days later, Hetta was having a drink with David Kidd in the middle courtyard. It was one of his last visits to the house before he and Aimee were to leave China forever. He was dressed entirely in white, wearing a white Panama hat, and with an ivory cigarette holder held in between his long elegant fingers. Hetta was wearing her blue communist uniform. She was telling him about their trip.

'My dear, it was a disastrous day. I had Jack Chen's little boy with us, as well as Mog and Jacob. When we got to the station no one wanted us on the train! The people Max had arranged with were different from the people in charge and they said if we hadn't got tickets it was impossible and you can't buy them in the ordinary way. Can you believe it?'

"No!" said David, "what did you do then?"

'Someone else said, oh just follow and get in the hell with it, and he grabbed the children and started running while we had our passes checked. Then he came running back with Jacob dripping with blood. The poor little dumb idiot had shut his eyes tight and run, and run into an iron pillar with an iron projection and cut his forehead clear to the bone.'

"My god! Is he all right?"

'More or less. I caught him up and ran to where they had first-aid and they bandaged him up. It looked pretty awful to me so I said I'd take him to hospital, then I went back to tell the others at the train, and they said Jake'd be madder if we didn't take him on the train than if he died from his wounds, and I was so dazed I said what the hell let's go.'

"Bravo! I'm sure that was the right thing to do."

'When we got there Jacob was alright but I had delayed shock and what with not sleeping and feeling in the wrong and guilty. Generally I was a pretty mess. I put the children on donkeys, and then had to run my guts out because I thought Jake would fall off and bust his head open again.'

"But you got to the Wall after all that, did you?"

'Yes, we got to the Wall and it was blowing a bitter wind and Pa found the most uncomfortable place on a steep slope to eat. I found somewhere out of the wind to open the Pai Gar and began to recover my nerve. Then all the donkey men crowded round and I find afterwards that I told them lots of stories about the Great City and the animal that is four different kinds of animal.'

"Had you drunk the whole bottle?"

'Don't know. The donkey men might have had some. They put me on a donkey too, but I fell off and they all laughed. The others went for a walk up the Wall, and I took the children back to the station and took the first train back. The American Drucker also came back and it was a nice empty train and he sang me American working-class ballads all the way. We got in at 7.30.'

"Did Jacob ever get to the hospital?"

'Yes, I took him to the PUMC and had two stitches put in his head. When I got back Pa thought we'd got lost or arrested or something because they'd got back earlier than us to find us gone.'

"My dear, let me get you another drink."

'Thanks.'

"Has he had his stitches taken out?"

'Not yet. He's due at the PUMC today to have them out this afternoon.'

"Have you seen Max since?"

'Oh yes. Next night Max took me and Eugene and a friend of his with sticking-out ears to dinner at Kieslings to eat a lot of prawns and then we went dancing till twelve.'

One day, not long after this Hetta took Mog and Jacob to the campus at Peita, and left them with their bicycles in the large central square of the university, known as the 'Democratic Ground'. She saw one of William's students, and left the boys in his charge while she went looking for William in his office on the second floor of the 'Red Building'. Jacob couldn't ride yet, and needed someone to hold the saddle while he pedalled. Mog was dashing about on his bike, showing off. The student was holding the saddle, and pushing Jacob along, going faster and faster. All of a sudden he gave the bike an almighty shove and let go. Jacob barrelled along, pedalling furiously, and found that he could ride after all. He never needed any further instruction.

For many years Jacob would tell his school-mates in England how they had steam-driven buses in Peking, where there was no petrol. All the stocks of petrol in the country were naturally requisitioned by the armies conducting the civil war. As he became more knowledgeable about steam engines, it became obvious that this was a ridiculous idea—one could never convert a petrol engine to run on coal and steam. He stopped talking about it, but the memory of the buses with their steaming engines on the back stayed with him. Eventually, listening to a radio documentary about alternative applications for powering combustion engines, the answer came to him—his memory was not at fault, but the description of the buses as being 'steam buses' was misleading. The steaming engine attached to the rear of the rear of the bus was in fact a furnace filled with burning coke. Water would be dripped onto this fire, and the gas given off—'water gas'—was a mixture of hydrogen and carbon monoxide. The chemical reaction involved is 'endothermic'—having the effect of cooling the coke and putting the fire out—so there would have to be careful control of the relative amounts of water introduced, and the bellows providing air to maintain combustion.

In any case, this lethally combustible mixture was then fed by a pipe to the engine at the front of the bus, and the water tap and the bellows were linked to the accelerator pedal. One can imagine that it would be a reasonable method of propulsion if the demand was constant—if the bus was proceeding at a constant speed on a level surface, but it would fail to respond quickly to an increase in demand (for acceleration or going uphill) and there would be a waste of gas when the demand reduced, with braking and slowing, as the rate of production would not reduce correspondingly. Presumably the steam that we saw was the result of vapours leaking from the improvisation. Almost certainly an extremely hazardous solution to the oil shortage!

Mog and Ickle Jacob would be hanging about in the kitchen with Guan Shi Fu, learning new swear words and bawdy, scatological songs, and listening to him lay down the law about what was right and what was wrong. One day he announced that he would take them to the cinema. So, on a Saturday afternoon they set off down the *hutung* and onto the main street, where Guan Shi Fu hailed a taxi. (Three of them would have been too many for a pedicab.) Taxis in Peking were typically American Ford V8s, with their very distinctive sloping backs, and this was one of those. They opened the passenger door to get in, and found that there were already three passengers on board, sitting on little stools. There were three more stools available, though, so they could all sit down. The driver kept the original bench seat, but the rear seats had been removed. (These cabs functioned more like buses than taxis, as people got on and off on demand, rather like the way 8-seater people carriers are used in third world countries such as Egypt to this day).

The cinema was packed, with soldiers with rifles shouldered, standing at the back and down the aisles on the side. This gave an additional excitement to the experience (although, with hindsight, perhaps these young men were being allowed an afternoon at the cinema for free). The film was a patriotic account of resistance to the Japanese invasion, alternating between being action packed and exciting, and then scary and tense, as poisoned steamed dumplings were being offered to the Japanese soldiers by the Chinese grandmother whose house they had requisitioned. When the greedy

Japanese soldiers ate them all, and lay about clutching their stomachs and groaning as they died, the whole audience was cheering and applauding.

There was a playground with a real Japanese warplane. You could get into the cockpit and play with the controls. One of them was on a rachet which you could run up and down, making an impressive noise of automatic gunfire. At the same time, the children outside could throw stones and bricks at the cockpit windows. These were impervious, being bullet-proof. The intention of providing the plane for children to play in was presumably to demonstrate the defeat of the Japanese and their technology. In fact it had the opposite effect on Jacob and his playmates—they thought the Japanese plane was terrific, and particularly admired the windows which could withstand bricks being hurled at them.

When they went out with servants they seemed to seek out the most crowded streets—perhaps on the basis that if there was a crowd there must be something going on that was worth seeing. In this way they joined in with the *lao bai xing* (literally, 'old hundred names', referring the limited number of Chinese surnames, and used as a slightly derogatory term for the general public). They went to the markets, and also to the streets specializing in specific products—for instance furniture, fireworks, or crossbows and bows and arrows. A few months before they left China Hetta and Walter took the boys to a shop in the crossbow street. The old man demonstrated how he could fire a clay pellet from a huge bow, miraculously missing his thumb. For the less adept, they could provide thumb-guards. They had crossbows of all sizes, and Mog and Ickle Jacob got one each, Mog's being the larger. They were loaded with clay pellets through a hole at the breach end of the barrel, and there was pig bristle to prevent the pellet rolling out if you were pointing downwards.

The winters in Peking were very cold, although snow was rare. It snowed only once while they were there. The lakes would of course freeze over, and the one in Bei Hai park with the island and pagoda in the middle was the one which was a designated skating area. The family would all go there together, Walter bringing his skates and reminiscing about skating in Michigan in the winter, and Hetta generally staying on the shore in her furs with a thermos.

In the summer there were family trips to the parks of the Summer Palace, with its lakes (and the wonderful marble boat). They had long boat trips among the giant waterlilies, and would picnic on the islands. Jacob learned to swim in the pool at the embassy in a fashion similar to his bicycling lesson, by being thrown in by Walter. They also went to the huge open-air public baths, which had small pools with mushroom-shaped fountains as well as the full-sized pools with diving boards.

After a brief spell at a French nursery the two boys eventually went to the *Kong De Xiao Xue*, a Chinese nursery school—starting there after the Liberation. They were taken there every day in a pedicab. The days began with the flag being run up the pole, and the singing of the national anthem. Then they sat in a classroom, and had lessons. Every day they were supposed to learn to write a new character (and were tested on all the ones that they were supposed to have learned already.) There was a memorable day when *Yen* was the character for the day. They already knew that one, as it was their family name, in Chinese, meaning 'swallow' (the bird). Curiously, the hieroglyphic for *Yen* contains the radical 'kou', meaning 'mouth'—so the idea of swallowing was associated with this bird in both English and Chinese cultures. Teaching was very traditional, and discipline was strict—or, more accurately, hardly necessary, since there was no question except that all the children should be attentive, quiet, and extremely respectful towards the teacher. After lunch every day they would have a nap, with everyone on their own little camp bed. As well as learning Chinese, they did arithmetic, and also had lessons on improving subjects such as agrarian reform.

To begin with, the other children assumed that they were Russians, with their Western looks and blond hair. Russians were still regarded as China's 'elder brothers', so it was disappointing to have to tell them the truth.

Mog and Ickle Jacob joined the Young Pioneers as a matter of course, and were proud to wear their red neckerchiefs. They both took their Communist duties seriously, but Mog especially so—one day he noticed somebody in the street behaving suspiciously, and he alerted the police, who made an arrest. After that he had the reputation of being well in with the secret police—the *Gong An Ji* (literally, 'Work Tranquility Office'!)

As well as going to nursery they went to a temple to learn shadow boxing. This was more like ballet than martial arts. One had to learn sequences of moves, done very slowly but in strict tempo and sequence, which were rather puzzling in their purpose. Jacob never really got the hang of it, although learning some moves, but Mog became quite advanced, and progressed to the stage of having two swords. He was allowed to bring the swords home, one day, to demonstrate his accomplishment with them to the grownups.

The servant who usually took them to nursery in the pedicab, Lao Chan, was to get into trouble with the authorities for black market offences. His punishment was to attend the police station once a week, to report to the sergeant and read aloud the diary he was supposed to have kept. This was to be filled with self-improving thoughts, and plans to improve his ideology. A dreadful punishment for a semi-literate—it was an example of the experimental methods that the Communist authorities were trying out to modernise the judicial system. Lao Chan evidently did not become completely transformed by this regime, as he was sacked, along with the housekeeper, in 1950, after which Mog and Jacob had to walk to nursery school for a while.

The story which made most impression on Jacob about the benefit of the new regime was the one about the city drains. The new government made a point of discovering where the ancient drains were, and, in the interests of public health, to clear them out and restore them to their former function, putting the shit carts out of business. As Hetta was to say in her introduction to the book *Contemporary Chinese Woodcuts*, 'Forty thousand soldiers and workers are being employed draining and dredging the lakes and the sewers, which have not been cleaned since the Ming Dynasty.'

While, in some ways, the new government revolutionized the judicial system, and experimented with novel methods of imposing law and order, in other ways they were to stick to traditional forms of punishment. Walter was to write from Shansi on May 21st, 1950,

> The streets were lined as far as I could see and everyone
> was turned in the direction of the center of the city as
> if they were waiting for something to come. At last a
> student told me in English that the govt. had shot three

people but he couldn't tell me any more except that they were criminals. Then a motorcycle came speeding along clearing the way. I looked up on the city wall and found it was jammed with people all looking in the direction of the Provincial govt. offices. The whole city had turned out. Just then I ran into one of my students who told me that they were <u>about</u> to shoot three sabattours (I know that's not right but its not in my dictionary) who had damaged the railway last July and caused a big accident. Just then the motorcycle came back again followed by two trucks the first with the firing squad all dressed up in their new brown hats and the next with the three condemned men thrust to the front of the truck, tied with their arms behind their backs and with white paper banners tied to their backs and sticking up over their heads. Horrible faces they were. The crowd only murmured as they passed. Then came three mule-carts loaded with twisted pieces of railroad track, two metal saws and some other tools. The carts had big signs probably describing the evidence. The crowd fell in behind the procession which moved very slowly out of the gate. I swarmed with several thousand others up the city wall which gave a perfect view of the place of execution about two li out of the city at the Fun river. I looked back at the city, a scene of complete desolation. Only a few children playing in the streets and all the ruins of buildings, desolate. On the outside of the wall the crowd soon got the holiday spirit. Little boys appeared selling icecream sticks. The top of the wall is fortunately supplied with urinals and people stood in line waiting their turns. (The most profitable concession at the

New York Worlds Fair was the pay toilet). It was like the bleachers at a ball game. I never did eat any lunch today.

Hetta had her own brush with the judicial system. In the early hours of the morning after an evening dancing and drinking at 'the Dump', she and Walter were leaving to go home. They found their way blocked by pedicabs, which had been parked to prevent anyone getting through, and the pedicab drivers were demanding exorbitant fees. So not only could they not get out, but a pedicab was out of the question at that price. There was an altercation, at the end of which Hetta became so impatient and enraged with one of the drivers that she smacked him in the face. (One of her smacks could easily fell a grown man.) All discussion stopped as the police were called, and then they all marched in a crocodile down to the police station. Hetta was questioned separately from the driver, and her interview with the young examining magistrate lasted until well into the morning. Every detail of the events outside 'the Dump' were laboriously considered, from every angle, all in Chinese. The facts of the case having been established, she was invited to discuss the rightness of her actions, to examine her ideology, and to criticize herself. Eventually, the magistrate told her that he was satisfied that there were wrongs on both sides, and that, provided she did not assault another pedicab driver in the future, she was free to go. Finally, he asked, in excellent English, 'And what do you think of our methods, comrade?'

David Kidd had a different experience, described in his own memoir, *All the King's Horses*. The Empson's original cook in Peking, Lao Yu, had gone to work for him at his house near Tsinghua University, but had not lasted long in the job—the head-banging on the rockery resumed, and David had let him go, fearing that this behavior might develop into a knife or chopper-wielding stage. He was now, post-Liberation, begging on the streets, handing out a card describing his misfortunes, in English on one side, and in Chinese on the other. By chance, he thrust one of these into David's hand without having recognized him. The card named him as an American imperialist who had forced him to work in fear and misery, and for nothing. They ended up before a judge, who asked Lao Yu why he had not filed a suit a year ago, when all this happened.

"But our Liberation Army hadn't come yet. The courts and officials were all on the side of the foreigners."

'I didn't think we were too bad,' said the judge, looking around.

"Oh, not you, Comrade!" Lao Yu cried. "I mean the corrupt officials we had before liberation."

'I was an official before liberation,' the judge said, 'In fact, I was a judge, right here.'

'Why didn't you quit when you weren't paid?' the judge went on.

This judge was most unsympathetic towards Lao Yu, but did not have the authority to dismiss the case—it had to be referred to the Central Ministry of Justice, with his recommendation, but with no guarantee as to how long a final decision would take. Lao Yu managed to drag David to one of the new People's Courts for a faster verdict. This court saw through Lao Yu at once, but suggested that David might give him a small proportion of what he was asking for, since he was obviously destitute, in return for a legal waiver of all claims.

The last that David saw of him was a few months later, when he was riding in a pedicab on the Avenue of Long Peace. The road was being widened to accommodate the triumphal parades planned to celebrate the inauguration of the People's Republic. Gangs of prisoners were carrying stones and pouring tar. Lao Yu was in one of these, singing one of the new Communist songs with the others. Presumably he had been picked up for begging, or perhaps for a less successful exercise in extortion from another previous employer.

When the Korean War started there were a lot of Chinese volunteers who went to fight the Americans, including many of William's students. Their new nurserys' part in the war effort was to collect money for presents for the boys at the front. Something went wrong with their collection—the money got lost somehow, and Mog and Jacob had in the end to give rather paltry presents—some pencils and a notebook. Their playground games with paper guns were always Korean War games, with the baddies being the Americans.

The authorities took the threat of a nuclear strike on Peking very seriously, and the nursery had its own atom bomb drills. During these the children got under their desks, put their thumbs in their ears and two fingers over each eye, and their little fingers over their mouths, to keep them shut. In fact there were indeed serious plans to attack China with nuclear weapons. John Foster Dulles was dissuaded from this by the U.S. military, who revealed to him that they only had four nuclear warheads at that stage. For all their destructive power their use against such a huge country would not have been decisive, and would only have caused a furious all-out conventional retaliation on their expeditionary forces in Korea.

Most foreigners left China during this period, and there were concerns for those remaining—Walter even received two letters from the U.S. government advising him to leave. One result of this was the paucity of people to socialise on the diplomatic circuit, and Hetta and William were surprised and pleased to be invited to a dinner at the Danish Embassy. On the appointed day they dressed themselves up and set off in a pedicab, arriving at the Dutch ambassador's residence, where they were received most graciously. As more and more drinks and nibbles arrived, and conversation stalled, it appeared they were the only guests. Finally, the ambassador's wife left the room, came back a few minutes later and whispered to her husband. He then said, 'We should not detain you any longer—I do believe that you are expected for dinner at the Danish Embassy!' It was a very small world indeed in Peking in those days.

The traditional role for the professor's wife, in England, would have been to support him in relation to his colleagues, for instance by entertaining, and being a charming guest. She might particularly cultivate the wives of his superiors. In addition, she would provide sympathetic advice to the wives of junior lecturers, on matters domestic, such as where to buy their first house, or how to furnish it. Female students might be advised on matters of the heart (including the practicalities of contraception). Hetta was never to follow this pattern, and much of this would in any case have been inappropriate in the context of Peking. She had her own part-time employment as a teacher of English at Peita. Also, as a Party member (albeit of a foreign Party) she was expected to attend meetings and to maintain a level of political activity. Before the victorious siege at Peking she had even been called upon to help academics and students escape from the KMT's (Kuo Min Tang's) killing squads. They were smuggled at night out of their dormitories in the university, sometimes to the Empson house at 11 Dong Gau Fan, from where they would be ferried to the safety of hospitals where they could be hidden by the medical staff. Having more than one entrance to the house allowed them to be taken in through one, and let out through another, to shake off any police or informers following them.

Hetta's foray into revolutionary theatre started as a Punch and Judy show. It turned out that Max had an accomplishment in puppetry, part of his background as an assistant in his father's fairground in Christchurch, New Zealand.

On 27ᵗʰ December 1949 Hetta wrote to Irene and John Vincent

> . . . 'Walter and I worked hard for a solid week before Xmas to make a real Punch and Judy show, because we discovered that Max Bickerton can do the manipulating and talking.'
>
> Max's father was a Federalist in New Zealand in 1899, whose attempt at communal life failed after some of the people stole the silver and ran away, and then the disapproval of the University (free love, etc), ended up turning the site, an island on a lake, into an amusement park, including a zoo and Punch and Judy.
>
> Parker made the booth for the puppet show with red and white stripes.
>
> 'Well we put it on for the Children's Party at the CLUB my dear and some little ones were carried away screaming, and sad Mrs Kandel looked at me regretfully with her great cow eyes and said gloomily, "We thought it would be something jolly." And Mrs Clubb said "We should have asked more adults". It was all a lot of crap, because it was a lovely show. Max made the Doctor say to Punch, "I can't

waste my time on lower middle class cases like yours" so
Punch poked him in his lower middle until he was dead.

The experience of putting on the Punch and Judy show inspired
Hetta to produce a more serious, satirical show, based on real-life
participants. These included General De Gaulle, Sigman Rhee, Mao
Tse Tung, General MacArthur in his dark glasses, and a two-faced
figure with the angel of peace on one side, the blackened skull of
nuclear war on the other. These were used to perform a series of
political sketches in performances for the students at Peita. These
figures became part of the Empson children's toy box for many
years to come.

Hetta had been commissioned to sculpt a life-size bust of the
Indian ambassador, Sardar Pannikar, in bronze. He therefore became
a regular visitor to their house as the work progressed. She made her
models in clay and it was eventually translated into bronze as an
impressive head. This was probably the most important work that
she ever did in her career as a sculptor, which never really took off
after their return to England.

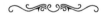

As well as these revolutionary, artistic and literary endeavours,
Hetta was engaged in a project with Walter to collect and export
Chinese pottery. Walter had found a source of interesting peasant
tea pots and cups, glazed in cream and brown, in Shansi. She also
planned to sell kites, 'unassembled, very nice, very chip, a dollar a
crack'. She was reliably informed by her friend Sid, along with Max
and David Kidd, that Americans never have more than one teapot
a lifetime, so the plan was to sell ashtrays, side plates, large plates,

bowls and saucers. Walter even tried to recall the address of a friend who was a big shot in a chain of New York dime stores, and was investigating the idea of exporting cheap jewellery. Walter wrote to her on May 16th, 1950

> I've spent the morning collecting samples of pots and what I say is its too good for peasants. I've got two of each item. There is a tea pot being made that I hadn't seen before which would appeal to the Americans much more than the others. The glaze is better and the shape though not as good will appeal more than the others. Regardless of what Sid says I think we should send tea pots. Lots of people have more than one, my grandmother for instance has about fifteen and can't resist a "cute" one. Anyway think of the people who haven't had one before and all the people just starting housekeeping. At 1,500 each I don't see how you can lose selling @ .25 or 35 cents and to Ye Olde Gifte Shoppe trade I'm sure they would sell at 75 cents to 1.50. There is a jardinière about one and a half feet high and as wide as that sells for 4,500 that I *know* would go over big as a fern and flower pot. It is the same cream glaze with brown, green and blue design of lotus, water weed and dragon fly, and it's got five character on the back. I think it's the nicest painting I've seen on peasant pots. I'm also sending some things that are probably to be had in Peking and some that probably have no market value but you can talk it over. What do you think of this black-brown bowl? Looks terribly Sungy don't it? Here is the price list.

Most of these pots were shattered when they eventually arrived in Peking, but they continued to plan this enterprise, and collected more and more crockery over the following year or so.

During one of the vacations when Walter was staying at Dong Gau Fan he came back from a night out (possibly at the 'Dump') with a puppy. He had found it abandoned in the mens' lavatory, and decided to rescue and adopt it. Putty, as she was known, became a permanent resident in their house. A typical Peking dog, she was short-haired, terrier sized, with black, white and brown markings, and a tail which stood straight up and then arched a little over her back. She had a puppy of her own in good time, and between them they made mischief. Hetta wrote to Walter in March 1950—

> A horrible thing, Putty and the puppy disembowelled the duck. I hate them both. It was her disgusting child incited her to do it. We haven't told Li Hsieh yet.

In the summer vacation of 1950 Walter also brought a snake back from Shansi University. It was not very big—slightly longer than a grass snake—and was not poisonous. It was probably a rat snake. He and Jacob spent many hours trying to catch lizards for it on the walls of the courtyard, using cups to trap them. Mog had a horror of snakes, and would have nothing to do with it. After this Walter and Jacob became a nature study group of their own.

For Jacob's sixth birthday he was given a monkey. She was a smallish rhesus monkey who had spent many weeks in a pet shop being jeered at by children. Unsurprisingly she did not take to him, and promptly bit his hand, making a deep wound in the ball of the thumb. Named Coco, she was provided a cage in the middle courtyard, and would be let out to run around, and to climb the tree. She was basically a wild animal, and something had to be done to tame her. Hetta's method, when Coco had done something particularly outrageous, was to take a hot flannel and hold it over the monkey's face, which seemed to induce a trance-like immobility. Afterwards, she clung to Hetta as though she was her saviour, and gradually began to behave herself. Coco stayed with the family for the next two years, until their departure for London. She gradually became tamer, and could be let out of the cage to join them after mealtimes, but was always more of a force to be reckoned with than an actual pet.

It was during 1951 that there was a rumour about rabies, and even that a girl in the compound (who did indeed have a scar on her leg) had been bitten by a rabid dog. Putty became a suspect. In due course a small van arrived in the *hutung*, and two men with nets on poles (like butterfly nets) came to catch Putty and take her away in the van. It wasn't until Jacob was forty years old that Hetta told him that Putty had never had rabies, and that she was taken away as part of a campaign against dogs in the city.

There was also a campaign against flies, and they had to fill jam jars with dead houseflies to take to their nursery school. It was amazing how many flies one could accumulate, with persistence.

The story-teller was a regular visitor to the compound. Over a dozen children would gather around, and he would sit on his stool and talk. These were often traditional 'Monkey' episodes, or other stories from the classical repertoire. There wasn't much audience participation or singing along—the children would all simply listen, and he kept their attention with all the dramatic effects that could be achieved by the human voice, and an assistant with a small gong to punctuate important points in the narrative. Cliff-hanger endings were usual, so they should be sure to come back the following week.

More elaborate entertainments—when a performance was actually ordered and paid for by grown-ups, included shadow puppet plays and the mouse circus. Shadow puppetry was performed in the evening, with a white cotton sheet forming a screen, lighted from behind. The puppets, made of transparent leather (or vellum) were held on metal rods against the screen, and moved about as the action took place. The plays were normally inspired by Peking Opera, with puppets with wonderful headdresses, and their faces coloured to indicate who they were (bright red, or white, and so on). The high-pitched wailing delivery typical of Peking Opera was performed by actors behind the screen. This was more than a childrens' show, and the grownups would be there in the audience as well.

The mouse circus was perhaps a unique genre invented by its entrepreneurial showman. The mice did all sorts of clever tricks, and acted out exciting little scenarios.

Watching the mouse performance with a friend

Mog and Jacob in the courtyard

Mogador and Jacob left the nursery school in August 1951, when Jacob was awarded his nursery school leaving certificate, which he still has. It is more impressive than either of his degree certificates.

Jacob's nursery school leaving certificate,
presided over by Mao Tse Tung

During their last academic year in China efforts were made to teach them English, so that they would be able to go to school in England when they got there. William still had hopes of his sons getting into his old school, Winchester, when the time came. Accordingly, when term started they went to an English school run by catholic nuns. This provided the first of a number of culture shocks that they were to have in the next year or so. Early in the term they came home to say that they had been learning about 'the farmer, the son, and the holy goose'—conflating the puzzling stuff they were being told with the lessons on agrarian reform they had had in the nursery. They had never been to a religious service, but this school had daily catholic prayers and hymns in their chapel. Above the altar hung Jesus on the cross, and the nuns made a great deal of fuss about him. Mog decided to test out the veracity of this Jesus person, and went into the chapel on his own one day, and prodded Jesus hard with his finger. He found that Jesus was (literally) a plaster saint, and that he had made a hole quite easily in him. When he reported back to Jacob it was obvious to both of them that the nuns were deluded, and that they were better off with their Young Pioneer ideas.

Walter then took charge of their English language lessons, but had a difficult time finding a suitable set of books for them—the 'Janet and John' equivalents were obviously too infantile for boys who had already had the facts of life explained to them. He found some Russian adult education booklets for learning English, which had little pin-men illustrations. The text was set in Russia, so they learned about things like how to tell the time by the big clock on the main Moscow railway station, and travelling on the Moscow underground. They already had a complete set of Peter Rabbit books, which had been sent by Aunt Molly to ensure that they had proper reading matter. Like much in their lives, this combination of reading material formed a puzzling mixture.

Jacob, Walter and Mog

The final preparations for their departure included finding a home for Coco, who was not going to be allowed to come to England with them. Walter took care of this, and made sure that Coco joined the other rhesus monkeys in the troupe in the zoo. He took Jacob there to say goodbye to Coco, but Jacob found it difficult to see her amongst all the other monkeys.

Hetta then discovered that the British Council, who were funding their journey, had provided for a six ton luggage allowance. This stimulated her into a frenzy of furniture-buying. In one of the shops in a furniture street she found a source for 'temple rosewood' furniture—the notion being that it was made from wood looted from temples. In fact it was simply a description of what we'd call 'reclaimed' wood. She chose an austere Ming style for this reproduction furniture, which was a warm red rosewood. Four large wardrobes, three or four small ones, half a dozen *dongze*, or square stools, two or three low coffee tables, some chairs and three or four camphor chests were ordered and then put in packing cases for the journey, together with furniture that she had bought over the five years in Peking, such as the large round red lacquered dining table.

On their last evening in Peking Guan Shi Fu took the whole family out to dinner in one of Peking's best restaurants. They sat in a private room at a round table, with Guan Shi Fu sat next to Pa, and Hetta on his other side. He had often found Pa difficult to please with his food, and would become quite distraught when Pa went for periods not eating but just working and drinking. So he took great delight in making sure that Pa's bowl was never empty on this occasion, selecting his favourite morsels from the dishes spread out in front of us to give him. Pa reciprocated, and it became a family legend that they each gave each other their own favourite foods, and receiving the foods that they respectively abhorred, but felt compelled to eat out of politeness.

The first leg of their sea journey was to be from Tientsin to Hong Kong. They duly took the train to Tientsin, where there was a problem. Pa was not allowed to leave the country. In the event, Ma, Walter, Mog and Jacob took the boat to Hong Kong, leaving Pa behind. He was not imprisoned but was allowed to stay at the Tientsin Club until the problem was resolved. He wrote briefly about this incident in his book, *Milton's God*,

'When I was emerging from Communist China in 1952 there was a midnight eve-of-sailing removal of my passport, never explained, which gave me an interesting peep for two weeks at the nerve-wracked foreign business community of Tientsin and its weeping but heroic bank managers.'[xiv]

Although he made light of it, Hetta always maintained that he had a fairly tough time with the police, who, according to her, had roughed him up at one stage.

The explanation for William's detention probably lay in his arrangement with a Burmese diplomat, Myint Thein, to take a suitcase of papers in the 'diplomatic bag', and to then send them on to him in London. These papers were drafts of a science-fiction novel which he never in fact finished—*The Royal Beasts*—and some other bits and pieces which were of no political significance, so it remains a mystery why he felt it necessary to resort to this plan. Somebody in the household—possibly a servant—must have overheard them talking about it, though, and alerted the authorities. Many years later Walter suggested to Jacob that it might even have been Mog who chattered to his friends in the *Gong An Ji* about his father's negotiations, probably being boastful and without understanding the import. He would have been by no means the first child to be taken advantage of in this way in the communist world, where information was as good as denunciation.

The boat was a freighter with some accommodation for passengers. The sea was rough, the ship small and they were all sea-sick. The cabins were at one end of the boat, and to get to the dining room they had to cross the deck on a walkway. It was pretty horrid. After they got to Hong Kong they heard that their ship had been intercepted by KMT pirates from Formosa on its way back to Tientsin, and all the passengers killed.

Hong Kong was a revelation in cosmopolitan life, compared to Peking. There was also air conditioning in the American library, which the boys had never come across before. The funicular railway was a big treat. Mog lost his water pistol, which was something which the two brothers obviously felt was a talisman of some sort, as it got mentioned more than once in letters Jacob was writing three or four years later. It was their defence against the capitalists. Otherwise, every day seemed like a holiday, with outings to the New Territories, down to the port to see all the junks, and floating restaurants, and so on. They went on a yacht trip with some friends in the archipelago of islands, some in very shallow water, and went swimming. Hetta was embraced and stung by a huge jellyfish—possibly a Portuguese man-o-war, and was brought on board to lie down on the deck with a great rash around her waist. All the men had to pee into bottles to pour on to the affected area, without it doing much good. They tried whisky too.

William was allowed to leave Tientsin after two weeks, to join the rest of the family, but it was another couple of weeks before they said goodbye to Walter, and embarked on the P&O Corfu, for the last part of their journey to England. Walter was to go to Japan.

The Corfu was huge compared to their little freighter, and they had proper cabins with clean sheets, and there were other families aboard. It was a six-week voyage, and Mog and Jacob made friends with other children, grownup passengers and with stewards while they were on board. It was a little floating world of its own. The ship stopped at Kuala Lumpur, where there was another funicular railway, but this one took one into the jungle. In Bombay they had an elephant ride. One day in the Indian Ocean there was a commotion on deck, and a lady in a sari pointed out a school of dolphins which were diving and swimming alongside their ship. The Suez canal seemed too narrow, but the ship managed to navigate it, and they stopped at Port Said. It was a source of resentment for many years that Mog managed to fit in a ride on a camel, while Jacob couldn't—they had to get back on board to continue on their way across the Mediterranean before he could have his turn.

Jacob remembers the day they arrived in England. It was his eighth birthday, the 30th September, and when he and Mog got on deck the ship was already in dock. It was so cold and damp that they could see their breaths, which was a novelty, and they went around blowing clouds of steam.

Chapter 4

Studio House: Early Days

Describing the arrival in London, Hetta wrote to Walter:

We got here on the 30th. John Wright, Aunt Molly and Uncle Arthur came to the dock which was London and drove us home. Stinking Pat Miles is still in one room (the largest) and we have to share the kitchen with her and Iqbal is coming back from India next week (too) so we have three rooms (small) one for me one for William (very small) one for the children. It's all much smaller than I thought or remembered and filthy dirty and the fireplace smokes. No job for William but he doesn't care and will go to USA next summer maybe for a year. The children go on Monday to a very "progressive" school where they have square dancing and no reading and writing if they don't ask for it themselves. It was the only one which could take them and anyway by next term they hope they'll read and write enough to pass the test to go to a normal school. The camphor chests came (two broken) with everything inside. The heavy stuff will arrive in two weeks (nowhere to put it) except the 24 things (all <u>confiscated</u>). Everything costs a lot and you have to stand in a line to buy rations (meat eggs butter sugar).

Food rationing was indeed still in force, and would be for another year. Meat and fish were in short supply, although whale meat was not rationed, and was regarded as one of the foods of the future. It was a dark meat with little fat, and Hetta made stews with it. It must have been a considerable shock, not only to have to cope with no servants, but to discover how difficult it was going to be merely to get something to eat.

Hetta was at the sink, and said to Pa,

'Do you know what the children do at that school? They spend their time lighting bonfires—Jacob even takes his own matches because otherwise, he says, it makes him so behindhand and then they jump through them. They haven't got any eyelashes now!'

William replied, "Well I don't suppose it will do them any harm, my dear."

Hetta added, 'One of the rules is they must call the teachers and head master by Christian names. They haven't got any other rules. Mog says the boys curse the teachers something awful and he has become rather puritanical so he hits them sometimes. He says he can hit them all—all except one girl who is very fat and she doesn't feel a thing, even if he hits her very hard, she's too fat.'

William temporised, "Well at least they're learning to swear in English."

The school (Burgess Hill) was indeed strangely libertarian, but as Hetta reported to William there were dancing lessons. Once a week a teacher came in to teach country dancing, and every child had to go. The Dashing White Sergeant was Jacob's favourite. Otherwise, one could choose what to do. Jacob enjoyed doing spelling, when he wasn't tending the bonfire.

Mog and Jacob were amazed at much of what they saw in London. The number and variety of cars was astonishing, and they lay on the top bunk with their heads stuck out of the window, playing I-spy with makes of car. They went on expeditions of their own, for instance on a bus. The conductor was a distinguished looking Sikh, and Jacob said to Mog—'Look, the capitalists are even making ambassadors work on buses! Just wait till we get home and I tell Ma!' (Of course, their only experience of a Sikh was the Indian ambassador to China, who used to come to the house for sittings for his bronze bust). They went to the cinema—the Odeon on Haverstock Hill, which was showing *The Benny Goodman Story*, with an aerial combat Korean War film as second feature. They were very impressed with CinemaScope, and Technicolour, but a bit puzzled about Benny Goodman. The war film was easily understandable, as the Americans were doing all the things that the American air pirates were known to have done. What was less clear was why they weren't ashamed of themselves, and why they were telling the story with such pride.

The packing cases arrived a few weeks later. Hetta was unpacking in the front garden, with the boys helping, standing in the mud, with a bonfire going of all the odd bits of wood from the cases. A neighbour peered over the wall and said he'd never heard of such a thing and was going to complain to the Borough Council.

'I'm a ratepayer', he said.

Once they found their crossbows Mog and Jacob left Ma to get on with it, but she got help from a passer-by, levering the cases open. When he noticed that one of her treasures was a small, half-empty bottle of Epsom salts he lost interest, leaving her to deal with the remaining fifteen giant cases. Finally she got everything upstairs into the sitting room—what was to be the new ke-t'ing, with Hetta's bed in the corner.

Jacob had accumulated a collection of little glass animals in Peking, which had been carefully individually packed in paper and put in a box. Unhappily for him, every one of them was smashed when they found them in all the other stuff in the packing cases. However the crossbows had survived the trip intact.

After a term of freedom at Burgess Hill School they were sent to Davies Preparatory School, which was just around the corner in Lyndhurst Crescent. They had proper uniforms, with blue blazers, grey shorts and ties, and they had proper lessons. While they were there, one day they asked if anyone wanted to be in a boxing match. Jacob was keen to show off some of his shadow boxing moves, and so raised his hand. Before long he was having boxing gloves put on his hands (to his complete puzzlement) and being propelled into a boxing ring. His opponent came up to him and punched him in the face. He was astonished, and then broke down in shameful tears—it had never occurred to him that they should hit him like that.

Davies's was not so much a normal school as a crammer, and after two terms they transferred to The Hall School, where they were to stay until they took their Common Entrance exams and went to Aldenham School, Mog in 1956, and Jacob in 1958. For Jacob, the five years at The Hall was the longest that he was to stay at any school. There were some memorable teachers: Mr Rotherham, who taught Latin, was a short Yorkshireman with a strong accent, well into his seventies. He had fought in the First World War, as he liked to tell us. He had all his hair, which was completely white—like a field of snow, as some boy had once told him. Jacob was so bad at Latin that he was later to have extra lessons with 'Rozzie', as they called him, to help prepare me for the Common Entrance exam. He liked to reminisce about The Great War, but also about his childhood, and his own teachers who managed to school him to a scholarship at a grammar school. Leafing through an autobiography in a second hand bookshop, many years later, Jacob was to find that he had also made a great impression on the young Clement Freud when he was a pupil at The Hall.

Another of the teachers was Mr Bathurst, who taught history. He liked to conduct his lessons as story-telling sessions, rather than trying to instil facts. He would sit on his desk in front of the class and tell stories which were historical in some way. Jacob saw him as being another sort of entertainer—like our story teller in Peking who came to the compound every week. He did not do very well academically at The Hall, consistently coming last in the class in all subjects. In his Christmas, 1956 report Mr Bathurst was to comment on his performance in History: 'Frivolous. He would be an intelligent companion for a weekend but he cannot settle down and work'. Jacob saw him many years later when he was in his thirties. He was on the descending escalator in a tube station, and Jacob was going up. He recognized him immediately, and wanted to shout and wave at him, but couldn't recall his name—it only came back to him when he'd reached the ticket hall.

Jacob loved the school dinners. After all that Chinese food it was wonderful to have shepherd's pie followed by spotted dick or frogs spawn, and he was always going up for second helpings if any were available. Lunches were served in a large hall (hence the school's name) which had the coats of arms of all the great public schools hung around—presumably to inspire the boys to work harder for their Common Entrance. Teachers sat with the boys in tables of eight or so, where they were encouraged to have proper conversations. One of them, Mr Earl, was a nice man with an inability to finish a sentence, and the boys would compete to find his final words for him. The French teacher was Canadian, and reputedly sweet on the music mistress, who was rather attractive. He seemed much more cosmopolitan than the others, and would entertain them with jokes and stories of French Montreal.

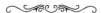

One of Ma's old friends was Clement Glock, who lived up the hill in Well Walk. Her daughter Oriel was about Jacob's age. The first time he saw her they were both nine years old, and she had rushed to the front door from her bath, with nothing on. Apart from not being shy, Oriel was remarkably enterprising for her age, travelling wherever she wanted to on the Tube on her own. Clement was a set designer at Covent Garden Royal Opera House. She had been married to John Davenport, famous for losing the only typescript of Pa's book *The Face of the Buddha*, in a taxi, and then William Glock, the composer and musical director at the BBC. Jacob visited her at her work with Oriel, more than once, when Oriel was most impressive in knowing her way around the backstage at the Opera House. Hetta also resumed some old friendships with Biddy Crozier, with Gwenda David, and others from the old days. There were others, such as the Shepherds, who had left London. She was not happy.

While Hetta's letters to Walter from Peking were frequently complaining about their being apart and full of schemes for him to obtain permits to visit Peking, her letters to him from London at this time are very different, in that she seemed to be in the grip of a depression which nothing could alleviate. Their life in Peking had been very circumscribed, but they did mix with intellectuals, with rising politicians and with diplomats, and there was the excitement of the developing revolution. The house in Dong Gau Fan was host to a multitude of guests, so that Hetta once said of it, that it was like being in a railway station, but with no trains. In London she was thrown on her own resources with very little money, in a city which was scarred by war and still subject to rationing. Her letters to Walter do tend to give a picture of misery throughout the forty odd years that she wrote to him. This is not to say that she had a dreadful life, but that when things got difficult or horrible she would resort to writing to Walter. However, there is a different quality to the unhappiness she was expressing in Peking, at his absence, from her unhappiness in London, which was close to clinical depression.

Early in 1953 William was enjoying some success. He had renewed old friendships in London, for instance with John Davenport, Rene Cutforth, and Louis MacNeice. He was being asked to talk about China, had arranged to go to the U.S. on another trip in June, and his book of essays was due to be published.

Naturally enough, he was looking for a permanent job—a Chair in English Literature. He had applied to the University of Hull, giving his old friend Alec Horsley as a referee (Alec was a hugely successful Hull businessman, with a dairy and a brewery to his name, who was to found the multinational Northern Foods). This would have been a congenial appointment, being so close to Yokefleet and his roots. Francis Klingender, a socialist art historian and old friend of Hetta's, specializing in the art of the industrial revolution, was also at Hull. However William was not short-listed or asked for interview, as the external assessor, a Cambridge professor, had made sure to have his name removed from the list of candidates. The long, vindictive arm of his *alma mater* had reached him again after twenty years.[xv] Sheffield University did not have the same assessor, and later that year they offered him the Chair of English Literature to start the following October.

The Morris Commercial

Hetta had not shown any enthusiasm for writing about China, which she had been invited to do, and her letters to Walter continued to be mournful. However, on 28th April 1953 she wrote to him to say, 'I bought a delivery van for forty pounds. Looked at England for ten days'. This development seems to have marked the end of her depression. The van had formerly belonged to a baker, and one could still read the lettering under the green paint on the sides, and the panel on the front above the windscreen. John Wright helped in the choice, and had travelled to Scotland with Hetta to give it the final once-over, and to pick it up. They said it hummed along like a sewing machine all the way down the A1.

William was easily persuaded to make an extended outing in the van. It was obvious that Hetta needed something to get here out of her moods, and they were both at a loose end. So they set off *en famille* to explore England. First they went to Oxford, staying a few nights, meeting old friends and visiting churches, colleges and pubs. They called in at Blenheim Palace, then made their way, with engine humming like a sewing machine, to Stratford-on-Avon to continue this tour with a visit to Ann Hathaway's cottage. They stopped at Stonehenge in the middle of the night, where the ticket office was shut, but one could wander around all the same. The drive through the Cotswolds included a sighting of the Uffington horse carved in the chalk hill, and they were on their way to Dorset. There they stayed with Kitty West, who had a nice house in a village. At a local point-to-point William won fifty shillings by backing outsiders. This exhausting progression continued with a visit to Tolpuddle to see the martyrs memorial cottages, then Winchester to show Mog what might happen to him if he was smart enough to be accepted when he became fourteen. Finally they drove back to London, without, as Hetta said, so much as a backfire out of the van after about a thousand miles.

A chance encounter with the Topolski family in Regents Park also picked her up. They had known Feliks and Tina during the war, when William had bought a small oil painting from him, which he always had next to his desk. Their house in Regents Park was handy for the rowing lake, where Daniel was already, at the age of ten or so, plying his oars. (He was later to become an Oxford blue, and the coach of a famous Oxford eight who won the Oxford Cambridge Boat Race against all the odds.) Things were at last looking up for Hetta.

The Coronation, in June, 1953, was the occasion of a visit across the road in Hampstead Hill Gardens, to watch the television. They had heard of television in China, but hadn't really believed it possible. However, there it was, all in black and white. The TV set belonged to Mr Elken Allen, an advertising executive, and his family, and they were to make regular visits to watch it in the following few years.

That summer they took off on a much more ambitious trip, taking a tent and crossing the Channel. They called in on John and Anne Willett in a village in Normandy, where they lived in an eighteenth century house set in its own grounds. John was a distinguished scholar of Bertholt Brecht, who had worked on the Manchester Guardian. Anne was bilingual, with a French mother and educated in Europe. She had in fact been flown into France on a secret Free French mission during the war. She was soon arrested, but managed to resist interrogation, and was eventually sent to a camp, where she became a leading light (even officiating at weddings, in the final days before they were all to be released and returned to their origins.) She was, and is, a local hero, officially recognized in being a member of the *legion d'honneur*. In their barns they had enormous floats which had been used in the recent village fête. Leaving the Willetts, they continued southwards, arriving at Cahors in the *massif central* in early August, and then to the Dordogne, where they visited the caves at Lascaux. In those days they were still open to casual visitors. They were highly atmospheric, if not scary, with dim lighting illuminating the extraordinary prehistoric frescoes of wild animals.

Their final destination was to be a small fishing village in northern Spain called Tossa del Mar, where they pitched the tent on a promentary overlooking the bay, and stayed for a week or more, reading, swimming in the sea, carefully skinning wild prickly pears and eating Spanish food—Hetta became a master of the paella, cooked on a little two-ringed camping cooking range, hazardously fuelled by petrol, and lent by John Wright. She loved the Mediterranean heat, the sun, and the parched landscape, which reminded her of South Africa.

Things changed again for Jacob and Mog once they were back in London at the beginning of term. William was now away in Sheffield and Hetta took the opportunity to 'hell around' as she was to put it. Kenneth Lo, the future restaurateur and food critic, was briefly a tenant in one of the rooms upstairs. He was to recall how he found Mog and Jacob cooking their own meals in the kitchen, with their mother out of action, or out of the house. It was during this period, early 1954, that her relationship with Peter Duval Smith developed, and her letters to Walter became infrequent. Peter was a great charmer, who looked Jacob in the eye as if he was somebody interesting to meet. He smiled a lot, and had an indulgent laugh. Hetta first mentions him in her letters on 6th December 1953—

> 'We're going to eat Chinese food and after to the Macneice
> for mulled wine—drinking (all anyone can afford). A
> mixed and not well-chosen party of seven with Kathleen
> Raine, Ableman and wife, young BBC man and Max.
> How trivial and straightforward her occupations are'.

Peter—the 'young BBC man' was to produce a half-hour program entitled *The Poems of William Empson* for the BBC Third Programme, which was broadcast on 15th December. He recorded the commentaries on the poems first, and then took William to a pub (probably The George) to drink a number of 'dog's noses'—pints of Guinness laced with white rum. The result was a remarkable contrast between the voice used to recite the poems, and that for the commentaries.

They went *en famille* to Yokefleet Hall for Christmas with Uncle Arthur and Aunt Molly and her husband Philip. Mog and Jacob felt that there were some reasons for having divided loyalties, here, possibly simply because Yokefleet was so very grand and obviously unsocialist. Perhaps Hetta was already voicing her hostility to the place, as part of her hostility to the British Raj, the British Empire, and THE BRITISH—a sentiment where socialist values combined with Afrikaaner grudges. At any rate, when the housekeeper Mrs Sellers served up the turkey on Christmas Day they declared 'We do not eat dead birds!' A week after their return, Hetta wrote to Walter, 'Pa and I have only just stopped talking at each other in the high-pitched screaming rolling eyes way that is habitual when addressing his relations'. Mog and Jacob had each been given a watch, and so was Pa. Hetta got a rayon scarf. A Cambridge friend, Desmond Lee, was to write in his memoirs about William, 'He was fond of his family . . . but his family found him difficult to understand, and he found communication with them difficult, saying to me once that fond as he was of them, when he visited them it was "like being in the company of steam engines". You recognised their merits but had little in common'.

Uncle Arthur was fourteen years older than William—born in 1892. He was the second of four sons, and had already made a career in the Army when his elder brother, John, died in 1914 in a flying accident. His father then died in 1916, making him heir to the Yokefleet estate—comprising about 2000 acres of very fertile arable land, and a large Victorian house, Yokefleet Hall. Arthur was in an Artillery regiment. He was wounded in 1916, but recovered well enough to return to the front, and was awarded the Military Cross and Belgian Croix de Guerre in 1917. The citation for his bravery has survived in the *London Gazette*. (All other records of citations for gallantry from the first world war were lost in the second world war, appropriately enough destroyed by enemy action). Oddly enough, he was awarded his medals for putting out a fire. Enemy action had ignited a store of camouflage, which was next to stored ammunition. It was assumed that the ammunition was going to explode. Arthur took it upon himself to put the fire out, at great risk to himself. His wartime letters show him to have been a stoic, very much as William was, in his own way. He was eventually to leave the Army in 1923 to take up the responsibilities of being a farmer and local squire. Being so much older, he was to take almost a fatherly interest in his younger brother. He never married.

Aunt Molly was only four years older than Pa, and had taken him under her wing when he was very small. She had been a keen sportswoman in her youth, winning prizes for her tennis, and regularly riding, despite being told that she had a heart murmur. Married in 1930 to Philip Kitching, she was told by doctors that she should never have children, as her heart condition would not sustain the challenges of pregnancy and childbirth. She was to remain childless all her life, although living until her late sixties. Her husband Philip was chronically ill with a lung condition, and although he was fit enough to join the family for Christmas that year, died in January 1956.

During the next few years Arthur and Molly were to take a more than avuncular interest in Mog and Jacob, as their parents' marriage became fragile, and they were, to a degree, neglected. They always had the best intentions.

Hetta's relationship with Peter was tempestuous. They both drank very heavily and would get into ferocious and violent arguments. Hetta would call the police. On one occasion Peter was kept overnight at the police station, where they found it difficult to subdue him. Jacob went into the bathroom next day to find him lying in the bath, with the water right up to the brim (excessive as always) with two startling black eyes and a broken nose—evidence of his struggle with the law.

Walter had been missing her dreadfully, and had been writing to her with plans for her to do a lecture tour in Japan on the emancipation of women, with introductions to women's clubs, and even a visit to a model women's prison. She did not reply, and he was writing again offering for him and David Kidd to pay her fare. David had suffered from TB in Japan, and, after a long convalescence, was now recovered and, with Walter's help, was writing his book about his experiences in China. He had given Walter a monkey for his birthday, called Mr Coco, who was better behaved than the Miss Coco that Jacob had been given in Peking. They both missed the Peking days, David writing, 'but Honey bun, what I wouldn't give to glide effortlessly with you in my arms across a polished dance floor in the intricate steps of the Fandango, just as they used to do. You would whisper sweet nothings in my ear, "Who the Hell is going to pay for this?" And, caressing your elbows, I would whisper back, "Not me!" . . . And afterwards being wafted gently home through the starry Peking night while the pullers chanted quaintly in their native tongue, "Ts'ao ni ma te p'i ku" (*fuck your mother, etc*) Ah, them dear dead days.'

During the summer Hetta and Peter became estranged, and she seems to have reverted to her former depressive state. At last she started answering Walter's letters. She had formed a plan to escape from London, at least for a while, either to join Walter in Japan or to persuade him to join her in Tangiers. This was even more impractical for him than for her, and he and David were now happier in Japan. He never agreed to meet her there. However, her letters became more and more insistent. In June she wrote,

> 'I've got an offer from the Macneices to take the children
> to Ireland from end of July till end of August and John
> Wright and Zoe will have them for a week beforehand.
> So I could leave around 20th July and be there by the 23rd
> if you can pay the equivalent of the boat fare towards the
> plane fare—I can find the difference and somehow make
> the return by writing—'.

More detailed plans followed, culminating in a telegram on August 10th, 'Meet me Tangiers'.

Walter did not meet her in Tangiers, although in the end she did go on her own. As for the boys, they had a most enjoyable and interesting time with the MacNeice family. Hedli and Louis

MacNeice, and their daughter Corinna (at that time always known as Bimba) lived in a large house overlooking Regents Park. There was an Italian servant, Restituta, formerly Bimba's nanny, but now a general help in the house. They also had a bull terrier called Phoebe, who was a very good-natured, friendly dog, as bull terriers often are. They looked forward to visits to their house, not least because of the relative normality and tranquillity that they lived in. Hedli was not tall, but she stood very straight, and had the air of one who knows how everything should be done. It was perhaps part of her stage presence, that she brought home with her. (She once explained that she had trained in opera, but her voice was 'broken' by an over-zealous coach. All the same, she had a wonderful singing voice, and regularly appeared in productions at the Players Theatre.) Hedli and Restituta in the kitchen were a lesson in certainty and order. Louis was of course the Irish poet, who had given up a career in academic life for his poetry and radio plays, and who worked at the BBC.

They left from the house in Regents Park, with the whole family including Restituta and Phoebe, and spent a week in a cottage in Suffolk—Holbrook, in the middle of 'Constable country'. There they were encouraged by Hedli to write a daily newspaper, partly at least because the weather was not good, and parts of this have survived to this day, in Corinna's house in Santa Fe. From there they travelled to Belfast, where they stayed for a night or two with relatives of Louis. Then they set off by car for Donegal, to stay in a cottage in Fintragh Bay, outside Killeybegs. Bimba was about Mog's age, and they were naturally matched, even at age 12, in a potential romance. Bimba teased Mog mercilessly, and he stood on his dignity. She was a provocative tomboy, a boarder at Hanford School, but soon to go to the Cone Ripman Arts Educational School, a leading stage school in London, whose most famous alumni included Julie Andrews. Bimba was most dramatic, and would cry, 'How IMPULSIVE!' at the drop of a hat. On one of the stops on the way they were left in a pub car park with their crisps and orangeades, and they noticed a donkey. Bimba challenged Mog to ride it, and soon they were taking turns to ride the donkey, which became impatient, and eventually threw Jacob into the air, and, as he was falling, lashed out with its hind hoofs. It caught him in the groin, gashing his pippy. Bimba joined Mog in the gents toilet to inspect the damage, which was quite impressive, although not actually bleeding. They never told the grownups, and it healed remarkably quickly.

Our newspapers, the 'Daily Mop' and the 'Daily News' included some diary items about trips to the beach, but also excruciating verse, and other items, such as 'Stop Press' or 'Advertisement'. There was a fifty line poem entitled 'The Church Cat'—repetitive, nonsensical, alliterative, in a word, childish! Also, an

Ode to Bim
There was a young lady of Holbrook
Who sailing one day lost a boathook
A man sitting by
Gave a blood curdling cry
For the strange young lady of Holbrook.

When they arrived in Fintragh Bay they went on a lot of walks, spent time on the beach, and also went fishing in the sea. Hanging a spinning metal lure on the end of a line was enough to attract the mackerel to bite, and it was shamefully easy to pull them out of the sea. Fried in butter the moment they got them back to the cottage, they were absolutely delicious. Hedli was a most accomplished cook, who would have her own restaurant in Ireland a few years later. One day they could see porpoises surfacing off the shore. This was thrilling, but they then discovered that the men with guns on the path with us were actually shooting at them—fishermen jealous of their catch.

Jacob, Mog and Bimba

After they got back Hetta and Peter had got back together again, and things went on as before. A big event for William, over that summer, was the preparation for the Queen's visit to Sheffield, which was going to include the university. The Vice Chancellor had asked him to write a masque, which could be performed for her by the students. This was going to be a tricky one, he could see, but he recalled his meeting with the Crown Prince of Japan, at a reception in Tokyo in 1932. Nobody had expected the Prince to turn up, so the diplomat who could speak the peculiar version of Japanese only spoken by royalty (and those addressing them) was not present. It was unthinkable for another diplomat to address him either in ordinary Japanese or in English, despite the fact that the Prince had been educated in England. William was therefore ushered forwards as an alternative. After greetings were over, William said to him, 'Why don't you start a pack of hounds here in Japan?' He did not need to say another word, as the Prince, entranced by the idea, spoke volubly about how wonderful it would be, although important to work with the peculiar fox-superstitions which the peasants held. As William was getting ready to join the conversation again, after having expressed nothing except cries of pleasure, he was yanked by the collar as the diplomat with necessary linguistic accomplishments had arrived. The lesson he learned from this was that royalty wants to be addressed in an unfrightened manner, so long of course as the manner is not impudent or politically wrong.

Hetta did not come to Sheffield to join the junketing, being pre-occupied with her love life with Peter, so William was left on his own to cope with the royal visit. The masque, a 13-minute performance in verse and song, told how the secret of making steel ('puddling iron') was given to the good people of Sheffield by a goddess who came down to them in a winged chariot. This goddess was of course the Queen herself. The director was the young Peter Cheeseman, then a student and later to achieve great eminence as a theatre director. William felt that he did a wonderful job, as did the cast of students who had been rehearsing through the summer vacation. Immediately after the performance William was delegated to speak to the Queen as the author, before the principal actors and director could join them, and she charmed him so utterly that he was converted into being an unselfconscious monarchist for the rest of his life. Although, as he said, she looked as cross as a camel when she was reading an official statement of approval of the University, once the show was over she had him in a state of abject devotion by her determined kindness to him, and then by the charm with which she greeted the actors. The Queen said she liked the play because it was so light. William thought, 'Come, come, mam, what degree of blasphemous flattery *would* you call heavy?' (But he did not say so). She also said that she had been watching the audience with great interest. By this stage it didn't matter what she said—William was in love.

A major change in the living arrangements in Studio House came when the family moved downstairs to the ground floor the following spring, in May 1955. Hetta was able to take over the studio, a room about 40 ft by 40 ft, very high ceilinged, with a skylight at the top. One end was set back, with conservatories on either side, forming a natural stage. It was here that she had a *k'ang* built, which she covered with yellow carpet. Traditionally, the *k'ang* was the communal sleeping area in a Chinese house. Built of brick, it would be sited over the stove, to be constantly warm. Hetta investigated the possibilities of having a stove underneath, but it seemed that building regulations, even in those days, did not allow it. She would sleep on a mattress in the corner of the *k'ang*. This was fine during the summer, but when winter came it was impossible to heat the whole room, and Hetta resorted to erecting a tent, with its flap going over the Pither (an anthracite stove which stood about five foot tall, and was the only source of heat.) There she held court in her Bedouin boudoir. The room next to the studio was also enormous, and this was partitioned into three, giving a kitchen, a bedroom and a passageway. Apart from the bathroom, they also had two bedrooms in the front of the house, one of which was Pa's. Mog and Jacob shared the new bedroom next to the kitchen.

Underneath the studio, and reached through a trapdoor in the floor, was another equally large room, which was full of discarded educational furniture, from when the house had been used as a Montessori school. Jacob discovered a human skull among all this, which he kept. Possibly because of this macabre discovery, the room under the studio was known ever after as the 'Christie room', after the murderer. Mog's trophy from this junk was an impressive brass microscope. John Wright still had his marionette theatre in the basement, in the very large room next to the Christie room, from which it was divided by large folding doors. John reinforced these, and made a sound insulation layer, by piling sandbags from floor to ceiling.

The studio had a very high ceiling—about 40 feet—so it became feasible to make use of the *huo guo*, or Mongolian steamboat, as it is sometimes called. A charcoal fired device, with a chimney running through the middle of a circular moat, into which one puts a thin stock. Theirs was quite an elaborate one, of decorated copper, and with wooden handles. (They were really a Chinese invention, to celebrate Mongolian cuisine. A traditional Mongolian cook, like the ones that Hetta encountered on her expedition to Inner Mongolia in 1947, would boil a whole sheep rather than messing about with a fondu set.)

Preparations would begin the day before, with a trip to Soho. The ingredients required for this Chinese cuisine were bought at the *Hong Kong Emporium*. This was the only Chinese shop in London at the time. Even there, some staple Chinese products were difficult to find. (This was when olive oil was only sold in Boots the chemist, in tiny bottles, for the purpose of treating infantile cradle cap.) For the sauce, one needed sesame paste, and peanut butter sometimes had to be used as a substitute. Root ginger was not always available, and Hetta tried grating lemon rind to give a similar flavour. Rice wine was never obtainable, and South African sherry was heated up and served from an authentic Chinese pewter teapot, into tiny jade cups, instead. Apparently it tasted very similar when warm, a bit like the contents of one's hot water bottle. Chinese restaurants were quite rare. There was one with a good reputation in the East End, whose core clientele were Chinese seamen, called *The Old Friends*. The same management was to open another, in central London, called *The New Friends*, but the days of high street Chinese restaurants, or of Chinatown in Soho, were years ahead.

The *bao tze*, or steamed dumplings, were enlivened with yeast, and needed plenty of time to rise. They would be steamed just before the meal was to start, and more could be cooked on demand. When Meifang was around, and could be dragooned into helping, she would make *jiao tze*, or diminutive Cornish pasties containing pork or shrimp, with ginger and garlic, which could also be steamed. Getting the pastry just right, and then being able to manipulate it into the right shapes, was an accomplishment expected of a Chinese young lady, but one very difficult to achieve. The lamb, both leg and liver, needed to be cut into tiny slivers, the thinner the better. The vegetables also had to be sliced very finely. Lastly, the sauce had to be prepared. The idea was that once the water was boiling, diners could choose morsels of meat, *jiao tze* or vegetables to cook in the broth, holding them with their chopsticks. These were then dipped in the special sauce before being eaten, accompanied by the steamed dumplings. By the end of the meal the thin stock had become quite substantial, what with all the pieces of meat and vegetable being cooked in it, and some lost by careless or unskilled chopstick users, and it was finished off by being drunk as a soup.

The advantage for a hostess is that once all the preparations have been made, everything is on the table at once, and there is no further need to leave the table. For William and Hetta, the further advantage was that, with the stock cooling off when too much food was put in, and having to heat up again, it meant that there were plenty of natural breaks to allow it to heat up, with further opportunities for drinking, or in having a cigarette. A meal which started as a late lunch could then last well into the evening, although William would normally have gone to his room well before the end. The journalist René Cutforth was invited to one of these *huo guo* parties, and became involved in a mock boxing match with Mog, and accidently hit him. Mog was outraged, and for ever after, René Cutworth was famous only for being the 'the man who hit Mog'.

At the Reading Fine Art Gallery exhibition of paintings by the Chinese artist, Ch'i Pai-Shih, left to right, Mr. Denis Matthews, Madame Chuang Yen Mr. Chuang Yen, and Mrs. Hetta Empson.

Cutting from a local Reading newspaper, June 1955
Photograph reproduced courtesy of the Reading Chronicle,
holder of the copyright. www.readingchronicle.co.uk

Hetta was still a Party member, and became involved in the organization of an exhibition of the works of *Chi Pai Shi*, a traditional Chinese water-colourist and long-term survivor, well-liked by the establishment in China, including Mao Tse Tung. (She had bought one large picture, and a number of smaller ones, purportedly by him, when they were in China. Jacob eventually inherited them, but Walter told him, years later, that they were probably fakes, knocked up by his assistants to raise cash during the uncertainties of civil war. They were among the collection of Chinese water colours, some of which were genuinely antique and interesting, which Hetta and William brought back to England. Prices were low in the late 40s and early 50s for these artworks, as Japanese collectors, who had driven up prices in the 1930s, had been forced to sell before they fled at the end of the war.)

The exhibition was held in June 1955, when Hetta was seven months pregnant—hard to believe from the photograph! This event was also notable for being the occasion when William met up again with Alice Stewart. They had met many years before, and while she had hoped for more from their relationship then, he had apparently forgotten all about her. On this occasion she must have made more of an impression. They began an affair which was to last, intermittently and at long distance, for fifteen years. She was divorced, with two children older than Mog and Jacob. Medically trained, she had been married to a schoolteacher at a public school, but was now resuming her medical career, and was based in Oxford where she worked as a medical epidemiologist at the university. It was she who identified Jacob's skull (from the Christie room) as having being prepared as a medical exhibit, with the hole drilled in the top of the cranium allowing the whole skeleton to be suspended, and the wires attaching the jaw bones. Also, from the wiggly nature of the sutures between the cranial bones she could say that the individual was elderly when they died, and from the general appearance and size of the face, that it was a female. Jacob thereupon christened his skull 'Mrs Urquhart'—for reasons which are obscure. However, she remained in his possession until late in his adult life, and was a useful teaching aid in the EEG/sleep lab in Hull, until his early retirement in 1999, when some well-intentioned cleaner disposed of her—presumably in the rubbish.

Hetta wrote to Walter on 10th August 1955:

> Ten days ago I started having the baby and then minutes after I got a temperature of 104 (quite unaccountable as I seem to do and it stopped the baby's heart—they put me to sleep till next day and I produced it normally and easily with another violent temperature—dead it was a girl.
>
> I'd got him (Pa) and the kids off to Wales the afternoon I went in to hospital—they're due back tomorrow and then the children go to Dorset to stay with Louis Macneice and family. I'm going to Scotland maybe for a little. This house is a mausoleum. It's been a bad year hasn't it. Maybe if they all stay quiet and mouselike for a bit—it will clear. I feel rather banged on the head but glad still to be alive. I'm going to get another small whisky now.

Her letter makes it sound as though she was completely without support, although Max had been to visit her in hospital, shortly after the still-birth, and after the baby's body had been removed. He wrote to Peter to tell him about her depressed state, and presumably he was popping downstairs to keep an eye on her, and to join her in the odd small whisky.

The boys' banishment to Wales during Ma's confinement was the first of a number of visits to Alice Stewart's cottage in Snowdonia, which was out in the wilds, with no plumbing or electricity. One got water by taking two buckets on a yoke to dip them in the stream. Lighting was by candle and paraffin Tilley lamps. Long walks, reading and housework took up all their time.

On their return to London Mog and Jacob were aware of what had happened, and were ready to blame the Whittington Hospital for their ineptitude in failing to prevent the death of their baby sister. Somehow, though, life simply carried on despite this, and they were packed off on our holiday with the MacNeices. This holiday in Dorset was memorable for the weather, which was hot, and the deserted shingle beaches and Bimba emerging from the waves one day clad only in seaweed. Phoebe was with them on this occasion, and so was Restituta. Hedli supervised another newspaper which they were all supposed to contribute to. Another reason for going to Dorset was that Bimba's school—Hanford—was there, and she was to be baptized in the school chapel.

Bimba's christening party at Hanford School
Hedli, seated on the left, Louis and Restituta standing on the right

On Jacob's 11th birthday, 30th September 1955, he was given a goat, instead of the python that he had asked for. They had been privileged to have access behind the scenes at the London Zoo, and handle the big snakes. This was probably through Bill Pirie, a biochemist who was a Fellow of the Royal Society, and with connections with the Zoological Society of London. A party comrade, he had been an admirer of Ma's for a long time. Jacob had been most taken with the warmth and strength of the large pythons, and demanded to have one of his own. In any case, Hetta decided that a goat would be a good idea for him. Gertie was a slot-eyed white Saanan, already in milk when she arrived, and she was established in the back garden in the garden shed.

On 25th November Hetta wrote to Walter:

> The kids still milk the goat. She got randy and I had to hire a van to take her to the billy. I sold my truck to the knackers for £10 because it finally stopped—very sad-making and no money for another one. An old-time flame of Pa's turned up in our lives as a successful doctor and I blackmailed her into loaning me her Daimler while she went to Russia so they were very grand for three short weeks with bowing and scraping all round—even from the coppers, but I only want a truck. Chinese opera came here from Peking and I took them around a bit. I've also been organizing exhibitions of Ch'I Pai Shih (the old painter) with scrolls from Peking through the Embassy

here. I don't want to go to Yokefleet for Christmas and Pa
says I needn't—he'll take the kids.

The trip to Gertie's stud—named Merrydown Pronto,
appropriately enough—was quite memorable. She was difficult to
get into the van, and was bleating all the way, whether from being in
heat or because she was protesting about the van they did not know.
He was huge, almost the size of a small pony, and very, very smelly.
When Gertie was put in his paddock he was immediately interested
in her, and was biffing her about quite roughly, which was worrying.
Anyway, he finally judged that there had been enough of that, and
mounted her briefly, after which he lost interest in her altogether,
and she in him, and she was taken home.

In the event none of them went to Yokefleet that year—the
responsibility of milking the goat was used as an excuse. The
Christie room gave direct access to the back garden, which was
handy for getting out to deal with the goat, who had demolished
most of the vegetation, including the laurels which were supposed to
be poisonous. Gertie was a boisterous and intelligent creature, who
Jacob used to take for walks to the Heath, to give her some grazing.
Dogs were a bit of a nuisance, as they were attracted to her, possibly
assuming she was another large dog, and she had to deal with them
by biffing them with her horns. All this distracted her from grazing,
though, and the solution he found was to take her to the children's
enclosure, which had a notice at its entrance—'No Dogs'.

She hated walking on the pavement—presumably her hooves
found the surface too hard—and would regularly go on strike by
lying down and refusing to get up. More often than not she did this on
the pavement in front of the Haverstock Hill Police Station. Pulling
on her lead and shouting at her had no effect whatsoever. The only

way of getting her back on her feet was to lie down with her, which she found quite disconcerting and out of order, and would scramble up immediately.

She occasionally got out of the garden, and then would make her way to Pond Street, where there was a greengrocers shop next to the Roebuck Inn. They would have all their vegetables spread out in front of the shop on the pavement, and Gertie would gobble as much as she could before being chased away. She became such a regular visitor that they knew the Empson household telephone number.

On April 13 1956, Gertie gave birth to a little billy named Dopey. Despite being a bit of a runt he had a lot of spirit, ever ready to play at butting, and seemed easily bored—he was always looking for attention. Jacob set up a course for him in the garden consisting of walkways across planks, leaps up to boxes, and so on, which he tried to train him to go around, and he took to it very quickly, even doing his routine when he was on his own. It was probably inspired by a complicated sequence of runways, drops and levers which John Wright had built for ball bearings to run down, as part of his puppetry theatre.

Gertie's milk output was such that they couldn't deal with it all ourselves, so they started a delivery service to the tenants. After a while Benty, the Spaniard in the tiny bed-sit in the basement, claimed that goat's milk gave him spots, and stopped his order for milk, and the other tenants followed suit. They then made a lot of cheese. The neighbours also got to know her and, in due time, her little billy kid (Dopey). Mr Elken Allen (whose television they went across the road to watch) even used a photograph of Jacob and Dopey to advertise a detergent—Oxydol.

Dopey and Jacob in their advertising campaign

Chapter 5

Separation and an interregnum

At The Hall School Jacob used to sit at the back of the class with Gareth Thomas, who was an irrepressible show-off. He had remarkable control over his bodily functions—he could fart to order, and produce the loudest belches. Jacob was impressed by Gareth, and proud to be his friend, and was disappointed when he was expelled. Gareth has of course had a distinguished career as an actor since those early days, famous for being 'Blake' in the TV science fiction series 'Blakes 7', but also much else. He was performing in Edinburgh not long ago in the Kings Theatre in 'Playboy of the Western World'. Another acquaintance was Matthew Spender, who was in a different class from Jacob—probably a higher stream, being groomed for Common Entrance to one of the more distinguished of the public schools whose coats of arms hung in The Hall. They sort of knew that both their fathers were poets, and acknowledged each other when they met, but it didn't go much further than that.

Nicky Hyman was a more conventionally reliable friend. Being a Hampstead prep school, The Hall had a very large proportion of Jewish boys. Jacob had never heard of Jews in China, and with all his political sophistication, drilled in our lessons at communist kindergarden, had never heard of the Holocaust. One day, when he had been having a conversation with the other boys about their families, it emerged that Hyman, Goldie, Leaver, and the others, had very few grandparents, or uncles or aunties between them, because they had all been murdered by the Nazis. Jacob was astonished and incredulous. To its credit, The Hall School had a small library in the main hall which was dedicated to Picture Post magazines about the camps. They then led Jacob to the magazine with its photographs of emaciated people, and corpses, and so on. This was a revelation to him, and very much a turning point. For many years it continued to inform his thinking about the world, and for him (and many others in his generation, in their later teenage years) Israel naturally accompanied Cuba as being one of the two nations of the future, of socialism and hope.

Being called Jacob, there was naturally a potential for ambiguity in his origins, and Nicky and the others would include him in invitations to their mothers' childrens parties—rather competitive affairs within Jewish Hampstead society. Jacob was most impressed by the grandeur of their houses, and was on the brink of being invited to a bamitzfah (and looking forward to it, although he probably had nothing suitable to wear) when one of the mums cottoned on, and he was blackballed from then on. The boys were highly amused. Of course it was a shared joke, and they all remained firm friends at school. Jacob had attached himself to the Jewish boys because of his own feelings of alienation from the other gentiles. His parents, and his home life, were obviously weird, and being friends with them, who were by no means weird in the same way, but were also somehow different, made sense to him.

The school did not have any playing fields immediately attached to it, and to play games they had to travel on the Metropolitan Line to Mitcham. This would take quite a long time, and was an adventure in itself. The carriages did not have a corridor, so each compartment was completely separate, and if the boys got one to themselves they could make as much noise as they liked.

The tenants in Studio House were an interesting group—some of them old friends from Peking days (or even before, such as John Wright), and others recruited by word of mouth. Max Bickerton had taken a room in the top of the house, sharing the kitchen, and he was to stay there until he died in 1966. He was already installed in the house before the family got back from China. He became a sort of Dutch uncle to the two boys. Max told them he had managed to raise the fare from Peking to London by selling his Phillips bicycle—British makes were obviously highly prized in China. He could not afford the most commodious passage, however, and was in steerage between Hanoi and Marseilles along with a lot of demoralized French Foreign Legionnaires, returning to Europe after their calamitous defeat at Dien Bien Phu in Vietnam. They were all seasick much of the time, so Max was in charge of the food and wine lowered down to them from the decks above. Max had a long history of seducing the military. In China he had been famous for persisting with his reckless seduction of soldiery even after the decadent KMT were replaced by the straitlaced PLA. He was in his element.

He also managed to infiltrate the upper decks, and get some decent food as well. This role, of being in-between with the authorities, was something he had taken on before, during his three years in Japanese internment camp, in Singapore. He would often reminisce about the war, as did many of the grownups of his generation, then and later. Max's fluency in Japanese had made him invaluable as a translator between the camp commandant and the leader of the internees. Max would attend their weekly meetings, and as a matter of courtesy, was offered a cigarette. Although he didn't smoke, he accepted this valuable gift, which he placed behind his ear to be bartered later in the camp. After a few months the Japanese commander insisted on having his cigarette lit for him, and Max was then obliged to smoke it, and put it out as soon as he dared, so that he would have a longish stub with which to barter. Despite the advantages of his privileged position, he still had a pretty thin time, for instance making a razor blade last two years by sharpening it on the rim of a glass.

For the rest of his life he remained a very heavy smoker, but could not finish a cigarette, leaving at least half of each Woodbine unsmoked, and stubbing it out in a gesture of disgust. He tried smoking smaller cigarettes (Weights) to economise, and even tried cutting the cigarettes in half, as he only smoked half. This was an unsuccessful experiment, and he ended up smoking more than twice as many halves of cigarettes than he would have done of halves of whole ones. For a few years he shared the kitchen with a Nigerian mature student, and then school-teacher, Yinka Oudebena, which was the source of some good-natured conflict from time to time. Yinka rather wittily bought him an ashtray in the shape of a black hand, so that he could take out his frustrations by stubbing out his half-smoked cigarettes on his palm.

John Wright was in the basement, which he had rented since 1944, with his puppet theatre. He was a South African Hetta had known in Cape Town before the war. He was a consummate craftsman, making wooden puppets with faces so expressive they were sculptural, and inspired by African art. At this time he only put on shows in Studio House on Sundays, and periodically took the puppets on tour. Hetta admired his work very much—particularly his skill as a wood carver. The rooms at the front of the house in the basement were occupied by Barry Carman, an Australian BBC producer who was to become one of the regular panellists on 'Round Britain Quiz'. (When they were planning this program they had recruited him to stand in, as he was an available body in the building, being an occasional producer of programmes. They then discovered that he could answer all the questions they had set. Barry's phenomenal memory thus earned him a permanent job.) He could not abide the English climate in the winter, and he was unfortunate in occupying the dampest part of the house. His solution was to spend the winters, or as much of them as he could, in Majorca, where he had made friends with the poet Robert Graves and his family.

A very small room in the basement (so small it had a fold-down single bed) was let to a Spaniard, Ventura Varo Arellano ('Benty'), who was on intimate terms with Max, so he spent most of his time with him in the attic. Benty came from Cordoba, in Andalucia. He told Jacob how his father had been a soldier in the Government army during the civil war, and had been captured and sent to a prisoner of war camp in Cordoba, his home town. He and his mother used to go to the prison every day with food for his father, until one day they were told not to come again, as he had been executed. This was one of Franco's ways of punishing the families of his enemies. Benty and his mother lived in poverty, to the extent that she counted out chick peas every evening, to leave to soak overnight. It was one of his memories of childhood, hearing them being dropped one by one into the pan while he lay in bed. Benty qualified as a school-teacher in Spain, but had come to England to escape the fascists and their homophobic persecution. He met Max on an escalator in the London Underground, and, as their relationship developed, he moved into Studio House. Max found him work as a language teacher in the same language school as his own, at very low wages since his qualifications were not recognized in the U.K. He then spent many years taking A levels, then a degree course at Birkbeck College, before becoming a legitimate teacher again.

On the first floor in the front there was a Chinese post-graduate student, Lo Hui Min, with his French wife Monique. Over time they would put up, if not shelter, a number of other Chinese academics and musicians who had turned up in London and were homeless for various reasons. Lo was to graduate to become an eminent academic at the Australian National University. David Hawkes (an academic who had been in Peking with the Empsons) was to say about him, at Hetta's funeral, that he was a man fluent in seven languages, but unintelligible in all of them. (He had an extraordinarily staccato manner of talking, as if his thoughts were so rapid his voice could not keep up.) The two rooms at the back, on the first floor, had a regular turnover of tenants during this time. It was a very friendly house, with most of the tenants being entertained at some point to Sunday lunch, or joining in at family gatherings.

When Pa was at home during the holidays, he would regularly feel it necessary to take the boys for a walk. He would typically walk in silence, although at times he would make a point of telling them an anecdote about some point of interest. A regular Sunday morning outing would be across the Heath to Kenwood House, where they would do a brisk tour of the rooms walking straight past most of the paintings. The Rembrandt self-portrait always deserved a fairly long halt, with moving about because it was hung so the sunlight reflected badly. A seventeenth century painting of London Bridge, covered in buildings, and with more buildings on either side of the Thames, was a particular point of interest. By the Dutch artist De Jongh, it only just failed to include the Globe Theatre, but if it had, it would have settled the long-standing academic debates about its architecture. The picture needed to be looked at carefully to confirm that The Globe still wasn't there after all. The Gainsborough portraits of Countess Howe and Lady Brisco also deserved inspection, and Pa liked to explain that the colour of the lady's frock matched the colour of the clouds in the background—a grey silk outfit and grey cloud for Countess Howe, and a bluish grey silk frock and bluish grey clouds for Lady Brisco. Romney's Lady Hamilton posing as a cottager with her spinning wheel was given a brief look and a smile. The Guardis, he claimed, were painted 'straight', with Signor Guardi then finishing the job off in cheerful fashion by whistling as he dabbed in the white patches for the waves on the Grand Canal. This could all be fitted in before Sunday lunch. A more ambitious walk would be to carry on over to the Heath extension, to visit the wallabees and the deer, and to gaze on the splendid palaces of Hampstead Garden Surburb. Even longer expeditions were to Kew Gardens, at least once in spring, to see the rhododendrons, and then in the autumn to see the autumn tints.

The Empson family would go on the little train from Hampstead station, down at South End Green, which William regarded as a family secret, and which took one all the way. The other secret, at Kew, was to do with the sensitive plant, which he believed was moved about to prevent people from knowing where it was. The object was of course to tease it. You couldn't ask one of the gardeners 'Where is the sensitive plant?' as they were under instructions to act dumb, and not to tell. You had to ask, 'Please, can you tell me where we can see the Mimosa *pudica*?' (stressing the *see*, and not letting on that you wanted to touch it in any way.) Once they had told you, and it was found, the Empsons could have a happy time taking turns to stroke its leaves, which would twitch and curl up when touched.

World political developments were to finally force Hetta's resignation from the Communist Party, of which she had been a member for almost twenty years. In February, 1956 Nikita Kruschev, then First Secretary of the Communist Party of the Soviet Union, made a secret speech to the 20th Party Congress of the Soviet Union, which was promptly leaked, and the gist of it was widely disseminated. The full text of the speech was eventually published in England in *The Observer* in June, 1956. A denunciation of the policies and government style of Joseph Stalin, it began with the words:

> We have to consider seriously and analyze correctly [the crimes of the Stalin era] in order that we may preclude any possibility of a repetition in any form whatever of what took place during the life of Stalin, who absolutely did not tolerate collegiality in leadership and in work, and who practiced brutal violence, not only toward everything which opposed him, but also toward that which seemed to his capricious and despotic character, contrary to his concepts.

Later during 1956 the Soviet Union was to invade Hungary and put down the popular uprising against the communist government. For a large number of Communist Party members across the world these events tested their loyalties to the limit, and there were widespread resignations from the Party.

Hetta had maintained her membership of the Party, and during the previous year had been making herself useful in escorting cultural delegations from China. However, her active role in politics came to an end in this year, and her Party membership lapsed. Her loyalty had never been blind, and she was well aware, during her time in Peking, of how the regime did not always live up to communist ideals. It was obvious that the transition to a communist system involved quite a lot of rough justice. She was also sure that the secret police had beaten up Pa when he was under arrest in Tianjin in 1953. However, she had kept her faith in the Party up to now. Her political convictions were to remain very much leftist for the rest of her life, but she was to drop any involvement in party politics. The sort of communist party which she had joined presumably suited her. Perhaps, to be simplistic, she was a natural Stalinist. She was to become active in the campaign for nuclear disarmament, and she reserved a particular hatred for South African apartheid, but democratic political parties held no appeal for her.

During 1956 Ma was to make friends with John Seymour, probably through Barry Carmen and the BBC. John had already enjoyed a variety of careers, including off-shore fishing, farming, as a sailor in South and East Africa, and as a soldier in the Kings African Rifles. He had travelled extensively in India as well as Africa. He was now working off and on for the BBC as a producer, but with no regular salary. Recently married with a small child, he was looking for a small-holding in which to settle down with his wife Sally when he came across Hares Creek Cottage, near Shotley, down the river Orwell from Ipswich. Without much land, it was too small for them, but he told Ma about it, and she went and rented it for 6/—per week. It became a refuge for her and Peter, as well as a weekend destination for everyone, and has survived in the family to this day. John and Sally went on to find a five-acre property, and attempted to live there as self-sufficient subsistence farmers. They supplemented their income with his writing and BBC programs, and Sally's pottery. Their book about this experience, *The Fat of the Land*, became the first of many best-sellers, and John was to become an international authority of the self-sufficiency movement.

Hares Creek was one of a pair of semi-detached game-keepers cottages, overlooking a two-acre field, pond, and the mud saltings bordering the broad estuary of the Orwell—a wonderful location. Once she had the keys, Hetta quickly furnished the house from the dump in Chelmondiston, the nearest village. There was no plumbing or electricity. There was an outside privy which had to be emptied periodically into a hole dug in the garden, and there was a pump in the outhouse which was the water supply. This outhouse also had a stove to heat the copper for boiling washing. You always had to leave enough water in a pitcher, next to the pump, to allow it to be primed, particularly if it had been left for a while. Otherwise one had to go next door to the Hailstones (he a Customs and Excise man with a motorcycle) to beg for some water to pour down into the pump to prime it. Lighting was supplied by candles, brass paraffin lights with wicks and tall glass chimneys, and, the most high-tech, a paraffin pressure light ('Tilley lamp') which required pumping up, and priming with methylated spirits to get the manifold hot enough to ignite the paraffin vapour. Even in the summer it would take well over an hour to get all the jobs done on arrival.

It was during this summer, with their trips to Suffolk, that the family got to know Nigel and Judith Henderson, who lived in a huge and very old water-side house in Essex. It had once been a pub serving the bargees and grain merchants who passed through as grain was shipped to London. The jetties were long since disused, and their little settlement had become quite remote. They had two daughters, Drucilla ('Jo'), about Mog's age, and Justin, a year or so younger than Jacob, and a very young son, Stephen. Nigel was an artist and photographer, teaching at the School of Art in Norwich. Judith presided over the rambling coach house inn, with its endless bookcases and stairs, a huge kitchen with a large range, with dogs and cats at her feet. Her literary connections included being a neice of Virginia Woolf. There were a number of cottages attached to their house, which they let out to other artists, including the young Eduardo Paolozzi.

In an addition to Jacob's list of accidents, during a game of hide and seek he was squeezing through two metal gates leaning together to form a fence, when the whole thing fell over, crushing his head between them. The back of his head received a heavy blow, which is what he was most aware of, but his two front teeth were broken, which were to become a life-time problem, with caps, then crowns, then bridgework and finally extraction forty years later. Paolozzi was acutely ashamed of this, as he was responsible for the temporary fence (and, of course, his sculpture was almost all in the form of steel metalwork, even when in bronze). In years to come when he met Ma in the street in Hampstead he would be asking after Jacob's broken teeth. (If only he had offered a small bronze in recompense!) Nigel had a brother, Ian, who lived not far away, and he and his wife Mae were also to be long-term family friends.

Mog had passed the Common Entrance examinations, and left home in September to board at Aldenham School. Peter Duval Smith also left England to take up a temporary, two-year post at Hong Kong University, arranged for him by William. For a little while Jacob had his mother to himself. However, this all changed in early December, when Ma gave birth on the 6th December to a son, Simon Peter. Again, the family did not go to Yokefleet Hall for Christmas.

Meifang Blofeld came to stay in Studio House early in December, 1956. She was the wife of the English ex-patriat John Blofeld, a linguist, translator and scholar who had lived in Peking until 1949, when he left for Hong Kong in advance of the Communist victory with his young wife. Their two children, James and Susan, were born in 1949 and 1950, and by 1955 had been sent to Darjeeling, to be in the care of nuns. They were not to see their mother for years. (When Meifang eventually turned up at the school to visit her, Susan didn't recognize her, and found the whole experience most upsetting.)

Meifang had come to England once already, to learn English, and now was making a second trip to improve her English, and learn shorthand and typing. She was given one of the rooms upstairs, to live on her rather small allowance of £5 per week from her husband. She could not know that her stay was not going to be the care-free jaunt that she may have hoped for, and she was going to be called upon to act virtually *in loco parentis* for the next eighteen months. To begin with, though, Meifang helped Ma look after Simon—she was not succeeding in breast-feeding, and Simon was constantly crying. Meifang came up with the old Chinese solution of giving the infant the water that rice had been boiled in. This did have the effect of quietening him, but of course was hardly nutritious. In any case, Simon managed to survive their combined efforts, and eventually breastmilk became available. Jacob tried to be helpful, too.

As the term came to an end, and Pa and Mog came home from Sheffield and Aldenham, there was what was to prove a false sense of normality. They had erected the tent in the Studio again, with its flap going over the Pither stove, and one of William's old Japanese students who had come to visit took a photograph of Jacob and Ma and Pa in the tent. The boys were not aware of the arrangements that the grownups were making, and Mog was back at school when Hetta left England in March, 1957, flying to Bangkok with Simon in one of the new BOAC Comet jetliners, with its large picture windows which were to prove its eventual (literal) downfall. They stayed with John Blofeld. Peter joined her there and they went on to Hong Kong.

In April Hetta was to write to Walter from Hong Kong:

> I flew from London to Bangkok last month, carrying Simon Peter (4 months) stayed a week with Blofeld and then we came here with the other Peter whom you don't know. He is at the University here for two years and met us in Bangkok. We are going to Japan at the end of June for the long vacation so—will you all be friends. I left Jake, Mog and Pa in the care of Mei Fang Blofeld in London saying I'd be away for a year. We're all friends and you'd like my Peter. We could have more fun and you must show us Japan and find me an amah for Simon while we hell around. It's heaven to be here, even if it is only smelly and rather hysterical old Hong Kong. We went to Macao for the weekend. I must say I'd rather like to live there.

Ma, Peter and Walter in Japan

Max Bickerton was in charge of collecting rents from the other tenants in Studio House, but it had been left rather ambiguous who was going to provide Mei Fang with the necessary funds to keep Jacob in bread and butter during term time. Hetta was not to return to England until August 1958. During this period Mei Fang and Jacob lived on their own in the ground floor flat in Studio House, joined during the vacations by Pa and Mog.

Life was ordered and quiet with Meifang in charge. There would be visits from the other tenants—Max, John Wright, and Hui Min. Meifang also had a girl-friend, Joan Higgins, who was a frequent visitor. They would sit and smoke (Bachelors cigarettes, the source of endless jokes about securing one) and listen to music on her record player. Joan's favourite singer was Alma Cogan—the girl with the laugh in her voice. Jacob gave Meifang a record storage box for her birthday on April 4th.

Soon after Meifang was left in charge of Jacob (and the house) Aunt Molly came down from Yorkshire to inspect the arrangements, which she could not reasonably fault. However, to be on the safe side she decided to take what was left of the family silver to the bank. (Hetta and William had been given a full silver service, with the Empson crest of a Maltese cross in a crusaders tent, as a wedding present. Much of it had been lost during the ten years that had passed, mainly in China. Mei Fang was certainly not to blame, and what remained would have been as safe with her as it was at the bank.) In any case, this was a most humiliating, and probably unselfconsciously racist gesture on Molly's part, although Meifang seemed to shrug it off.

So far as Mog and Jacob were concerned, this was obviously a critical time in being abandoned by their mother, particularly since their father was so abstracted, if not positively distracted by the turn of events. He did his best to make arrangements for them in the holidays, but was able to leave term-time care to Meifang (for Jacob) and Aldenham School (for Mog). Jacob wrote to Ma saying how he couldn't remember much about Hong Kong, 'except I remember Mog losing his water-pistol and he was sure that the capitalists had stolen our only means of defence, at the time I believed him. So if you find it please send it back. I think he lost it when we moved.' The idea of them being jointly in defiance of the capitalists was wearing a bit thin, and Mog and Jacob were spending increasing amounts of time apart. The first of their holidays without Ma, Easter, 1957, was spent by Jacob with some friends of Joan Higgins, who lived in Kent. It did seem odd to be staying with total strangers and he wrote to Ma to say, right now I am in Kent, in a place called Groombridge, near Tunbridge Wells, with some friends of Joan Higgins . . . . My hostess is named Mrs Rodgers, and the border between Kent and Sussex is at the bottom of the garden.

Mrs Rodgers has got three dogs and two sons, the elder son is seventeen years old, and is in Holland for Easter. The younger one is here with me, he is twelve years old and rather like Hugo Davenport—he thinks he knows everything, but otherwise he is O.K . . . . On the Saturday before Easter, I learnt that they had the custom of giving presents for Easter, so I had to go out shopping. I bought Mrs Rodgers a tea cosy. Then I bought Pierz (the younger son) a box of chocolates. I was outdone, however, for Pierz bought me a magnet and a book, and Mrs Rodgers bought me a tie.

He wasn't with the Rodgers for the whole holiday, for they spent some time at the Creek, with Joan and her friend Eric, going there in the trusty Morris Commercial van (presumably one of them could drive, as Meifang did not have a driving license at the time.) Mog and his school-friend Wynn were with them for some of the time there. Paul Massie, the actor, was a lodger with Mabel Sharpe. He was starting his career in the cinema, with Alexander Korda as his mentor. He was to make a couple of British thrillers, but will perhaps be best remembered for his role in Tony Hancock's *The Rebel*, when he played the diffident artist whose work was plagiarised by the ambitious Hancock.

Meifang, Paul Massie and Joan Higgins at the Creek

Max Bickerton became concerned about Jacob being too solitary, and wrote to William to suggest that he should become a weekly boarder. In fact Jacob wasn't aware of being very lonely, and on a Saturday would take the tube down to Knightsbridge to go to the Natural History Museum. They provided stools, pencils, paper and sketchpads for children to go and draw the exhibits, and he was particularly attracted to the dinosaur fossils. One memorable day he over-stayed after closing time, and the lights were all turned off, leaving him in the dinosaur room with the Tyrannosaurus skeleton, amongst others. It wasn't really scary, but provided a tale to tell his schoolmates. He also had a friend, McDermott, who played with him at weekends, when they took their bikes on the Heath, or back to the McDermott house on Fitzjohns Avenue to have their favourite sandwiches with 'Kraft Dairy Cheese'. They took long bike rides over Hampstead Heath, and all across London, in the hot summer of 1957 when the smell of the ubiquitous privet was overpowering. Jacob never found out whether he had problems at home as well, or why he was prepared to join him on these excessive long trips with little purpose.

William made an effort to pay more attention to his sons, as he was now in sole charge, and took Mog on trips to the British Museum and the War Museum, and Jacob for a long walk in and around Missenden. Jacob discovered an abandoned pair of cow horns in a ditch, which he carried home. Joined in the middle with a wooden yoke covered with false fur, they would have hung in a butcher's shop. He has one of them still, with the end cut off so it can be blown to produce a cow-like mooing noise. In any case, Pa decided that things weren't so bad as to warrant boarding, and Jacob carried on as before.

The long summer holiday posed a greater problem for Pa and Meifang to keep the boys occupied. Some of the time was spent with the family of the historian A.J.P. Taylor, on the Isle of Wight, where they went with the Davenports, John and Marjorie, and their two sons Hugo and Roger. The Taylors had a house close to the sea, where one could go shrimping. Taylor himself was rather scary when he emerged from his study, too pre-occupied to notice children. His daughters were not there to begin with, having gone on holiday in France, and when they returned they were polite but not very interested in playing with boys. Jacob got into trouble with one of them, Amelia, who said to him in a very threatening way, 'I've got a bone to pick with you!'—it turned out that he had used her shrimping net without permission, while they were away, and had *ruined* it.

They spent some time at Yokefleet with Uncle Arthur, and were taken there by Uncle Dick, by air. Uncle Dick (Richard Atcherley) had been a famously flamboyant aviator before the war, with his twin brother David, also a pilot. They had succeeded in joining up by Dick taking the eyesight tests for both of them, and David doing the written exams. They were both successful pilots and famous in the R.A.F. for their practical jokes and derring do. Dick had the honour of being in the team which won the Schneider Trophy in 1929, in the Supermarine seaplane, a fore-runner of the Spitfire. (Although achieving the fastest time around the course, he had unfortunately flown inside one of the pylons, instead of going around it, and so was disqualified.) They had also bombed the Egyptians in Cairo with bags of coal to show their displeasure at some diplomatic slight or other. He could fly upside-down and pick up a hankerchief from the ground. The twin had died, disappeared over the Mediterranean in a Meteor in 1952.

Uncle Dick had never married, and had no children, so he was to join the team of well-intentioned relations looking after the abandoned Empson boys. By this time (1957) he was an Air Vice Marshall, in charge of all Air Force training, and based at Camberley. He had access to a number of aircraft, including a twin-engined Anson and a De Havelland Dove, reputedly belonging to the Queen's Flight, and normally flown by the Duke of Edinburgh. We always called him Uncle Dick although he was in fact a cousin on my grand-mother's side (a Micklethwaite.)

The 'Supermarine' seaplane which gloriously won the
Schneider Trophy in 1929

The flight with Uncle Dick was very exciting. He had taken the
Anson on this trip, which climbed to what seemed a great height,
above the clouds, but below another layer of clouds. We were
surrounded by clouds, although flying in clear sky. It seemed like
a cathedral of cloud. It was wonderful to think that this world was
up there all the time, and one only had to have an aeroplane to get
up there to appreciate it. This was the beginning of Jacob's love of
flying. Mog never admitted to being impressed.

That September Mog was taken to board at Aldenham, where
he went for a lot of solitary walks during his first term, collecting
conkers which had fallen from the huge horse chestnuts which lined
the football pitches at the far end of the playing fields. Conkers
were prized possessions at prep school, where everyone played
competitive conker bashing every break and lunch-time and a good

supply was essential. So Mog collected as many as he could. He had amassed a whole shoe-box full before somebody told him that *nobody* played with conkers at Aldenham—that was kid's stuff. This explained the huge number of neglected windfalls. On his first exeat he brought them home and gave the whole shoebox full to Jacob, who was hugely greatful. When he took them to school the following Monday he was to find they were an embarrassment of riches, and ended up giving them away by the handful to increasingly confused boys. What should have been rare and desirable specimens were now so abundant that they seemed common, and the games of conker-bashing actually diminished. Initially, Jacob's hoard had given him some status, but gradually the boys began to view him rather quizzically.

That Christmas vacation was spent at Yokefleet Hall, where Uncle Arthur took a particular interest in Mog, teaching him to shoot. The house was (and is) huge—tall Victorian Gothic, surrounded by large trees which came quite close to it, and was approached by a half-mile drive through woodland. It was a pretty forbidding prospect on arrival. The first room after the small entrance hall was the billiard room, dominated by the full-size billiard table, with a wide open staircase leading up to the first floor, with carved wooden balustrades. Around the dusty walls of this room were hung black and white prints, dedicated to various causes, such as 'Floreat Etona', and so on. (A bit reminiscent of their prep school, in fact). Double doors led into another, smaller room, with floor to ceiling windows onto the garden. On the right was the dining and on the left was the 'Morning Room'. The house had most recently been furnished by Arthur's mother, with mainly Victorian furniture, which was moved into the new Yokefleet Hall after it was built in about 1890, replacing an eighteenth century house which had burned down. Uncle Arthur had changed nothing. The Morning Room contained eighteenth-century furniture which had belonged to his grandmother, including a small piano. The place was thus a bit of a time capsule—in retrospect, a sort of baronial Munster's house.

Uncle Arthur was very much the local squire. He farmed about 1000 acres himself, and had about another 3000 acres let to tenant farmers. He was proud of his agricultural innovations, such as the grain dryer, which he would allow the tenant farmers to use when he had finished with it every season. His greatest achievement on the farm was to have revived the practice of 'warping', where, for a whole season in the early 1950s, the waters of the Humber were allowed to flood the land, bringing valuable silt with the brackish water. Although it left the land too salty for crops for a year or two, it was said that the benefits of this tricky manoeuvre would last a generation. On Sundays he sat in his pew at the front of the church in Blacktoft, where a number of his relations, including his elder brother John, were buried, and would normally read a lesson. He was a local magistrate. He was tall, and very large—in fact too big to be able to ride any more, so he had given up riding to hounds. Mog and Jacob listened to accounts of all these accomplishments, and were very impressed. A formidable person, although very much the avuncular old chap with a twinkle in his eye.

One day, after lunch, Pa slipped and fell on a loose rug in the dining room, breaking his arm. He spent the rest of the time in bed, which was particularly excruciating, he claimed, because they had put him in the best bed with a feather mattress. This had the effect of making any small movement a major upheaval. With Pa temporarily out of action, Aunt Molly took the boys to Scarborough. She had owned the hotel at Hayburn Wyke, a stop on the railway line between Scarborough and Whitby, where she and her husband

Phil had also invested in a caravan park. She always talked about it as though it were very grand, so it is a disappointment to visit the place today—with the railway long closed (after Beeching), the outbuildings derelict and no caravan park left, there is simply rather a run-down pub clinging on by holding karaoke nights and providing a mini-bus service to and from Scarborough. When it came time for them to return to London Uncle Dick flew them back.

With Aunt Molly in Scarborough, 1957. Mog is wearing
Jacob's school tie (he was already at Aldenham)

Despite having his arm in a sling, Pa insisted on sticking to the plan to go to the Scottish Highlands, to stay with his colleague Murray who had a croft in the deep interior, near Loch Fionn. They took the train to Fort William, and Murray picked them up in his Landrover for a very long drive. He had a curious lump on his forehead, which he said was a family trait—the mark of a true Murray! His wife took charge of the boys while the men talked office politics, or literature, or whatever. They went on scouting expeditions to look for deer, and were told all the best ways of seeing one—not looking where you expect to find it, for instance, as a movement at the corner of your eye is noticed better than in full vision. They never did see any, however, and it was another holiday of exposure to weather, coal fires and carrying water.

In October 1957 Jacob was to write to Ma,

'We went to see Uncle Dick again. He flew me to Blackbush (Near his home) on Saturday morning. Mog was to arrive on Sunday. Aunt Molly and Uncle Arthur turned up for dinner. But before that, after lunch Uncle Dick took me 'for a flight'. We went to the Isle of Wight. It was a twin-engined, duel controlled Ansen. When we came into sight of Blackbush again, I knew more or less how to guide it. For I had been watching him. He let go of his joystick, and shouted above the noise of the engines, "I'll use the pedals, you bring her in!" I was terrified. I expect you're expecting me to say that I brought it in wonderfully, and stepped out amid roars of applause from the Control Tower and Officers Mess. But I didn't. I couldn't see the lights. When I found them, I was off course. So I had to swing around in a circle. Just then Uncle Dick pointed out something. It was a red Very light. So he brought it in. As you may have guessed, half of this is made up. But I did drive it a little bit. It was like having a racehorse under control. It was so full of life. I was not at all sick.'

The dinners at Uncle Dick's house were very formal, with RAF stewards attending, and serving the food and drink. The first time, when they had finished their pudding and everybody seemed to be getting up, Jacob did so as well, which was quite the wrong thing, as only the ladies were leaving. He was supposed to stay and watch the chaps pass the port, and talk manly things, like tales of breaking the sound barrier, or how the cannon barrels on a Canberra expanded when they got hot, so that the rounds would spin head over heels as they emerged, and then stick out of the target like a pincushion, instead of destroying it.

It became a mission of Uncle Dick's to recruit Mog and Jacob into the R.A.F. His nephew, Sam Keys, was already an R.A.F. officer, and was well into his military career. One way of getting a boy interested in aeroplanes is to send him up in a jet fighter, which he duly did. In February 1958 Jacob was to write to his mother,

' . . . . On the 18th I went with Aunt Molly and Mog to Uncle Dick's. I went up in a Meteor—a jet fighter—trainer. Have I told you all this before? It was wonderful above the clouds. Just like at the North Pole, for the clouds looked like pack-ice below us, and in the gaps between them it looked so blue that I could hardly believe that I was not looking up. I had to be dressed in a flying suit to go up, with an oxygen mask and earphones for speaking to the pilot. I was sick, but it was worth it. I don't think the pilot had many chances of going up in jets (he was about 56) and he determined to enjoy himself. For the rest of the day my enthusiasm for aeroplanes was sumwhat damped.'

The Meteor was Britain's first operational jet fighter. It had a jet engine on each wing, and, in the training version, two seats fore and aft. Mog and Jacob were both dressed in pressurized flying suits, with flying helmets with microphones, earphones and oxygen masks, while they waited their turn in the plane. The pilot, it seems, had been told by Uncle Dick that the boys were expecting some exciting manoeuvres, so, when it was Jacob's turn he took the plane up to a great height and then stood it on its head to return to earth. Jacob was sick after they levelled out, but did remember to remove the mask and use the paper bag. The flight crew had made him promise not to make a mess of the mask, as he said it would be his job to clean it out. After these aerobatics the Meteor flew to the Isle of Wight and back, all in less than half an hour.

Their previous flights had been fairly low level, compared to this—the Meteor took one up well above all the clouds, and the permanent sunshine up there just took Jacob's breath away. It was wonderful to think that whatever the drab, damp weather one was having down below, the Meteor pilot could always be enjoying the sunshine. Jacob had definitely been successfully recruited, although Mog remained determinedly unimpressed.

The Gloster Meteor trainer

Uncle Dick lived in the style befitting an Air Vice Marshall, in a large house with servants in air force uniforms. He had lots of memorabilia from his escapades—bits of pranged aircraft, shrunken heads from Borneo or somewhere, and, in pride of place, a silver model of the Supermarine—the beautiful little seaplane in which his team had won first prize in the international Schneider speed trials. He gave Jacob a walking cane made from the centre of a plywood propeller blade, with the ply swirling around the head with its silver top. It was a treasured possession for quite a while. He had to be kept informed of any important developments, so that occasionally a batman would come into the sitting room to tell him something—for instance that Flying Officer so-and-so had just broken the sound barrier in a Hunter. 'Good show. Send him my congratulations!' Or else, Flying Officer so-and-so had a bad landing. 'Bad show'.

On one occasion Uncle Dick was taking Jacob in the Dove from Hendon Aerodrome to Elstree Aerodrome, next to Aldenham School, to go and pick Mog up for a flight, and to take him out for lunch.

It was one of his Sunday 'exeats'. They flew around the aerodrome repeatedly, but every time they made an approach a red Verey light was fired, indicating that they should not land. (There was no radio communication at Elstree, where 'air traffic control' was conducted by amateurs.) Uncle Dick was swearing and exclaiming at their stupidity, and tried every permutation of approach, but to no avail, and they had to return to Camberley, telephone the school to warn Mog that they were going to be late and do the trip all over again in a limousine. When they arrived the whole school was in chapel, attending the morning service, and Uncle Dick and Jacob were hanging about in the entrance lobby, with its wall covered with coats hanging up. Uncle Dick started picking boaters off their hooks trying them on, and eventually throwing them for Jacob to catch, despite his pleas for him to stop, and they must have been heard by the whole school. He just couldn't help being playful. Years later Jacob met a bloke at a party who was boasting about how he had prevented an Air Marshall from landing at Elstree Aerodrome, on the pretext that he had circled on the wrong side of the landing strip.

They went to Yokefleet again for Christmas. Uncle Arthur and Aunt Molly made an effort to make things special for the boys. They were each given a bicycle, which they rode around the lanes. Aunt Molly taught them how to play 'fives' on the billiard table, which consisted of hitting the ball with your hand so that it bounced off the top and side cushions, and you tried to hit it so hard that your opponent missed their turn. This involved a lot of running around the full-size table, and probably damage to the cushions, but was much more fun than trying to hit the balls with a cue, and an ideal activity for a rainy day. After New Year they had an expedition to Hull, to see the pantomime at the New Theatre, where Uncle Arthur had booked a box. They took a hamper with lots of food packed by Mrs Sellers, and had a very merry evening shouting out 'He's behind you!' and so on. Mog and Jacob were beginning to take to the British way of doing things by now.

The next Easter holiday was spent in Wales, with Pa and Alice Stewart. She had a cottage in a remote part of Snowdonia, where there was no electricity or plumbing. They had to fetch water from the stream, using a yoke and two buckets. Alice was a good sport, who didn't try to be mummy, but seemed to know what a little boy might want—presumably a trick learned from her years not only as a mother but as a head-masters' wife. They climbed Snowdon, and played cards in the evenings by lamplight. Mog was allowed to not join the party, but to take off with his friend Wynn to France on a hitch-hiking holiday (on condition that he joined the Youth Hostel Association).

Any 'normal' marriage would undoubtedly have ended in divorce by now, with Hetta's persistent infidelity, her bearing a son by another, and, indeed, leaving the country with him. She had raised the issue during 1957, in a letter from Hong Kong. William had written back without specifically objecting to the idea, but restricting himself to talking about the financial arrangements that may have to be made. He also pointed out she would be best advised to start proceedings before her return, and that on her return she would not be able to stay in Studio House. In a letter to his brother Arthur, later that year, William was to say,

> As to divorce, Hetta wrote from Hongkong and offered
> an undefended divorce, because it crossed her mind
> as a high-minded thing to do only, I am sure; but we
> high-minded characters are accustomed to feel that we are
> safer if we have made the alternative offer quite firmly.

I wrote back earnestly offering to arrange a divorce if she expected to earn so much money as a sculptor that it would save money on our joint tax, and explaining that I could not possibly marry the woman I now love, divorced or not, because we both earn salaries which would be cut in half if we married. As lovers nobody objects to our appearing together, but if we married all informed persons would feel that the craving had become a bit sordid. Hetta really is, as I said to Molly some while ago, as strong as a horse, and as brave as a lion, and I only hope she can manage to carry off her bet or fantastic choice and make something of Peter.

Oddly enough, I am almost as much against divorce as a Catholic, because I want to behave like an eighteenth century landlord. I wish I had a third child, but as I am going I couldn't have afforded that. As long as Peter can afford it, I have nothing to grumble about; but that, as we will soon find out, may become a difficulty. I could not arrange to leave Hetta alone with a difficulty by telling lies to satisfy a disgusting law.

William's ambition for a marriage which included sexual relationships with others had worked well when they lived in China, where Walter had been a willing and agreeable accomplice. This had now obviously failed, as Peter Duval Smith was only interested in Hetta having an exclusive relationship with him. William, however, obstinately stuck to his guns, refusing to believe that it was all over. In the event, Hetta changed her mind about divorce, and elected to stay with her complaisant husband with her boys, assuming, presumably, that she would be free to have what sexual relationships she chose at the same time.

Eventually the day came, in June 1958, when Hetta returned from exile—although not by jet airliner as when she left. Hetta did not have a return ticket from Hong Kong, so she had to find the fare to come home. Rather than travelling by air, she had saved up enough for the boat from Hong Kong to Marseilles, and then by boat train to London. Peter, it seems, was unable to help financially, and she was resorting to a number of schemes to raise money. One of them was a commission to create sculptures to decorate a millionaire's new mansion, being built high up on the slopes above Hong Kong. Apart from decorative pieces, such as fineals and gutter ornaments, she had planned a couple of 'watchers'—monumental figures thirty feet high, facing the sea. She brought a model of one of them home with her, made in lead, showing it as a plain figure, with its head slightly doglike, although without features. Unfortunately her millionaire suddenly went bankrupt, so she was one of many, including architects, builders and tradesmen, who were left unpaid for their efforts. Eventually Pa sent her some money to contribute to her fare, so, all in all, her return was anything but triumphant.

Pa, Mog and Jacob all met her at Victoria Station. She managed to make the best of what anyone else would have found a humiliating situation, coming home on her own and broke, after her break for freedom. She got off the train with a familiar figure, who was the actor Miles Malleson—a portly character actor in films, instantly recognizable. It turned out that he had also been a life-long Communist, and they had known each other for years. He was on the train quite by chance.

At any rate, she advanced down the platform in some style carrying Simon on her hip, with Mr Malleson trailing behind her manfully struggling with her bags, and the family was all happily re-united. There was no sign of Peter Duval Smith.

Chapter 6

Boarding School, Josh

There was a second flight in a Meteor, organized of course by Uncle Dick. Hetta and Pa had both come to take Mog and Jacob to Camberley, leaving Simon in Meifang's charge. Again, the pilot had been instructed to do some acrobatic stunts, and Mog and Jacob were both sick. After the boys' flights in the jet the family took off in the De Havelland Dove, with Uncle Dick at the controls, to fly to Yorkshire for a weekend with Uncle Arthur. Jacob was still feeling queasy after his time in the Meteor, and, sitting in his window seat in the smart plane, with the air smelling of rubber blowing out of the vent above his head which only made things worse. He'd had enough of aeroplanes for the day. There was an incident to enliven the proceedings, though. Uncle Dick was rather taken with Hetta, and she with him, never being averse to a dashing aviator, and half-way through the flight, and having had a few drinks, she was standing with another one in her hand at the front of the passenger cabin with the door open to the flight deck, and said, 'Why are we going to bloody Yorkshire? Why don't you fly us to Brussels?' Uncle Dick put the plane into a steep right turn, with the right wing pointing at the ground, taking her at her word. 'No!

No!' she cried, hanging on to the door frame, and started pleading with him to stop. On this occasion she had met her match in being outrageous.

Jacob had taken his Common Entrance early in 1958, and did sufficiently well to be accepted to join Mog at Aldenham School the following September, so a home had to be found for Gertie and her new kid, this time a nanny. The Hendersons agreed to take them both, and called the little nanny Henrietta, after Ma.

A new school meant a trip to the school outfitters to be fitted out with a complete new wardrobe of the smartest clothes Jacob had ever dreamed of. This included a grey suit with long trousers, half a dozen shirts, a grey blazer, dark flannel trousers—not to mention the sports clothes. He hadn't had new clothes in a while, what with being in Meifang's charge, and her budget didn't run to anything like that. Anyway, this was very exciting. Mog had been having a very good time at Aldenham, so Jacob was all set to go and enjoy himself too.

It turned out that Mog had been given the responsibility of being the House boiler-man in his first year, and Jacob inherited this job, which was shared with another new boy, Handley. Handley asked him, 'I say, Empson Minor, what's your Christian name?'

"Jake", replied Empson, "What's yours?"

'My parents call me Tommy, after the comedian'.

So they both had assumed names. They had two furnaces to keep filled with coke, and emptied of ash, which had to be done twice a day. One of their games was to open the door to the furnace and throw a shovelful of water onto the white-hot coals. They would turn black, and then there would be an almighty bang as the water gas generated by the mixture exploded. They had no idea about carbon monoxide, hydrogen, and so on, but it was a mighty good thing to do, and impressed visitors to their little kingdom. Boiler-men also had a secret cache of *Health and Efficiency* magazines, hidden behind a brick in a hole in the wall, passed on from generation to generation. (These were ostensibly naturist magazines, with photographs of graceful young ladies playing tennis with no tops on). Hetta had given Jacob 400 cigarettes to take to school with him, and these found a hiding place in the boiler room too. They were a very mild brand (*'Mink'*) she had brought with her from Hong Kong which made them suitable for a young man like him. She had also given him an air gun, which was impossible to hide, and was confiscated on his arrival.

Hetta and Pa both came to Aldenham to take Jake and Mog out for the day on their first 'exeat'—an opportunity for parents to take their children out to lunch on a Sunday.

Pa and Ma in a pub garden, with Mog in the background
stroking the pony

The school was divided into five 'houses' including two (the 'school houses') in the main buildings and three others in their own. Mog and Jake were in Beevor's House. In the late 1950s Aldenham was, like almost all other boys' public schools, operating on the traditions developed during the nineteenth century. The older boys were given considerable authority over the younger, including powers to inflict punishments and canings. There was also the system of 'boying', in which chores had to be done for the older boys. Since Jake (now known in the school as 'Empson Minor') already had responsibility in the boiler-room he was let off some of this, although he still had to tidy and clean the Captain of House's study, clear the grate, light his fire when required, and to run errands for him. It was said that some house captains even sent their 'boys' to sit on the toilet to warm the seat for them, but Empson Minor was never required to do that. Minor infringements included having the wrong buttons done up on your jacket, or straying onto the lawn reserved for older boys. These were punished with 'changing cobs', where you had to run up and down the stairs to the dormitory, in and out of sports clothes and day clothes, and having a chit signed by a suitably senior boy every time. More serious infringements, such as insolence ('lack of respect') or smoking cigarettes, were punished with beatings.

The head of house was a history teacher, Chris Wright, who seemed a thoroughly civilized, progressive sort. It was difficult to reconcile all this with the system over which he presided. His deputy, Palmer, was also a historian, who, again, seemed a most sympathetic sort, and who took time to hold special tutorials for boys with particular interests in history and current events.

There was a brief service in the chapel every morning, and on Sundays there were two services. The chapel had as its altarpiece a large painting of the crucifixion by Stanley Spencer. (Somebody on the board of governors had had the foresight to commission the great artist to paint two pictures for the school during the early 1950s.) Hetta thoroughly approved of these works of art, and she felt Aldenham had demonstrated a level of good taste in acquiring them—making up for its other deficiencies. The crucifixion was a very scary painting. The executioners nailing Christ to the cross were draymen (a reference to the school's origins in a bequest from the Whitbread brewing family), and they were grinning, hanging on to the cross on top of their stepladders, with huge nails in their mouths, ready to be hammered in. One of the thieves was unconscious, or at least slumped, while the other was leaning forwards with his mouth wide open, screaming with rage. This uncompromising depiction made a great impression on Empson Minor, and it never lost its power during his three years at the school.

He had been placed in the lower set, consistent with his rather poor results at Common Entrance. By the end of the academic year he had done better than expected in class, and was transferred, with another boy, Griffiths, to join the clever set, although a year younger than them, in September 1959. There didn't seem to be much sense to this, as they would still be taking GCEs at the same time, but possibly it meant that they were timetabled to take English Language a year early, allowing time for Additional Maths. Griffiths and Empson Minor came jointly first in the end of term exams, which entitled them to a prize of a book each. Hetta suggested that Jake should ask for John Reed's *Ten Days That Shook the World*, his eye-witness account of the October Revolution in Saint Petersburg. When prize day came the distinguished visitor, handing out the prizes, gave Empson Minor a piece of cardboard instead of a book, and he had to go and buy the book at Colletts Bookshop in Hampstead himself:

the school had not been able to bring themselves to purchase such inflammatory literature.

The school played football in the Christmas term, hockey in the spring term, and cricket and athletics in the summer term. Jake wasn't much good at any sports, although he enjoyed hockey and running. He was not entirely happy at Aldenham. One day he reflected how the school had so many advantages—a nice library, a swimming pool, all the sporting facilities, and so on—to be a complete paradise. However, all the regulations and arbitrary punishments by the older boys made life so unnecessarily unpleasant. He particularly didn't like the 'boying' system, and the way the sixth-formers could beat the younger boys, and didn't want to become involved in it as he progressed through the school. One could see how some of the sixthformers did in fact opt out of the system, simply keeping to themselves and not bothering about enforcing petty rules (and avoiding becoming prefects) but there were plenty of others who revelled in it. Mog ('Empson Major') was, it turned out, one of the latter, becoming head of house. There was a convention that elder brothers didn't communicate with their siblings (to avoid favouritism) and Mog and Jake generally avoided having much to do with each other at school.

The whole public school tradition was becoming obviously anachronistic. The boys were not going to run the Empire. They were not even going to be Billy Bunter, idling in the Remove in the certain knowledge that a private income awaited them when they left. The world was changing, and they had access to it, even in term-time, with their transistor radios. Even the old Bakelite radio set in the Common Room could be tuned to pick up Radio Luxemburg, which brought them into touch with the music of the United States. Eddie Cochrane, with his subversive 'Who cares? C'mon everybody!' was just one example. The good thing was that the boys were united in resisting the old regime, to greater and lesser extents. The bad thing was that they were still isolated from the real world during term-times, and whenever it liked, the school regime could turn and impose its weird authority in the form of beatings and punishment 'cobs'. It was a toxic combination, but for once Jake didn't feel that he was unusual in feeling displaced.

There were comings and goings with Peter Duval Smith during this first year at Aldenham, after his return from the East. There were the usual drunken arguments, and it was a relief for Jake when they were taken off to Aldenham in the van with Mog at the beginning of term. It was during this term at Aldenham that Peter smashed both their crossbows during one of their rows. Mog and Jake found that very difficult to forgive. In fact they never totally forgave him for it—they represented their Chinese heritage. Fortunately they didn't see a great deal of him after that. It also marked a cooling in relations between the MacNeice and Empson households. This was probably a result of an incident when Peter disgraced himself at their house. He had kept Louis up drinking when he was due to be up early to broadcast the next day, and refusing Hedli's pleas to go home. Eventually, on being thrown out of the house, he took the rest of the bottle of brandy they had been drinking with him, and drank it on the pavement before throwing the empty bottle through their sitting room window. (Peter had known the MacNeices for a long time, having lived with them briefly in Greece in the early 1950s).

By now, Louis and Hedli had their own problems, which were to end in separation and divorce during 1960 and 1961. Corinna was at her theatrical school in London, and doubtless had many other friends, and, of course, Mog and Jake were to be in boarding school. They were to take up with her again in their late teens, when

Corinna was sharing a flat with Maro Gorki, both of them students at the Slade Art School.

Hetta had replaced Peter with another young man, Michael Avery, or, as she like to call him, Josh. Josh was an ex-sailor who had been knocking about in Soho, having been picked up by Daniel Farson, the television journalist. Farson was on intimate terms with the painter Francis Bacon, and with other artists and photographers who drank in the York Minster (the 'French pub'), the Gargoyle and the Colony Club. Josh had presumably obliged Farson sexually during his months spent with him, but was essentially heterosexual. He was striking to look at, with a large head, curly dark hair, rather thick lips and a dark complexion—suggesting an exotic, perhaps even piratical, background. He was rather stocky, and athletically built. He would make an impression because of his looks, but also carried a presence which was greater than could be accounted for by them on their own. From his days as a boxer in the navy he had learned a certain belligerent carriage. Also, having been a devoted fan of the Swedish heavyweight Ingmar Johansson, he emulated him by acting big. That is, he would for instance approach a door sideways, as if his shoulders were too broad to get through straight on. He exaggerated muscular effort, whatever he was doing, even if it was just hoisting up his trousers. He was, perhaps unintentionally, naturally a little intimidating on first acquaintance, but would dispel this with his distinctive laugh and toss of the head. A very different kettle of fish from Peter, being practically one of the children, not so much because of his age (in his late twenties), but his complete lack of education. Pa rather approved of Josh, saying that he had fine feelings.

Josh was an orphan who had been brought up by a series of foster parents, and then sent to the Royal Navy boy sailor school in Shotley, Suffolk—HMS Ganges. He had a short career in the service, being trained as a gunner and a middleweight boxer, before absconding and finding his way to London, and being picked up in Soho by Farson and his friends. There, on being introduced to Francis Bacon, he first announced himself as being a painter, then, on reflection, given the hilarity that his claim had caused, that he was a poet. With no source of income, and still on the run from the Navy, he was reliant on Farson for everything, sharing his bed in his flat in Soho. He was treated rather well, being taken to Devon to stay with Farson's parents, and to visit aristocratic friends in Wales (where he was even set up in a little cottage for a while, to help him write his poetry). A proposed trip to Italy required a passport, and Farson arranged for a false one so that he could travel to Venice with him. The trip was a disaster, with Josh getting angry when he felt slighted by a waiter, and smashing up a bar. In his own memoir, Farson recollects the moment that he was finally out of sympathy with Josh being when he refused to look up from his comic book when they were first approaching Venice by train—on of the greatest railway views of the world.

On their return the photographer John Deakin was using Josh as a model for an advertising campaign for Players cigarettes. Deakin's assistant, Cecelia, was to give Josh the opportunity to escape from Farson, and to develop an alternative career as a ladies man, when she took him back to her Hampstead home with her. It was possibly Farson who informed on him to the police, and he was picked up and spent a few months in military prison, for desertion. (They never found out about his false passport.) This part of his life was documented in a rather hero-worshipping book, *Dog Days in Soho*, by the journalist Nigel Richardson.

During 1959 Peter was periodically turning up at Studio House, sometimes on the pretext of seeing his son, sometimes just wanting to get back with Hetta, and there were a number of confrontations between him and Josh, who treated him with contempt, on one occasion saying, 'Why don't you just piss off?' By December Josh was well established in the house, and Peter had apparently given up on Hetta. (He had actually married Jill Neville in August of 1959, although this was a very short-lived marriage). There was a family Christmas in Studio House with both Josh and Alice Stewart. When reasonably sober he was a good-natured bloke with an ironic sense of humour. When drunk he was worse than Peter, getting furiously angry at the complacency of Hampstead intellectuals, the hypocrisy of the Left, and so on. You could say he had a chip on his shoulder.

It was at a party given by Elizabeth Smart that Josh first became violent towards Hetta. Elizabeth lived in Paddington, with her two sons and two daughters. A talented poet and journalist in her own right, she had encountered the poetry of George Barker in the late 1930s, and became besotted with him. She had eventually sought him out, to have an affair with him which lasted over ten years and which produced four children. (George was to be the father of about fifteen children eventually, with various women.) She was now working in the advertising business as a copywriter. Her two sons were about the same ages as Mog and Jake, but rather more dashing, and they went to a posher public school, playing rugby and not football. Georgina was tall and very beautiful, and training to be a dancer. Rosie was a precocious twelve or thirteen-year-old, already an expert smoker.

Josh became incensed for some reason, and attacked Hetta before leaving the party on his own. Later, Hetta and Jake left Mog there and she drove back to Hampstead, where she went to bed in the bunk above Simon, with Josh asleep in the studio on the k'ang. Jake was woken by a terrible noise, and went in to find Josh on top of Hetta on the floor, with his hands around her neck, obviously attempting to strangle her. He dashed off to get his new hockey stick, and, standing over him, swung it in a perfect shot. If his head had been a ball it would have travelled the whole length of the pitch just twelve inches above the ground. Josh collapsed on the floor, but then recovered after a minute or two, and shambled off, to leave Jake to comfort his mother as best he could. Josh returned later in the night, and Jake was summoned again, although he couldn't get a good angle on him with his hockey stick, as he had got in the top bunk with Hetta. All the same, waving it at him, shouting, and hitting the parts he could reach did have the desired effect, and he went off to bed on his own again.

Hetta had a broken rib and a black eye, as well as the bruises around her neck, when she drove the boys back to Aldenham shortly afterwards. Josh had been banished, first to the Creek, and then altogether, and Hetta was in a state of terror. Her cousin Helena Crouse, a clinical psychologist, was in London, and she came and stayed in Studio House to keep her company.

Josh's disgrace did not last very long, and he was back in Studio House by the Easter vacation. For the next ten years or so they maintained a pattern of violence and reconciliation, with periods of relative calm in between. Josh could be good company, enjoying quirky little jokes. His rages would be precipitated by his feeling that he had been slighted—that his lack of education or any significant accomplishment—was being commented on and derided. Then of course his only accomplishment, his use of his fists, would come into play, normally directing his aggression at another man. Drink certainly played a part, but particularly whisky. Pa was to explain, in a letter to Ma in January 1960, soon after she had told him about Josh's violence,

> He is deeply upset by not being educated enough for his pretensions or for what he wants to do, and whenever he goes out and meets a large party he feels the other men don't take him seriously enough, as they couldn't do, so then he takes it out on Mum. This I am afraid is the basic thing, and the only way out for him is to buckle down and learn something he wants to know; it needn't be much more than a technical skill, but he must be proud of his skill at something before he can come away from a party with the people he likes to meet without feeling assertive and miserable.

Of course the problem of domestic violence towards women is not confined to the rather exotic household that my parents constituted in Studio House, and is unhappily prevalent throughout society. A typical conversation down at the police station could go like this:

> *Police*: 'Why do you do it?'
> *Wife beater*: 'It's the drink.'
> *Police*: 'So what happens?'
> *Wife beater:* 'I go down the pub, have about eight pints with my mates, go home, and then I hit her. It's the drink.'
> *Police*: 'If it's the drink, why don't you hit your mates before you go home?'

While about 80% of cases of domestic violence involve men attacking women, a sizeable minority, 10%, involve women attacking men. It was certainly true that Hetta was normally capable of defending herself, and sometimes initiated violence against Josh, for whatever reason. She rarely humoured him in his exquisite sensibilities, and could sometimes be accused of winding him up by jeering. It was around this time that she developed the affectation of a Southern American accent—emulating both Blanche Dubois *and* Stanley Kowalski from *A Streetcar Named Desire*, as somebody once wittily remarked. She carried this on almost all the time, so it was a sort of expression of defiance—and of her complete alienation from British polite society. Her cousin Helena, for one, could not stand it, complaining to me, 'But she can sound like an ambassador's wife if she wants to. Why does she talk in that ridiculous affected way?' But Hetta had found a voice which she felt comfortable with. In the years since their return from China she had suffered from depression in post-war London, then seemed to find a cure in the joys of the open road with her first van. With Peter there was the promise of another life—perhaps even being an academic's wife again, but married to one who was at least faithful to her gender. With him proving totally unreliable, she was now to make her own life all over again, and it was in the role of a social provocateur. 'This is my paramour!', she would announce when introducing Josh, and then carry on in her affected drawl.

William was endlessly tolerant of Josh, and this was in spite of the occasional outburst being directed towards him himself. The pattern of Josh's disgraces, and banishments, would be for him to promptly go to William for some money to see him over until he could hope to come back, and Pa always seemed to oblige him. William was convinced that when he was taken away by the police (as regularly happened) he would be playing snooker in the police station basement until it was time to go home again. Perhaps this story was one that Josh had told him out of bravado—it did always sound a bit far-fetched. John Haffenden's biography has an extended explanation of what William was trying to achieve in his sexual life, with his ambition to share his wife with another man in order to please her. Over the following ten years or so Mog, Jake and Simon were not aware of these complex motivations, however, and, while he could be good company on a good day, Josh's continued presence remained inexplicable to them.

One consequence of all this was that, even in Hampstead, the Empson household was regarded as being bizarre if not dangerous, and Hetta and Josh acquired few respectable friends. They were regulars at the Roebuck in Pond Street, at the end of Hampstead Hill Gardens and in easy walking distance. They would quite often bring fellow drinkers back after closing time, to finish up whatever there was to drink in the house. Hetta referred to them as the 'pub dregs'. This assortment included a Canadian from Montreal, Donald MacDonald, whose claim to fame was that he had been treated, after a road accident, by the neurosurgeon Wilder Penfield, whose work Jake was to hear a lot about years later in university. (He was a pioneer in experimenting on patients whose cortex was exposed, under local anaesthetic, stimulating different spots on the surface and asking them what they experienced. These low voltage impulses often evoked vivid memories in the patients, making Penfield believe that he had found where memories were stored in the brain.) There was the playwright Paul Ableman and his wife Tina, who loudly claimed to have discovered oral sex. Jake was curious about what they meant, but never go around to asking them. Jon Rose, the rather vulnerable scientologist, who was spending his every spare penny (after what he had spent on beer) on further and further 'auditing' sessions in his gradual progression through the hierarchy. 'Ashcan', the ballet choreographer, whose passion for music was such that he would play the spoons with what was left of the Yokefleet silver service, and get everybody dancing. (There was no such thing as a musical instrument or even a record player in the house.)

In a way, the drinking was fairly moderate, as it was confined to beer in the pub, and then possibly more beer afterwards, or some wine. This was almost always what was described as 'Spanish Burgundy'. It was a rough red wine sold in half gallon bottles, as well as ordinary sized ones, having little in common with either Rioja or Burgundy. It was, however, an indication of the new cosmopolitan tastes of the dawn of the 1960s. When Pa was home for the vacations he would normally have provided a half gallon every day, which was made generally available, although his own supply of brandy was not, and kept in his study.

Jake once babysat for the MacDonalds' two children, in their small flat opposite Belsize Park tube station, and was astonished to find a house that was even dirtier than his own. It was probably the concentration of dirt into a smaller area that made it seem worse. In Studio House there was plenty of room in between the filth. Hetta rarely spent any time cleaning, and nobody else did unless she nagged them into it.

There were two annual parties which were the highlights of their social life—the Boat Race Party and the Christmas Party. The Boat Race party was given by Julian Trevelyan, an artist and contemporary of Pa's at Cambridge, with his wife Mary Sedden, at their studio in Hammersmith, Durham Wharf. It had a terrace with a fine view of the river, and, like at a Studio House party, the teenagers and the middle-aged mingled amicably.

Mog and Jake developed a tradition of providing the turkey for the Christmas lunch, by waiting until the last minute on Christmas Eve, after the pubs had shut, and then driving down to Smithfield to get a bird at a give-away price. Mog drove the Morris Traveller. It was a festive scene at the market, with the pubs still open, as they were every night and morning for the market workers. The traders were shouting their prices, eager to get off and back to their families, and Mog and Jake would wait to the last minute before buying a bird, then load it in the car to drive back to Hampstead, in triumphant mood. The Christmas Party itself was given by Ewen Phillips, the art historian and auctioneer, on Christmas Day in the evening. It was a tradition begun by his mother in the 1930s that the family should provide a meal for the poor on Christmas Day every year, and then to hold an extravagant party for their friends in the evening. It had developed into something of a scrum, as its reputation had spread across North London. What with the charitable side of things earlier in the day, it obviously became difficult to distinguish gatecrashers from the deserving poor. All the same, it was always a good end to an otherwise rather boring festivity.

Jake's enthusiasm for a career in the RAF continued, but it became clear that he was short-sighted, and would probably always need glasses. Pilot training would be out of the question. For a little while he was hoping that the Fleet Air Arm would be less particular, but this was an unrealistic idea. Also, with a promotion to full Air Marshall, Uncle Dick retired from the Air Force so there were to be no more free flights courtesy of the Ministry of Defence. He took up a job with Folland Aviation, who produced a small jet fighter called the Gnat, as an international salesman. (He had been Commander of the Royal Pakistan Air Force for a couple of years after independence and partition, so would have had many useful contacts in Pakistan and elsewhere in the Middle East.)

The school took a dim view of Jake's prospects in the GCE exams—particularly in science subjects. They also assumed that he would be taking Arts subjects for A level, while Jake rather wanted to get into doing science—particularly biology. What with his disenchantment with the school, he asked his Ma and Pa if he could leave, and go to a day school in London to do science subjects. At the same time he started working quite hard on his own, taking his books to the library rather than trying to revise in the communal rooms in Beevor's House. Hetta consulted Mabel Sharpe about the relative merits of schools in London, and she recommended Westminster City School, as she had had a lodger who was an English teacher there, and had spoken highly of it.

Jake—Empson Minor no longer—therefore started at Westminster City School in September 1961, having passed all his O levels, and in fact having done rather well, so there was no question of re-taking any, and he was enrolled in Zoology, Botany, Chemistry and Physics. The 24 bus from Hampstead went all the way to the Victoria Road, taking about 40 minutes in the rush hour every morning and evening.

The boys at Westminster City were a very mixed lot, from all over London, and in fact from all over the world. There was a lugubrious Armenian—Gulvanessian, from whom Jake learned that all Armenian surnames ended in 'ian', like Gulbenkian, the millionaire who lived at the Savoy Hotel. Vidar Strand was an Icelander, his father a consultant psychiatrist who lived in Gloucester Road, between Kensington and Chelsea. Richard Abbott was a cockney from Cable Street, where his parents had a café. Tony Gatcombe was another Londoner, from Notting Hill Gate (which was by no means the fashionable address that it is today.) There were two very bright Jewish boys, Goldschmit and his friend, who did the Telegraph crossword every morning, and who liked to boast that they didn't need to go to Maths or Physics lessons because they could derive all the equations whenever they chose. To begin with there were some other Jewish boys—completely beyond Jake's experience—from the East End, who would throw you out of a fourth floor window as soon as look at you. Very hard. They didn't stay very long in the lower sixth, but went off to work in their family businesses.

The headmaster was a tall imposing figure, Dr Shutt, a chemist who occasionally took sixth form classes. A Yorkshireman who had retained a strong accent, he told the boys studying Chemistry about his PhD work on optical isomerism in the crystals of sulphides. Preparing the crystals involved boiling solutions of sulphide down, and their smell would linger on him long after he got home every day, he said, telling this tale as a lesson in the importance of self-sacrifice in the pursuit of knowledge. The biology teachers were Mr Marshall and Mr Hunt. Marshall was an enthusiast, particularly for botany, and an inspirational teacher. A graduate of Durham University, where he was not ashamed to tell the class that he had got a third class degree, he encouraged them to apply to go there for the rugby if nothing else. Hunt was rather a bumbling character, but a good sort when one got to know him, and with a genuine love of his subject. With these good teachers, and plenty of facilities, there was really no excuse not to do well.

While still at Aldenham Jake had arranged one summer to go off on a cycling holiday with the boy who had been his fellow boiler stoker, Handley. They took their bikes to France, and stayed in youth hostels, returning in about two weeks. When Jake arrived in the kitchen in Studio House Pa looked up and said, 'What, home already?' It was a brief trip, but he had got the taste for it, and it became the first of a number.

Ma had bought a 3-ton ambulance at auction, sold off after a life-times service in the emergency services. Powered by a large Perkins diesel engine, with its stretchers and their trolleys (and the siren) removed, it was a very stable platform for touring, and, with the wooden double bed that she had built into it, a comfortable mobile home. The bed was a bit like the *k'ang* in the Studio, going right across the width of the ambulance and fairly high, so that, lying on the bed one could stick one's head out of the tinted window on the side, and have a fine view of the countryside. Otherwise, sitting in the back could be a bit sickmaking, with the swaying motion and the lack of a clear view out. She, Josh, Simon and Jake took a trip to the south of France in it, first of all returning to the Dordogne and its caves, staying in campsites, where they slept in the ambulance and Simon and Jake had their own tent.

The Daimler Perkins Diesel 3-ton ambulance

They called in on an old friend of Hetta's from China, a British spy, now knighted, Sir Vere Redman. He lived in a remote fortified farmhouse, which had a central tower. Redman had always been a diabetic, and was one of the first to be successfully maintained on insulin injections. The story was that when he was actively engaged in his work in China he always maintained three independent supplies of insulin, to prevent his enemies from seeing him off by cutting him off from any one of them. Redman's routine in retirement was to drink cognac, after an insulin injection, until it was time for a nap, and then, on awakening, to have another insulin injection. Hetta went up into the keep to drink cognac with the great man while Josh, Simon and Jake stayed downstairs in the kitchen with his mother, drinking cooking wine and juice. Josh might have got cross and created a scene, but chose to show another side of himself—his uncanny intuition. With nothing much to talk about to the deaf old lady, he leaned across to her and loudly asked, 'Where do you want to die?' This hit the nail right on the head. 'In England!' she cried, and started wailing. The cognac party upstairs was disrupted, Hetta and Redman coming down to see what the problem was, and the ambulance was soon on its way again.

The next port of call was on some French friends of Mabel Sharpe, the Delpeche family, who were spending the summer in their house in Marcorignan, a village South East of Toulouse, between Carcassonne and Narbonne—a part of France called Languedoc. They stopped there one afternoon, to be greeted with great warmth, and with an English tea. (Mabel had warned them that Hetta might be dropping by.) This went on until it was time to open some bottles of blanquette from the cellar (it seemed that the house was in fact a brewery, and they had extensive vineyards.) Then it was time for dinner, and there was no question of leaving. With their traditional, extended meals (each vegetable being served as a separate course), there was little time between meals, and the addition of an English tea in the afternoon meant that they were effectively trapped there indefinitely. One would hear the occasional pop from the cellar, as another bottle of blanquette had spontaneously burst its cork, so of course it would have to be brought out and drunk up. It was a very enjoyable stay.

The following summer Hetta arranged to visit again, but this time as part of a house-swap arrangement, so the Delpeches could visit London, and their old friend Mabel. Ma, Pa, Mog, Simon and Josh were joined by Biddy and Blake Crozier. Jake cycled down independently. He had bought a superior touring bike from Vidar Strand, the Icelander at school, an original Claude Butler. Vidar used the proceeds to buy a shortie mack, which were all the rage for young men about town. Staying in youth hostels, Jake cycled to Paris, then south to Chartres, discovering on his way what a large country France was. To speed things up, and to avoid the challenge of negotiating the Massif Centrale, he took the train from Montlucon to Cahors. From there it was mostly downhill to Toulouse. He discovered that he enjoyed being solitary, with a legitimate purpose, and would obsessively count the kilometre stones as he went, stopping about every fifteen kilometres for a smoke (always Gitanes in France) and sometimes a drink of wine or wine and water. He aimed to do about 100 kilometres every day.

Jake joined the family in Marcorignan where they had been taken under the hospitality of the vineyard steward and farm manager, Gilbert, who, in the absence of the Delpeches, took responsibility for seeing that they were taken on tours of the vineyards, shown where to swim in the river, and so on. Gilbert was very taken with Hetta, and was persistently asking her to join him in the vineyards.

Josh took it upon himself to drink Gilbert under the table, Simon remembers, as his way of keeping him from having his wicked way with her. Mog and Jake got to know the local boys, and learned to speak French in the distinctively accented way of Languedoc. The village fete was the social event of the year, when a marquee was erected, a live band was brought in, and the girls all dressed up in their best. It was something anticipated with great relish, and the event itself went on all night and into the following morning. In fact Mog and Jake had gone to bed at some late hour, but were woken at about six o-clock in the morning by a group of boys who had been up all night, throwing stones at the windows and calling for Mog to get up and join them.

There was a third and final summer holiday in Marcorignan, and Jake cycled more or less the same route, although taking the train to Paris, as he had found the plains of Picardy were rather dull. On his last day on the bike he decided to do it all in one day from Toulouse, about 150 km. As he approached the local large village of Lezignan there was a sign directing all traffic to the bypass, which he ignored, being tired, and carried on through the centre of the village, where crowds were lining the streets. On spotting him with his saddlebags and (presumably) obvious English appearance, they cried, 'Simpson! Simpson!'—the reason for the diversion was that the Tour de France was due to come through town.

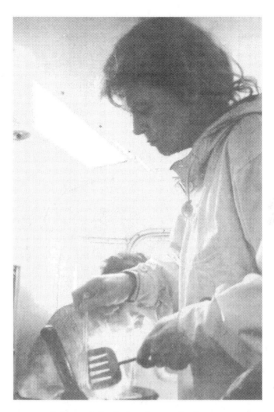

Ma and Josh in the ambulance

During term Jake's evenings and weekends were rather busy, what with one thing and another (although he rarely did any homework). His new friends at Westminster City would tell him about parties in various parts of London, which often took hours to get to on the tube. In the week he generally went out to have lunch in a café with Richard Abbott, who was another smoker. They shared an interest in Botany, in saving the world, and therefore in Agricultural Botany, mainly inspired, in Jake's case, by Bill Pirie and his mechanical cow project. Pirie, a close friend of Ma's and a Fellow of the Royal Society, had given up a promising career in pure biochemistry (some have said that he could have become a candidate for a Nobel prize) in order to develop a method of producing cheap protein directly from grasses and other vegetable matter, as a way of dealing with what was widely believed to be an impending crisis in food production in the world, and especially in poor, developing countries. Hence his 'mechanical cow'. This device was loaded with grass (or any other vegetation which was available) and eventually, after a number of artificially induced digestive processes, produced a rather sandy-textured green powder, tasting a bit like seaweed. He was convinced that Hetta, as an expert cook, would be able to devise a way of preparing this material to make it palatable, and would always bring another sample of it when he came to call at Studio House.

The winter of 1962-3 became the coldest since records began, and the deep snow prevented any traffic, even on Haverstock Hill, the main road in front of Studio House. The silence was eerie—first of all, from the lack of traffic, and then from the deep snow absorbing any of the sounds that were made. Peoples' footsteps were almost silent in the snow, and their voices had no resonance, simply falling into silence. One day Mog and Jake, with Hetta and Josh and Simon, were walking towards the Heath with a toboggan when a figure emerged from his house in Downshire Hill, waving at them to stop. It was Freddie Uhlman, a Viennese jew who had been Hetta's landlord at one time during the war. He came back out with two pairs of skis, which he gave to Jake and Mog. Mog's were Austrian, and fairly short, blade-shaped, while Jake's were long, narrow, Norwegian walking skis. Both pairs had the old system of attachment to the boots, with the heel free while the front of the boot was clamped down. He didn't have any ski sticks. They took them home and Ma told them how to wax them—ironing on candle wax to give them a smooth finish, and dug out her old ski boots from her year in Munich in 1936. These fitted Jake, and were compatible his new acquisition. Barry Carmen turned out to own a pair of ski sticks, so Mog and Jake shared them, as well as improvising broomhandles. For the next week or so they were skiing down Parliament Hill, becoming reasonably proficient at slow speeds. (Mog had found a way to use a pair of army boots, whose deep wide soles were good enough for the clamp to grip and hold them.)

They even went onto the Heath after the pub closed at night, to ski and toboggan by moonlight, joining a number of other drunken winter sports enthusiasts. Josh had commandeered a half-bottle of brandy, taken from Pa's study, and was not sharing it—or, at any rate, had finished it by the time the party got to the top of Parliament Hill. When it was Jake's turn to set off from the top of the hill he felt a bit of resistance in the ski, but once under way everything seemed all right. It was when he got back up to the top that he discovered that Josh had been standing on the back of one of his long skis, and his push forward had thrown him off balance. He had fallen over and broken his leg. Mog and Jake set off to the nearest houses to call for an ambulance. When it arrived they walked with them and their stretcher up the hill to find that the patient had gone—some other people had put him on a toboggan and towed him to civilization.

Josh was not a good patient, with his leg in a cast for weeks. However on this occasion Hetta tolerated his moods, in a way that she was not to five years later, when he broke his leg again.

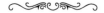

Rich and Jake applied to do Agricultural Botany at a number of universities, and were both accepted at Bangor, with conditional places. After their A level exams they decided to go on a cycling trip together to Stockholm. Taking the ferry from Harwich to Hook of Holland, they cycled across North Holland, discovering that it was not all as flat as all that, and then Germany, to Hamburg. The *Top Ten* club was where the Beatles had performed the year before, before becoming famous, and they had heard that you could actually stay there all night if you bought a cup of coffee. This they did, listening to an endless succession of bands from Liverpool wanting to emulate the success of the fab four.

Going up to Copenhagen was quite a long trek, and when they arrived there at the youth hostel, they took stock, and realized that they were only half way to Stockholm. There was no way that they would be able to do the trip before term started. So, in the morning they took the bikes around the back of the youth hostel to park them and took their panniers on their shoulders to hitch their way to Sweden. They succeeded in reaching Stockholm, but with some difficulty. It seemed that there was not a great tradition of hitchhiking in Sweden, as there was in the rest of Europe at the time. However, when drivers did pick up a hitchhiker they would sometimes take them home with them (which happened to Rich and Jake twice). The first time they were picked up by a middle-aged couple, with their young daughter, and had to squeeze in with her in the back of the tiny Saab. They were very friendly, but drove off the main road onto local lanes, laughing uproariously every time the car hit a bump. They spoke very little English. It turned out that they were hoping that these two English boys would improve their daughter's English, while staying in their farmhouse with its own lake. Rich and Jake managed to get away after a couple of days. The other one was a boastful playboy, driving a convertible, who wanted to tell them about his sexual conquests and to show off his beach house in Halmstad, where they stayed one night.

Coming back to Copenhagen one evening ten days later they found their bikes right where they had left them, although the youth hostel was full. There was nowhere else they could afford to stay in Copenhagen, so, when they'd had something to eat, and the coast was clear, they tossed a coin for front or back seat, and climbed into somebody's VW Beetle in the car park to spend the night under their towels. Up at dawn before anyone was about, they set off on their way to Germany and home.

Rich had done well in his A levels, and would be going to Bangor, and on to greater things in Botany (he is now the Professor of Evolutionary Botany at the University of St Andrews), while Jake had failed his, and would have to go back to school.

The following September, turning up again at Westminster City School, Jake was pleased to see Vidar Strand, who had done almost as badly as him in his exams, and was also having to take them again. They became close friends for the rest of that year, doing a lot of drinking in pubs, both in Hampstead and Chelsea.

Another curious development of this time in London was that, through Josh, Jake became friends with an aristocratic circle. Dan Farson, during his time with Josh, had introduced him to Lady Rose MacLaren, the daughter of a marquis, and a widow who occasionally made forays into Soho. On one of these outings she ran into Josh, with Hetta. She promptly invited them, and Jake, to one of her cocktail parties at her house in Smith Square, in Chelsea. She had two daughters, Victoria and Harriet. Victoria was the older one, very pretty, blond and pink, and a little plump. At the cocktail party there was nobody for her and Jake to talk to except one another, and after spending a couple of hours together, she agreed having an evening out with him on their own. On their first date Jake arrived at their house to find Dan Farson was there, who gave Jake a five pound note to take Vicky to the pictures. Jake was not too proud to accept it. They went to the Leicester Square Odeon and saw *The Guns of Navarone*—hardly an auspicious beginning for a romance. It was however the beginning of over a year of being her boy-friend, with plenty of sexual charge in their relationship, but no question of consummation. It was thoroughly romantic.

Jake was invited to their house in North Wales, in the grounds of Bodnant Gardens. As they arrived, he saw that they had ponies in the field, and exclaimed, 'How marvellous, we'll be able to go for rides!' Vicky and Harriet were not enthusiastic. They had got tired of their ponies years ago, and they were only kept on to give employment to a Polish ex-prisoner-of-war who looked after them. Jake wasn't the only young man in the house party, and they were joined by two chaps from Eton College. One of them was also doing Botany A level, and he and Jake took their 'Floras' with them into the gardens to identify plants. They got on rather well. Eton sounded dreadful.

Vicky was to 'come out' as a debutante, which meant that she had to go to parties which were part of the 'London season', and, in the end, to have a coming-out ball of her own. Jake went to a couple of the parties with her, and then she told him that he would be her beau at her coming out ball. This was a considerable privilege, so Jake had to find the appropriate clothes to wear. Barry Carmen came up with a dinner suit for him to borrow. It had lapels which extended to his shoulders—very much in the 1940s tradition. Surprisingly, it fitted fairly well, so that was it. In the event the other young people thought that it must be the latest fashion. There was a marquee, champagne all night, and the Ken Ball jazz band—it must have cost her mother a fortune.

Mirabel Fitzgerald, daughter of C.P. Fitzgerald, who was in Peking in 1947, was in London attending the Byam Shaw art school, and it was with her that Jake was to have his first grownup affair, during 1963. She was a very different proposition from young Vicky, with her own flat, and half-way through her degree course. Jake and Mirabel swore they would never get tired of one another and there seemed a special bond with their shared background in China. They spent their first night together in Studio House and in the morning Pa insisted on coming in with two cups of tea. When Mirabel tried to hide under the bedclothes Pa reached under the blankets to tickle her toes. He was very pleased for them, and determined to establish that it was a Bohemian household.

Vidar Strand (in the middle) with me and Mirabel in
Studio House. Josh with his back turned. The occasion
must have been Mog and Linden's wedding party.

Despite his love for Mirabel Jake was not discouraged from also taking up with Oriel Glock, whom he had known since childhood. She had been living with her father, stepmother and her children from the age of about six, although she regularly stayed with her mother in Well Walk, where Jake was a a regular visitor. Clement committed suicide when Oriel was about twelve, and he saw less of her, although after coming to London to go to Westminster City he would call around at her father's house in Holland Park, or they'd meet in Hyde Park in their school uniforms. He was never invited back to the house, and got the impression that all was not well there. When she got a place at Sussex University Jake went down to Brighton to visit her in her shared flat, for a weekend before the General Election of 1964. She had another friend staying, Gerry Silverman, nephew of the Labour back-bencher Sidney Silverman, and a medic going through his internships. He proudly announced that he was a venereologist, that month. Gerry was an excitable enthusiast, and got Jake to help him with his canvassing on behalf of the Labour Party in Brighton. They were invited in more than once by lonely pensioners, but it was clear that this constituency was a lost cause to the Left. At night he took barbiturates as sleeping pills, and on one night in the early hours of the morning he got everyone up in the flat, having woken up in a state of hyper-activity—a case of a drug having a paradoxical effect in a high dose: instead of acting as a sedative, his barbiturates were now making him even more hyper. He sat on Oriel's bed and they talked to him until the sun came up.

Oriel was pleased to see Jake in her new life, but very undemanding, and he felt that this was going to a life-long friendship. He was so very sad when she died in 1980. He had always assumed that he would get back to her at some point.

Oriel Glock

Chapter 7

The Empson ménage, and boating

T hings had settled down considerably in Studio House since Josh's eruptions of the early days. They had a routine of going to the Creek, probably every other weekend, and on the others there would be people calling in and staying. Jeffrey Craig and his wife Penny were frequent visitors. He was an Australian—originally introduced by Barry Carmen. He worked as an advertising art director and photographer. He had been in the Australian Air Force during the war, and it was obvious that he was still suffering from the experience of being the rear gunner in a bomber. He was twitchy, and hated the Japanese. Otherwise, he was educated, sane, a gifted artist, and an elegant, catlike, man. Penny was beautiful and glamorous. They worked hard during the week, living in a flat in Peter Street in Soho, and when they came to visit always brought at least one bottle of extravagant cognac. Jeffrey had become addicted to Philip Morris cigarettes when he had lived in Paris, and Penny now joined him in chain-smoking them. They weren't obvious country types, but they enjoyed the Creek, going to the Butt and Oyster at Pin Mill on a Saturday night before being driven home by Ma in the ambulance and then drinking some more and playing bridge until late. The following morning they would be lying about reading the Sunday papers until lunch, and then the trip back to London.

For a number of Hetta's friends, it seemed that a visit to her, even in Hampstead, was an escape from the pressures of life in central London. John Deakin was another who would take a break like this. He was a photographer and Soho habitué, friend of Dan Farson and his circle, including Francis Bacon. He was famous for being mean—never buying his round—bitchy, but also occasionally genuinely witty. He was another veteran of the war, when he had learned photography in the RAF. One of his jobs had been to take pictures of young airmen in hospital in Malta to send to their mothers. Some of them were badly burned, so it could be a difficult exercise in getting angles right to present the best possible representation of what may have been a pretty disastrous face. He told Jake how one of them had been unconcerned about his appearance, but begged Deakin not to tell his mother the truth—that he had loved to shoot the Germans down, and then to follow them, watching them burn. Stories about the war were a favourite topic of conversation.

Jake had acquired a new Russian camera, the cheapest SLR on the market, and Deakin was very kind in giving his comments on it—mainly to the effect that it seemed a splendid device, but it was what you did with it that mattered. His own camera was always a Rolleiflex, although he had bad luck with them, losing one for instance to a young man on crutches who he had picked up in Soho and taken home with him. Next morning he woke on his own, and found that his camera, which he'd hidden under the bed, was missing, and had been replaced by the crutches. Others had been pawned, and never retrieved. Jake found that his Russian SLR did indeed have an excellent lens, but the pictures were always blurry when taken a slow shutter speed—which he attributed to his 'familial' tremor. It seemed, though, that there was a design flaw, at least in this one, in that the mechanism for moving the mirror out of the way to take an exposure rattled the camera.

Josh was working pretty regularly as a painter and decorator, much of his time working for Ron Weldon. Ron was a painter and musician who was running a decorating business to supplement his erratic income. He was married to Fay, who at that time was a copy-writer in the advertising business. As Jeffrey Craig once said, she and Elizabeth Smart were the two best copy-writers in London. One job that came Ron's way was to redecorate a shop, and convert into a picture gallery. He was too busy, and Josh was left to it on his own. The story was that during 1963 Fred Reid, another French Pub regular, had formed a partnership with a pornographic bookseller, Bobby Katz, to arrange an exhibition of the paintings and drawings of Stephen Ward, the osteopath involved in the Christine Keeler/ Profumo affair. Fred was a small, weaselly man in a shabby mac, and Bobby was larger, suited, and with a big sweaty face. Fred was another air force veteran—known as 'Fred the Wing'—who was an antiquarian bookseller. Again, rather twitchy, he rarely talked about anything else except the ghastliness of his time in Bomber Command, when they had routinely drunk sixteen pints of beer to obliterate their memories, and sedate their terror. Ward was facing trial, and needed money to pay for his defence, and was selling his pictures, many of them of his patients, and many of them of notable people, including royalty. Fred and Bobby leased a shop in Museum Street, a stone's throw from the British Museum, to hold the exhibition. Vidar and Jake were roped in as decorators to help Josh get the premises presentable, and Penny Craig was employed as the glamorous receptionist. Bobby explained to Vidar that his business involved buying pornographic books which he then sold to the British Library. (A law-abiding printer would have registered every book with a number, and supplied the 'copyright libraries' with complimentary copies—the back street printers producing pornography had no such compunctions). In the interests of ensuring a complete collection of British publishing the British Library resorted to dealing with the likes of Bobby. He and Fred had also operated as book thieves, targeting Foyles bookshop in Tottenham Court Road because of its multiple entrances. One of them would act as a distractor, being an obvious thief, while the other one was filling their capacious poacher's pockets in a more discreet fashion. Whether he had ever sold pornography to the British Library is open to question, although it would have been the sort of thing that would have amused him a great deal.

One lunchtime they were all in the Plough, a pub halfway down Museum Street which had a tap room with no access into the rest of the pub. To get to the toilets you had to go out into the street, then in through the public bar. Bobby could not see the point of this, and when he got up to order another round he set his pint glass, full of piss, on the counter, and said to the landlord, 'Get rid of this, will you?' He was truly astonished when he was ordered out of the pub, and he, Fred, and their employees were all barred.

Josh, Vidar and Jake worked long hours to get the shop transformed into an art gallery in time for the grand opening of the exhibition and sale of works. There was a small back room which they had to get ready as a priority, and Fred and Bobby were being very mysterious about it, keeping it locked when they had finished. Vidar got in once, and saw a collection of rather conventional sketches of royal subjects such as Princess Margaret and Prince Philip—presumably done from life. There were two notable visitors before the exhibition was due to open. One was Miss Mandy Rice Davies, famous for coining the phrase, 'Well he would say that wouldn't he?' when challenged about something in court, and being Christine Keeler's fellow courtesan. She came in when Jake was up a ladder, pointed at a self-portrait by Stephen Ward, and screeched, 'I painted that! It's mine!' Jake came down and offered her one of his Woodbines, which was spurned, and she flounced out. The other visitor was someone with a briefcase monogrammed with the royal crest, who wished to see the pictures in the back room. Having seen them, he made Fred and Bobby a cash offer for them, on condition that he could remove them immediately (he was an emissary from the Palace). Naturally, they felt compelled to accept, out of patriotic sentiment.

In the event, the exhibition was cancelled, as Stephen Ward managed to take a fatal overdose of barbiturates in prison.

Although, in comparison to the early days with Josh, life was really quite pleasant, it didn't always seem like that to an independent observer. Robert Lowell visited the house during 1963, and wrote to Elizabeth Bishop:

> They live in 3the edge of Hampstead Heath. Each room is as dirty and messy as Auden's New York apartment. Strange household: Hetta Empson, six feet tall still quite beautiful, five or six young men, all sorts of failures at least financially, Hetta's lover, a horrible young man, dark, cloddish, thirty-ish, soon drunk, incoherent and offensive, William . . . red-faced, drinking gallons, but somehow quite uncorrupted, always soaring off from the conversation with a chortle. And what else? A very sweet son of 18 [Jacob], another, Hetta's, not William's, Harriet's

age. Chinese dinners, Mongol dinners. The household had
a weird, sordid nobility that made other Englishmen seem
like a veneer.[xvi]

Josh was obviously at his worst when there was someone in
the house who might possibly judge him by some standard of lofty
achievement. At least nobody got hit. Lowell was taken on the walk
across the Heath to Kenwood House, and Jake went along. Perhaps
he'd given William a lot to think about, as he was not talking much
on the way, and Lowell and Jake were left to talk to each other. He
listened to Jake's explanations of the Heath and its woodlands quite
patiently. Once in the house, of course, Pa launched into his repertoire
of comment and anecdote about the various rooms and exhibits (and
about Lord Mansfield himself, who was famous for pronouncing in
1772 that slavery was unsupported by law in England or Wales. The
case against an escaped slave thus failed).

It was about this time that Jake became aware that his father
was not only an eccentric, and a very clever man, but that he was
regarded with awe as a genius by some people. His reputation was
not wide—he wasn't a 'telly don' like Jacob Bronowski, one of his
Cambridge contemporaries. But people like Bronowski, or Bill Pirie,
the biochemist and fellow of the Royal Society, who sometimes
came to the house, would let slip the truth on occasion. So it was
a secret that William was a genius. Over the years this knowledge
became a source of empowerment for Jake. 'Little do you know,
but my father is William Empson', he would hold to himself, when
challenged by the ignorant of this world. The other secret was the
way in which William had been ill-treated by the Establishment.
Hetta felt this most acutely, and it was difficult to work out whether
this was simply part of her general anti-Establishment pose, or

whether she really had something to say about it. It was a secret about ill-treatment conflated with his being financially ill-treated by his family. One was curious about these things, but not so curious as to actually ask about them. Gradually the truth about his fall from grace at Cambridge came out, little bit by little bit, when Hetta was in a confidential drunk state. Also the revelation that he had wanted to go to China 'for the boys'. This was a bit astonishing, not because he might like boys, but that he had any sexual inclinations at all. The secret about William being a genius was definitely the main one, followed by the disgraceful treatment by Cambridge University. The Yorkshire Empsons might or might not have cheated him financially, but he obviously didn't care, so that didn't matter.

The fact was that William's reputation was curiously isolated—so that he would be discovered by clever undergraduates, who had read his difficult poems, or *Seven Types of Ambiguity* or *Some Versions of Pastoral*, and he would be their secret. With his years of exile he did not have that natural academic reputation based on a continuous interaction with his peers, even though he had a good published record. It was therefore not just a family secret, but one shared by a succession of brilliant young admirers—whether John Wain, Christopher Ricks or Jonathan Raban. Of course all this reinforced the family secret, making it all the more powerful.

William the arch cerebral had been expelled from his natural home—Cambridge University—where he could and perhaps should have spent the rest of his days. Instead of enjoying the tranquillity of college life he had been propelled into a world of travel, adventure and difficulty. Despite his abstraction, he seemed able to cope with this, albeit at some cost. He was forever losing his wallet (and even, on one occasion in China, all his clothes), but managed to survive every setback, perhaps, in part, by appearing obviously harmless. By the time of his rehabilitation into English academic life, after twenty years or more in the wilderness, with his appointment as Professor at Sheffield University, he was making a virtue of his worldliness. His inaugural address was full of his experience in China. He was to continue to twit and tease his academic colleagues and rivals with his superior knowledge of the world in the years to come. He had turned a catastrophic failure into a great strength, and would say how glad he was that he hadn't been trapped into the same world as Leavis. He would obviously have developed into a very different person if he had, and a much less interesting one.

Jake's 'flashbulb memory' of the JFK assassination was in the Studio, where the small Radio Rental TV was turned on, with nobody watching it. He was passing through when there was a news flash that President Kennedy had been shot and wounded in Dallas, Texas. Josh and Ma were incredulous when he told them, and eventually they gathered around the TV set as more news came in. Surprisingly, Josh already knew the name of the vice-president, from his close reading of the Daily Express, and was also well-informed enough to know that Lyndon Baines Johnson was to become President of the U.S.A. in the event of Kennedy's death.

In a bid to keep Josh happy, Ma decided to sell her Henry Moore bronze and buy him a boat. The maquette, about two feet high, was a figurative study for a larger sculpture, a mother with a child on her knee. Presumably she had acquired it from the artist during the time when the Hampstead Artists Council were renting the ground floor of Studio House—Henry Moore was a principal trustee. The boat she got was a 28 ft barge yacht. Today her bronze would be worth at least three or four of them. It had a main mast, with a foresail and a lug sail, and a mizzen mast with another lug sail. Flat-bottomed, and only drawing about two foot, it had leeboards on either side which could be lowered to allow sailing with a wind which was anything but from behind. The sails were terracotta—one of Ma's favourite colours. It had been owned by somebody with Air Force connections, and the main cabin had a round domed Perspex roof-light taken from a bomber. There was a built-in engine, and, internally, it had built-in bunks, a galley, and even a toilet.

Ma sold her Henry Moore to pay for a barge yacht. Her
small maquette was even more beautiful than this, the final
full-sized version, being a bit more figurative,
more 'Michelangelo'

She hadn't consulted Josh about this idea, and it turned out that he hated boats, so the venture was initially not a success. However, Mog and Jake were enthusiastic, and Josh was induced to take part in playing with it. It was moored at the Creek, where it could sit on the mud at low tide. They had got the engine going, and had been up the river to the Butt and Oyster, but had never put the sails up. John Seymour was asked to come over to inspect it, and take it out on the Orwell to test it out. John had owned a large Dutch barge, the 'Jenny III' in which he had sailed to Holland, and around the broad canals of England. In a previous life he had been a fisherman in the South Atlantic, off the coast of South West Africa. So he was something of an expert. He had them pulling on sheets and tying knots, and letting the leeboards down, and the boat was made to heel over hard, as he sailed her into the wind. Ma became hysterical—'We're all going to drown!'—but he was enjoying himself and would not stop. He despised the engine, and kicked it when it wouldn't start, and kicked it again when it did start.

A few weeks later they set off on a more ambitious trip, having arranged to meet up with the Hendersons at Walton-on-the-Naze to then sail up the Hamford Water to their house at Thorpe-le-Soken. They hadn't seen the Platanna, so it was agreed that the boat would fly a red flag to be easily recognized. It was a beautiful sunny day, with a light breeze. Biddy Crozier, with her daughter Blake, Pa, Ma, Josh, Simon, Mog and Jake made up the crew. Pa was sitting on the deck in his underpants, doing the Times crossword as they sailed down the Orwell and out to sea. Heading south past Harwich towards Walton they were in the open sea, with the leeboards down and Mog at the helm. Ma was becoming upset, certain that Mog was taking them too far out to sea. 'You're taking us to Holland!' she cried. Mog stuck to his guns, and didn't want to give up the tiller, so Pa was made to come down from his seat at the bow to persuade Mog to allow Josh to steer. Josh headed them back towards the coast, where they struck a sandbank and went aground, so, after raising the leeboards which were stuck in the sand, the boys had to get out and push the Platanna into deeper water. The water was warm, and it seemed to them that they were getting on top of this sailing malarkey. (Mog and Jake had had some experience of sailing dinghys, for instance at Alice Stewarts cottage on Anglesey). It was all going swimmingly, with the breeze from off-shore pushing the barge along at a good rate, and they eventually came in sight of Walton. Here the breeze freshened and it became apparent that they were headed for the pier, rather than the beach where they wanted to moor, and Josh tried to turn the boat a bit more into the wind. She was having none of that, and persisted in sailing sideways toward the pier. 'Chop down the mast!' screamed Ma, as the pier got closer and closer. 'Start the engine!' she cried, and Josh started pulling the starting cord. The engine refused to start, and they carried on towards the shore, eventually hitting the pier with the stern of the boat. The impact broke the mizzen mast off half way up. The most probable reason for her reluctance to steer across the wind was that they had forgotten to put the leeboards down after having gone aground, so, with no keel and only drawing its meagre two foot of water, the boat had virtually no purchase against the water when being propelled by the wind.

At that point the engine started with a roar, and they were heading up the side of the pier out to sea. Unfortunately for them, the anglers lined up on the pier had their lines picked up by the rigging as the boat went, and there were loud and indignant shouts. As they rounded the top of the pier a lifeboat came into view, which came up and insisted on towing them into port. They had been launched when the red flag had been noticed—apparently it could be interpreted as being a distress signal, which explained their timely arrival. Everyone assembled in a dockside pub, and Ma had to pay quite a large sum to them for their services, and to compensate the fishermen on the pier, before they finally managed to pick up the Hendersons and continue on their way.

The Platanna did not make any more ambitious expeditions like this, and in time she became neglected. At one point two boy sailors who had run away from HMS Ganges at Shotley got on board, broke the compass and drank the spirit. They then did the usual things that boys do in these circumstances, such as rummaging for anything of value to steal, and pooing on the table. They were caught not long after, quite locally, and the neighbourhood policeman, PC Love, brought them back to the scene of the crime and made them get overboard and search, up to their knees in the mud, for things that they might have thrown off the boat. It wasn't long after this that Ma sold the boat, presumably at a substantial loss, to a man who wanted a houseboat to moor at Pin Mill.

This was not the end of their sea-faring adventures, though. Firstly, John Seymour asked Mog to crew for him in a new boat that he had just had built in Filey, in North Yorkshire—the Willy-Nilly. It was a traditional coble—a fishing boat of the North-East coast. The distinctive shape of the boat — flat-bottomed and high-bowed — was intended for stability at sea, but also ease of beaching inshore, when the long tiller, attached to the backwards sloping stern, would be knocked out of its bracket as the boat hit the. The design was said to contain relics of Norse influence. Normally, these days, they are about 25 feet long and powered by a large onboard engine. This was just 18 foot. It had a single mast with a curiously arranged lug sail, with a boom at the top which could be on either side of the mast, depending on wind direction. Changing tack involved lowering the boom altogether, and moving it bodily to the other side of the mast. John had the sail made to order, out of a very thick, heavy canvas which would hang straight down whatever the wind. There was no engine. They were to go to the Baltic, starting by crossing the North Sea to Holland, and then heading up to the Kiel Canal. In the event they had a very rough crossing, and Mog didn't do the whole trip to the Baltic, but gained valuable sailing experience. John wrote up the expedition in his book *Willy-Nilly to the Baltic.*

At the end of his voyage John left the Willy-Nilly in Burnham-on-Crouch, being looked after by the editor of the magazine *Yachts and Yachting,* a friend of his. When he wanted the boat back in Suffolk he asked Mog and Jake to go and get it, and to sail it up the coast to the Orwell. They went and spent the night on the floor of the office of the magazine, before getting up at day-break to set off, equipped with an admiralty chart, lots of sandwiches and a thermos flask. The Crouch, a broad estuary with multiple waterways, was absolutely flat calm as they set off at about five o'clock, with a low mist, and a light breeze barely moving the lug sail. It was a very magical morning. Mog was on the tiller, and Jake was sitting amidships holding the main sheet and in charge of the chart. Heading northeast, once at sea, it was obvious that they would lose sight of land as they crossed the broad estuary off West Mersea, before they came on to Clacton, Frinton and Walton, and heading north for Harwich, and the joint mouths of the Stour and the Orwell. What happened was that the wind freshened, the waves got higher and higher, and they did not see any land on their port side (facing West) as they had expected. Eventually Jake spotted two smudges on the horizon, close together, which, consulting the admiralty chart, he identified as two factory chimneys just south of Harwich. They turned and headed for them.

By this time the waves were very high, and when they were in a trough they could see nothing but water, but had a fine view when on the crest of a wave. On occasion, the coble surfed pell-mell down from the crest into a trough, and Mog was hanging on to the tiller for dear life. Jake was blissfully unaware of the danger, and thought it great fun. When they got close enough to his two smudges to see them for what they were, it turned out that they were ancient military sea-forts, dating from the Napoleonic wars, and presumably not marked on the admiralty chart in order not to give their presence away to the enemy. Looking west, when on the crest of a wave, they could see land now, but just as far again, so, with visibility at about fifteen miles, they must have been over thirty miles off shore when they first saw smudges. Sailing as close to the wind as they could, they headed inland, still thinking they were headed for Harwich, as Jake had by now spotted another pair of smudges which he thought were the factory chimneys marked on the chart. As it happened, he was quite wrong, and they had sailed further north than he thought. These two smudges turned out to be radar towers—again, left off the Admiralty chart so as not to give them away to the enemy. When at last they came to see an estuary mouth it was the Deben—a narrow entrance, and the last feasible landfall (apart from beaching in the middle of nowhere) before Southwold, many miles to the north. They headed straight for the entrance, and the boat seemed to bolt through, before they tied up at a jetty, and got off. A local spoke to them, saying, 'Got in on the eddy, did you?' They didn't know, but apparently it was a notoriously tricky matter getting into the Deben, and it had been sheer luck that they had approached at just the right angle, or they would have been swept out to sea. It was now about six o-clock in the evening, and, completely unaware of how close they had come to being lost at sea (at least on Jake's part) they tidied up the Willy-Nilly before leaving her and setting off to hitch-hike home. They were lucky with their lifts. They found out later that the weather they had experienced was a force 8 gale, despite the fine sunny weather.

Having got the boat into the wrong river, it became necessary to bring her back to the Orwell, and Josh, Tony Snoaden, and Jake took on that job. (John Wright, together with his new partner Lindy, had removed his puppet theatre from the basement to a new premises, the Little Angel Theatre in Islington, where it is to this day. Tony had recently taken over the room vacated by John. It was very large, and had once been the billiard room.)

On that occasion they found out how vicious the eddy was when leaving the Deben, when there was no wind, and they were taking turns at rowing, two at a time, with the third man on the tiller. It felt as though the oars were being plunged into something solid, the water was so resistant. Somehow this malevolent tide seemed to continue all the way past Felixstowe, until eventually they hoisted the sail with a following wind to enter the Orwell estuary. It hung straight down, with no sign of the wind having any effect on it, but they did seem to be moving, so they rested on their oars and enjoyed the scenery. They then saw, ahead of them, a magnificent yacht with its thin sails and spinnaker billowing out in front, and, lo and behold, they were catching up with it! Despite their flat hanging sail, they actually passed them, and, as they did so, they sailors on the yacht called out, 'Ahoy there, Willy-Nilly!' *Yachts and Yachting* had featured the boat in their previous month's edition, with an account of her trip to the Baltic, and the Willy-Nilly was now famous with yachtsmen.

In spite of this glorious end to an adventure, it was the last time that any of them ventured out onto the sea in an open boat.

Although Mog had passed his A levels sufficiently well to matriculate, his grades were not brilliant, and his performance on Cambridge entrance exams not good enough to get him a place at Magdelene. He spent a gap year taking another A level, in Chinese, and improving his spoken Chinese by having lessons with Meifang. So, during 1963 Mog was accepted on to a course at Leeds University for a four-year course in Chinese and Economics. The professor, Owen Lattimore, was an old acquaintance of William's from China days before the war. He was reputedly a victim of the Macarthy purges in the 1950s in the United States because of his left-wing sympathies, and had been dismissed from his post at Harvard University.

One reason for Mog not being involved in this last trip on the Willy-Nilly was his increasing pre-occupation with his love-life, in particular with his developing relationship with Linden Zilliacus, daughter of the back-bench Labour MP, Konni Zilliacus. The Zilliacus family had a cottage just a mile away from the Creek, right on the river bank, called the Clamp, and it was in the Butt and Oyster at Pin Mill that Mog and Linden first met.

Mog and Linden got married at the Hampstead register office. Linden had always been a favourite with the Daily Express, being the glamorous young blonde accompanying her leftist father on fact-finding trips to Yugoslavia, Cuba, or the Soviet bloc. He was a personal friend of both Tito and Castro, and generally well thought of behind the iron curtain. The press photographers were therefore out in force on the pavement outside the register office, which gave a good sense of occasion.

Alice Stewart had bought a house close to Leeds University, as an investment and as a way of helping the young couple, and they were to stay there as her tenants while Mog was studying at the university. Their first son, Saul, was born in December 1963.

Chapter 8

Wales, Leeds and Sheffield

S tudio House had been bought in 1944. Hampstead was always an expensive place to buy property, but the war and the constant possibility destruction by enemy action had depressed house prices, and with the help of a legacy from his mother, William was in a position to afford to buy this huge house on a long lease. By the mid sixties, with the Victorian 99-year lease due to expire in 1970, it was becoming increasingly urgent to find an alternative place to live. Rather than look for an alternative property in London—perhaps the prices were prohibitive—William and Hetta made the astonishing decision to buy a house with land in Wales. The idea was that after Pa retired they would move there permanently, and he would be able to catch the bus to Aberystwyth to work in the National Library of Wales. Ma would develop her horticultural side in the large garden. Josh would find work as a decorator. They bought Stradmore Mansion—close to Newcastle Emlyn, a small market town. The house was on a hill with its own drive leading through woodland down to the main road. It came with fishing rights on the river Teifi, flowing down the valley on the other side of the road.

During the summer of 1964 the whole family decamped to Carmarthenshire to put the house in order, together with various friends and helpers who came and went. For a while Jake shared a room with Ariel Levi, a Hampstead friend of about his own age who was trying to find his way into the movie business. Although not tall, he was strongly built and full of energy, and worked from dawn to dusk decorating inside the house, and clearing the overgrown garden. He had driven from London in his American army jeep, bringing Simon, which took all day as, despite being a striking mode of transport, it was not capable of any speed. Ariel felt it was crucial to have a distinctive vehicle in the movie business, so if he could not afford an expensive car it must be something out of the ordinary. At one point he had a black cab taxi.

Alice Stewart arrived, bringing her petrol rotary mower, which cleared some paths through the brambles. The house had not been lived in for some time, was suffering from damp, and the garden really needed a flame thrower. It was a white-painted, double-fronted house, rather grand looking. It was only on close inspection that one realized that the front was clad in corrugated iron—the result of an arsonist attack against the previous owner, a judge, by a disaffected criminal. They had no furniture to speak of, and the boys were given the job of making tables and chairs from wood reclaimed from the garden. On market day they made a trip into town, where the local farmers were getting drunk in the pubs. On that occasion they were invisible, the locals carrying on as if they didn't exist. Whenever else they went into a pub, conversation would cease, as the locals watched them until they gave up and left. They weren't exactly welcoming and friendly.

The idea of having fishing rights was very exciting, and there were plans to catch salmon, and particularly sea trout, for which the

Teifi was famous. Nobody knew how to catch fish with a rod, and in any case they did not have time and patience for anything like that. Josh advocated dynamite, which he had once used before in his navy days, but was over-ruled. Netting was illegal, but Ma managed to acquire a long net, three foot deep, and one night they went out into the river on a secret fishing expedition. With one person on each bank, Jake was deputised to hold up the net in the middle. This wasn't easy, in the dark, with the water flowing quite fast (and after a few pints of beer), and he kept losing his footing and began to think that he might drown. Eventually they caught something, and with much excited shouting and shushing hauled it in to find it was an empty can of beans. That was the end of their efforts at fishing.

Rather surprisingly, a fairly near neighbour turned out to be an old friend of Ma's from Soho, the jazz singer and surrealist art expert George Melly. One of the reasons for him having a house in Wales was to indulge his passion for fishing, as well as to provide a base for rest and recovery from the London scene. He came over a few days after the abortive netting attempt with his long waders and flies, and managed to catch half a dozen trout, which Ma made into a soup. Melly was to write in his autobiography, *Hooked! Fishing Memories,*

William, the famous poet and essayist, his dashing South African wife, stylishly dressed in the sado-masochistic mode, and hippyish young people ad lib, some of whom were their children, or perhaps stepchildren.

It was a truly Bohemian setup in the Augustus John tradition. There was for a start very little furniture; the ageing poet, his fine head partially framed by a long white beard growing from *under* his chin, sat in an otherwise empty room in a deck-chair reading, with calm concentration, a copy of *The Times*. The kitchen, however, presided over by his glamorous and lively chatelaine, was as restless and noisy as a troop of the bandalog. When it was time to eat, Empson carefully folding up his *Times*, we sat at a huge table on long benches (although our host and hostess had proper chairs at each end). As it was getting dark one of the youngsters was dispatched to bring back a light bulb—they were apparently at a premium in the house—and, once it was plugged in, Madam served us huge helpings of pig from a great cauldron suspended over a burning tree. She told Diana [Melly] they'd bought a whole dismembered pig from a farmer, head and all (probably slaughtered illegally) and bunged the lot into the cauldron with a daily boost of vegetables. It was, while one couldn't help but wonder what part of the pig's anatomy had landed up on one's plate, delicious. Afterwards there was the rolling up and smoking of what Private Eye then called 'exotic cheroots', although I can't remember W.E. indulging. Indeed he was almost silent throughout the evening, but just now and again he would make an enigmatic if seerlike announcement, e.g. 'In Mandarin Chinese the word for "Atlas" is the same as the word for "Hurrah"'.

It was a memorable evening but not to be repeated, as, very soon, although they hadn't been there long, they sold the house by auction. This was perhaps a wise move, as it was clear the Mrs E was a stranger to brushes, brooms, mops, soap and especially a flush brush.

Melly, the author of *Rum, Bum and Concertina*, and one of the leading bohemians of the Soho scene, sounds almost priggish here. He must have kept his Welsh life completely separate—to enjoy his fishing and relative sobriety in his retreat in the country. He didn't enjoy the idea of Soho coming out to Newcastle Emlyn, showing him up and possibly tempting him into dissolution.

The immediate neighbours, in the farm behind the house, were the Lewis family, who were, unlike the locals in the pubs, very welcoming. When Ma sat in Mrs Lewis's kitchen, talking to her, she would gradually acquire a Welsh lilt, until she was practically doing a Peter Sellers impersonation. Jake found it very embarrassing to listen to, although he didn't believe that she was aware of it—her natural linguistic talent just kicked in, and she inevitably started talking like that. The Lewis family kept sheep, of course, and when one of them died of 'a broken heart' (an attack of maggots in its rear end) they were proposing to give the carcase to the local hunt. Ma wouldn't hear of it, and they dragged it back into their kitchen, where Josh and Jake were given the task of skinning it and cutting off the parts which had been affected by the maggots. The skin provided a costume for Simon to wear in a local show, the Pembrokeshire Eisteddford, appearing as a cave-boy, and he won third prize.

By then end of the summer it must have become fairly obvious that Stradmore Mansion was never going to be an agreeable place to live. The locals were hostile and the house and garden were grimly challenging. As George Melly said, they had little or no furniture in the house, and were even resorting to making their own, from the trees that had been cut down. It was unclear why they didn't visit the local dump, following the pattern for furnishing the Creek, but perhaps in Wales they did not throw away serviceable furniture. The plan for Pa to catch a bus to Aberystwyth to the National Library of Wales also proved to be impracticable. Despite all this, they carried on with the project to re-decorate the house and clear the gardens. That September Hetta and William were to go to Ghana on a sabbatical term, leaving Josh in the house in Wales to continue the good works (and, presumably, to stay out of trouble in London). Jake got the news that, although he had at last passed his Botany A level with a reasonable grade, he had failed the other two yet again, and a university place was out of the question. He was therefore to join Simon in going to stay in Leeds with Mog, Linden, and their young son Saul, and to have another, last attempt at university entrance. Vidar had passed his exams sufficiently well to get a place at medical school at Reykyavik University, his father's *alma mater* in Iceland.

Josh wrote Hetta a few letters during his exile at Stradmore, complaining about his isolation in the Welsh countryside. In one of them he described getting to know some of the locals:

'The only people I've met is Danny the Dog, Willy the Ferret and Billy the Bullet the last named because he's so slow. Haven't talked to a woman, go to a pub in Cardigan about twice a week. The men don't take their women out. Willy said he would take me out ferreting tomorrow you know, that's when you send a sort of big rat into a rabbit hole to chase them out, I don't expect he will though. Also had a chat with clerk of the court, he used to visit 'Stradmore' when a judge lived here. The reason for the corrugated, is that that the house was burned down, the rumour is that it was arson, probably an ex-convict or poacher the judge had sentenced, anyway when people find that I am living here, they always say, 'On your own?' which sounds very ominous. It does seem less friendly now.

Simon and Jake travelled to Leeds with Mog in his little converted Ford van, which Uncle Arthur had given him. With no motorways, it was a long trip in those days, and they seemed to make a tour of race tracks—names they were familiar with from Ma's efforts, informed by the Daily Worker's racing correspondent's recommendations, to win money on the horses. (She had always had an account with Ladbrokes.) Mog and Linden lived in the ground floor of the house in Windsor Terrace, which was usefully placed right across the road from the university, and they sublet the rooms upstairs. There was a bed for Simon in the house, but Jake was moved into the rooms above the double garage behind the house. There was a large room under the sloping ceiling, and a small workshop which he used as a bedroom, and in which he built a bed, assisted by Simon. He had a paraffin heater, and a table and a chair in the larger room. Pa had arranged an allowance of £2 per week to be paid into his account, and to begin with he was looking in the small ads in the local paper for jobs to supplement his income. He had a couple of interviews for jobs as lab assistants, but was unsuccessful. In fact he found that he could live quite comfortably on his allowance, plus the 10/—per week that he could get by renting out the garages under flat, so it did not matter.

Enrolled at the Leeds Technical College to retake his Chemistry and Zoology A levels, Jake was curious to meet his new classmates. It seemed that they were all employed, and taking these courses (which paralleled similar HNC courses) on day-release schemes. When there was a practical class, such as a chemical titration, they could all get it done in the first twenty minutes, with perfect results, leaving Jake struggling to complete his version of it, while they were all having a fag break. They weren't unfriendly, but were obviously from a very different world: with their wages they were pre-occupied with things that Jake had no access to, such as their motorbikes, cars, and nights out in clubs, and he did not make any particular mates. These part time courses left him plenty of time to work on his own. For the first time, he made a point of establishing exactly what was on the syllabus in each of his subjects. He then systematically listed all the topics in his notebooks, and organized notes around them. He was very proud of his efforts, writing to Vidar in Iceland that Chemistry was in fact 'quite interesting'. When Christmas came and he was back in London for the vacation he made a point of going upstairs to show Max how thorough he was being.

Life in Windsor Terrace was well-ordered and tranquil, compared to Studio House. Simon was enrolled in a local primary school, where he would stoically walk every morning, after Mog had fixed him a breakfast. His comment on the other children was that they were 'triangular'—it was never clear what he meant—and his memories of Leeds in later life totally monochrome. That winter term was presumably rather a shock for him. Jake would go into town, if he had no classes, and work in the public library next to the art gallery, which had a couple of Stanley Spencers, and a Colquhoun and a MacBride to make him feel at home. Sometimes he had lunch in town, at the Ceylon Tea House, but more often would come home, where he or Linden would collect sandwiches and fruit pies from Ainsleys the bakers opposite the Brotherton Library. In the evenings, they would sometimes get up the road to the Eldon, then a very traditional pub where you could ring for the potman from your seat, and have your beer brought to your table. Mostly, though, they were models of studiousness, with Mog working on his essays and Jake on his notes in the evenings.

Mog and Lin had the van, so at weekends there were expeditions to local attractions, such as Kirkstall Abbey. They also made a trip to Wales, to visit Josh at Stradmore, where he was still decorating and repairing, in the beginning of November.

Jake could cook in his little flat, using the paraffin heater, which was one of those chimney-pot shaped ones, with a circular flame at the bottom, and all the heat coming out of the top. One could balance a kettle or a saucepan on it. He bought Katherine Whitehorne's *Cooking in a Bed Sitter*, which provided the absolute basics of cooking, as well as recipes for a more ambitious, continental cuisine. She advocated a rather experimental approach, using processed foods in ways that were not intended for them. For instance, you could use Campbell Condensed Soups as sauces, allowing you to concoct dishes which seemed quite sophisticated. For Jake this was a revelation, although, in retrospect, they must have tasted vile. During that first term he had a visit from Mirabel, who admired his makeshift arrangements in the flat above the garage, and shared the experience of Katherine Whitehorne's *Cooking*. She was to return to Australia, so it was in the way of a farewell, although they were to continue their relationship by letter for years to come.

The Empson family were all invited to join Alice for Christmas at her cottage outside Oxford. In the event Mog, Linden and Saul were not to go, but Ma, Pa, Josh, Simon and Jake duly arrived in Oxford by train, and took a taxi to Alice's house, set in a village a couple of miles out of town. On arrival, Ma and Josh quickly found that they were not being made as warmly welcome as they wished. While Alice did open a bottle of champagne, she kept a tight grip on it, and there was only one glass each. This was not a good start. It then turned out that that Josh, Ma, Simon and Jake were to be billeted in a farmhouse down the lane. Alice had some Hungarian refugees in the house, so there wasn't room for the whole family.

At bed time they made their way to their billet, where tempers got worse and worse, as the farmhouse was cold and without any drink. Ma sent Josh out to find firewood, and he duly went out in the dark, coming back with armfuls of wood. It seemed that he had pulled up a fence. He quickly built a nice big fire in the bedroom. He was then sent back to the house to get through a window and find the bottle of Marsala that was his Christmas present for Pa. Once the marsala had been all drunk up, Josh was sent back to find more to drink. He returned with a bottle of whisky. Feeling more and more outraged, Ma started to kick the furniture to pieces, to provide more firewood.

What with all the upset, Simon wet his bed (and so did Ma and Josh, with the upset and the bottle of whisky). Pa came over in the morning, on Christmas Day, to see how they were, and tell them that lunch would be ready soon. He tried to tidy things up a bit, and got Josh to help in turning the mattresses, and tried to smooth Ma's ruffled feathers. It was not a very jolly Christmas lunch, and as soon as it was over there was a mad dash to the pub to get there before closing time.

The following morning Alice had been told about the farmer's fence, and had been over to inspect the other damages. She made it clear to Pa that they all had to leave. There was no public transport back to London, so David Hawkes was telephoned, and he came to take them into Oxford to stay at his house in Woodstock Road.

"I'm sorry, but I can't get you all in my car, Bill," David told Pa, "I'll take Ma, Josh and Simon, and come back for you and Jake."

So they were ferried into Oxford in his rather small Austin. It was a relief to be with the Hawkes family—Jean was always so wonderfully sane—and Josh and Ma relaxed and had a laugh about it all. The day after Boxing Day the buses were running, and they got one back to London, and a very chilly Studio House with not much food.

There were faults on both sides, but it was futile for Pa to hope that the ladies were going to get on like sisters. After this disaster his relationship with Alice continued, but without any further attempts at involving her in his family life. It was the last Jake saw of her until Pa's funeral.

The rest of the Christmas vacation, for Jake, was a round of going to the pub with Ma and Josh, and staying in Studio House. Mirabel had gone back to Australia, and he didn't have many friends to get in touch with very easily. When he showed Max his independent workings on the A level notes he could also boast of become proficient in some of the Zoology dissections—for instance, finding out that one could expose the cranial nerves of a dogfish by twisting its head sharply (after skinning it), when the formaldehyde embalmed muscles would simply fall away from the bone, leaving the nerves nicely behind. There was a danger of doing catastrophic damage to the head, but in that case one was allowed to ask for another fish, and, since the operation was so speedy, it didn't matter. Back in Leeds he continued his systematic approach to his studies. He was beginning to doubt his commitment to Botany as a subject at university and was drawn towards the social sciences which he had not heard about when at school. Mog was in his second year of his course in Chinese and Economics, where the Chinese group was very small—fewer than ten—and Jake got to know them quite well. Mog's classmates gave him introductions to other, first year, social science students, so he was able to find out when and where the psychology and sociology lectures were taking place, and mingle with the others. He was impressed by psychology's scientific approach, and resolved to take it up, although he had already made his University entrance applications for Botany and Agricultural Botany, as usual.

As it happened, his A level results were enough to secure entrance to a good university, and, ignoring his offers for Agricultural Botany and so on, he set about applying for Psychology courses by telephone after the results had come out, late in the summer vacation. He was invited to Durham University, where they gave him an intelligence test before he was interviewed by Professor Fred Smith. Fred seemed intrigued by Jake and his story, and was sympathetic in an avuncular way. He told him that he could offer him a place, but that he might not get a room in one of the colleges (halls of residence) at such short notice. He was also offered a place at Sheffield University, so he decided that it would be good to be at the same university as Pa, and accepted that one, arriving there as term was starting in October 1965.

His first weeks in Sheffield were a bit chaotic, as he hadn't made arrangements for accommodation. One of Pa's colleagues, Derek Roper, put him up for a couple of nights, and then the university accommodation office found him a room in digs. This was with a family consisting of a father, who was always out, two very young boys, and a youngish Irish housekeeper, who was very lonely and persistently asking Jake if he didn't like going out dancing. This wasn't a very happy arrangement, and Pa made enquiries among his graduate students, one of whom then volunteered to rent him their attic rooms in their house in Broomhall Crescent. This was Derek Guyton and his wife Rose, a couple of Trotskyites who had inherited some money, and, despite Rose giving most of it to the Socialist Labour League, was expelled from that organization for her bourgeois tendencies—she had committed the crime of using what was left of her money to buy a house. Derek's bourgeois tendencies had manifested themselves in his work with the youth wing of the party, where he had been more concerned with their education, and with rehearsing for dramatic productions, than with dragging them along to demonstrations. He was also expelled.

On the top floor of their house Jake had a bedroom, a sitting room, and a kitchen. Another lodger on the first floor (in just one room) was a young Nigerian called Danny who worked as a lab assistant. We all shared the bathroom on the first floor. He gradually furnished his little flat from the Sheffield auction rooms—his most successful bid being for a large brass bed, which cost £5.

On his first arrival he was just in time for the last couple of days of 'Freshers Week', when the student societies put out their wares and tried to recruit first years. He gravitated towards the CND stall. This was not manned, but there was another first-year there, looking tall and bewildered. This was Brian Turton, a Mancunian also on the psychology first year course, who Jake was to have a lot to do with over the next three years. Since nobody seemed to be doing anything about CND, they resolved to take matters in hand themselves. Brian was very much the activist, and over the following weeks he organized a film show to drum up members. He managed to acquire the hard-hitting Peter Watkins film, *The War Game* as well as *Fail Safe*, with Henry Fonda playing the president of the United States in his usually assured manner, presiding over nuclear catastrophe.

A couple of students left in tears during *The War Game*, and Brian managed to chase after them to sign them up. The evening ended with quite a respectably large membership for a student society.

Jake was enrolled in Politics with Professor Bernard Crick taking the first year course, in Psychology, with Professor Harry Kay doing the same, and in Physiology, which was taught in a very large class, including dental students, and with practicals on Saturday mornings. He was unique in taking Politics as well as Physiology, which made timetabling for tutorials quite difficult—possibly a reason why Saturday mornings were involved.

During term-times William lived in the damp basement of a tall terraced house in Broomhill, a suburb of Sheffield much admired by the poet John Betjeman, who described it as

> 'the leafy district of Broomhill on the western heights of Sheffield, where gabled black stone houses rise above the ponticums and holly, and private cast-iron lamp-posts light the gravelled drives. Greek, Italian, Gothic, they stand in winding tree-shaded roads, these handsome mansions of the Victorian industrialists who made their pile from steel and cutlery in the crowded mills below. They lived in what is still the prettiest suburb in England.'[xvii]

Pa had found one of the seediest houses in Broomhill to rent a small flat. He had one bedroom, a kitchen in the corridor, and access to a bathroom upstairs which he rarely used. He could pee outside, and of course had access to more salubrious toilet facilities in the University Arts Tower, where he worked. The entrance was through the back yard, where he tried to grow herbs. Across the road there was an off licence—Broadhursts—which sold everything he needed, including tinned meat pies and half bottles of brandy. He called the flat his 'burrow'. Jake got into the habit of calling in at the burrow once a week in the evening when he would sit on Pa's bed, or on the only chair, drink his whisky out of a cup, and chat about the university, or politics. The room was a shambles of books and papers, on every surface. For light reading, and in a pile close to the bed, he had a collection of the works of Rex Stout—Nero Wolfe detective stories, as well as other detective stories in the English genre. A favourite author was Michael Innes, the *nom de plume* for an old friend of his, an Oxford don called J.I.M. Stewart. His detective John Appleby was forever visiting country houses, and being involved in the intricacies of English social niceties and murderous scruples. Jake would be allowed to borrow the odd detective story.

This was not the first of Pa's lodgings. When he first arrived in Sheffield he had found a good dry room on Western Bank, very close to the campus. Disaster struck, however, when Ma came to visit him and to see his arrangements for herself, soon afterwards. The landlady refused to believe that this lady was his wife, and they were both asked to leave. She was far too glamorous.

Towards the end of the first term Harry Kay set the first year class a test, and gave out the results the following week. It was as much a test of general knowledge of psychology as of anything they had been taught in particular, but it was very gratifying for Jake to find that he had come top of the class. He proudly reported this to Pa, and he fished around in his wallet to come up with a pound note as a reward. He was very pleased for his son. It was a turning point in Jake's translation from feeling he was a bit of a fraud, endorsing him as a legitimate student, and at last, if not yet a success, at least an 'ex-failure'.

Pa was pleased that Jake had decided to join him in Sheffield, although he was probably doubtful about whether they would have a great deal to say to each other. His poem about his own mother, *To an Old Lady*, dealt with the whole impossibility of communicating with a parent:

> Ripeness is all; her in her cooling planet
> Revere; do not presume to think her wasted.
> Project her no projectile, plan nor man it;
> Gods cool in turn, by the sun long outlasted.
>
> Our earth alone given no name of god
> Gives, too, no hold for such a leap to aid her;
> Landing, you break some palace and seem odd;
> Bees sting their need, the keeper's queen invader.
>
> No, to your telescope, spy out the land;
> Watch while her ritual is still to see,
> Still stand her temples emptying in the sand
> Whose waves o'erthrew their crumbled tracery;
>
> Still stand uncalled-on her soul's appanage;
> Much social detail whose successor fades,
> Wit used to run a house and to play Bridge,
> And tragic fervour, to dismiss her maids.
>
> Fears her precession do not throw from gear.
> She reads a compass certain of her pole;
> Confident, finds no confines on her sphere,
> Whose failing crops are in her sole control.

Stars how much further from me fill my night.
Strange that she too should be inaccessible,
Who shares my sun. He curtains her from sight,
And but in darkness is she visible.

William had been particularly proud of this poem as a young man because, when he showed it to his mother, she thought it was about his grandmother.

Tante Helena had suggested, over the summer, that Jake should seek professional help in deciding on his career plans, as he seemed so aimless—disaffected with his first enthusiasm for Agricultural Botany, and drifting toward the social sciences. By the time that his appointment with the National Institute of Industrial Psychology arrived he had already voted with his feet and gone to Sheffield to enrol in Psychology. It was late December when he went to their premises in Welbeck Street, W.1 for his assessments. There were ten different tests of attainment and ability, and although he did slightly below average on a test of checking speed for numbers and of knowledge of arithmetic, he was well above average on all the others. Their report arrived at Studio House during the spring term. They identified his strengths in verbal fluency, with an aptitude for practical-technical applications, and commented that their estimate of his ability was that it posed no limitation on academic achievement. This was an endorsement of his decision to take psychology as his main subject, as well as being confirmation that he was not thick—all in all he could put academic failure behind him.

William continued to take a close interest in Jake's studies. He particularly wanted to know what was being taught in Politics: for some reason he imagined it was going to be about local government, and how to become an alderman. Jake's politics tutor was a chain-smoker, who began the tutorial by lighting a Players, and then lighting another one at precisely fifteen minute intervals, so that when the fourth was stubbed out it was time for the students to leave. For one of his tutorials Jake had to write an essay about 'political parties', and was puzzling about how to begin. William suggested that he should compare them to the Babylonian chariot teams—the blues and the greens—and see how far he could get with the analogy. He did this, and the tutor wrote 'Brilliant Stuff!' on his essay, making him feel a little bit of a fraud again.

In the physiology practical classes he was put in a group of three with Janet Beard and Geoff Blowers. They had what must already have been obsolescent equipment for doing recordings of the electrical activity of the rabbit heart, or frog leg muscle, or whatever, on a 'kymograph'. This was a rotating smoked drum with a needle wiggling up and down, driven by a valve amplifier attached to the preparation, which would leave a trail on the smoked paper. They then had to immerse the recording in paraffin, or something, to make it permanent. The rabbits were killed by technicians who held them by their hind legs, swung them, and belted the back of their heads on the edge of the bench. The frogs were 'pithed' with a needle into the base of the brain. 'Starling's laws of the heart' had to be demonstrated with the sacrifice of a dog brought down from the roof, and sadly dispatched by Dr Barry himself, with the class watching on closed circuit television. This did seem gratuitously unnecessary, and he seemed genuinely upset by the procedure—probably more than most of the onlookers, but it was obviously regarded as being an essential part of our education, particularly, perhaps, for the budding dentists who were going to be brutalised further as their course progressed.

Janet with Arts Tower in background

Janet was registered on a general science degree course, taking zoology and chemistry as well as physiology. These courses were normally a prelude to a teaching qualification, and a career in the classroom. One day Jake was sitting on a step with her, before a lecture, and they shared some of their experiences of home. Oddly, she was as much an outsider, a misfit, in her own way as he was. Her parents came from Hartlepool, and, as her father had progressed in the Inland Revenue, had come to live in Rickmansworth, a London suburb, where Janet and her two brothers were brought up. She and her elder brother Phil became the rebels in the family—possibly not so much in action as aspiration, as both of them did well at school, and proceeded to a good art school and a good university. In any case, Janet joined Jake in being a member of the university CND society, with Brian Turton as its chairman and him as secretary. They also signed up for some Marxist classes with the Trotskyites, which began with a study of the Communist Manifesto, and carried on with Lenin's *The Family and the State*, followed by the works of Rosa Luxemburg, at which point they dropped out. It was, however, a political education of a sort.

Janet and Jake were soon an item, and they decided for her to move in to his little flat. Jake went and helped her move her huge trunk from her hall of residence.

Pa enjoyed walking, and Sheffield was (and is) fortunate in having the Derbyshire countryside on its doorstep. In addition, the peculiar industrial development of the manufacture of steel, which found Sheffield such a perfect site, required plenty of water power. The rivers and streams which powered this industrial revolution flowed from the hills into the heart of the city. One could therefore walk from the city centre (for instance, Hunters Bar, near the university) out into the countryside in continuous parkland. A complete circumnavigation of the south of the city is possible—entitled the 'round walk' and is a demanding fifteen miles. A less ambitious outing follows the same route to Ringinglow, a village on the outskirts of the city, lunch in the pub, and a bus back (instead of continuing through Ecclesall Woods and Graves Park, and back to Hunters Bar).

Pa walking in woods. A dark room accident
inadvertently caused the special effect.

It was on one of these walks that Pa, who often walked in silence,
told Janet and Jake the story of the 'Ringinglow Murders'.

'There's an interesting story, which Richard Wilson told
me, about the newspapers in Sheffield.' (Richard Wilson was his
opposite number, Professor of English Language.) 'There used to
be two newspapers in the town, the Sheffield Star and the Sheffield
Telegraph, and they were in fierce competition with one another.
Then the editor of the Star noticed that the Telegraph was employing
fewer and fewer reporters, even though they seemed to be getting
the news as well as his team did. He made enquiries, and came to the
conclusion that the Telegraph had a spy in his offices, who simply
carried the stories back to the Telegraph, to be copied. '

'So the editor laid a trap, do you see. He invented a sensational
front page story—the Ringinglow Murders. Two people horribly
killed, and the murderer still at large. Blood everywhere. He

calculated that Ringinglow was just far enough away for the Telegraph editor not to bother with the cab fare to send someone out to check for themselves. They set up the front page with this story, and awaited developments. At the last minute, before the presses started to roll, they swapped this front page for the real one, with the banner headline, "Sheffield man in small earthquake in Chile". In the meantime the presses across the road at the Telegraph were turning out the sensational news about the dreadful murders.'

'The outcome of all this was huge embarrassment for the Telegraph, and ruin as the truth came out, so that it was taken over by the Star, and, to this day, there is only one newspaper in Sheffield, the Star and Telegraph.'

'What would you like to drink, now, my dear? Mine's a black and tan.'

Pa also enjoyed visiting country houses, so that a walk and a visit to Chatsworth House, for instance, combined two pleasures. The walk from Chatsworth to Haddon Hall was another favourite. He liked to point out that the practice of being shown around the grand house went well before the days of mass tourism: during the nineteenth century it would be perfectly proper to call in at Chatsworth, at the back door, and, if the owners were not in residence, for one of the servants to show you around for a small fee.

'But, Pa, why is it owned by the Duke of Devonshire, when we're here in Derbyshire?'

"Just a case of the King being deaf, Jacob. Make him Duke of Devonshire, then! he said, when they'd told him what a wonderful house he'd built in Derbyshire."

It was during this period, after his sixtieth birthday in 1966, and the disastrous attempt to please both Alice and Hetta at once, that William increasingly took on the role of 'old buffer'. This was made easier by his succession of ailments, whether affecting his eyes, his teeth or his stomach, but it was probably a conscious decision. At the same time, he was quite likely to refer to himself as being 'at the height of his powers', meaning, of course, his intellect.

However, what started as a pose gradually became more of a reality over the next ten years or more, and he even seemed to welcome this. For instance, a hernia was allowed to go untreated, giving him the appearance of even greater corpulence than was necessary. His teeth were neglected until dentures were inevitable. In the late 1970s the Canadian guru Marshall McLuhan was to remark that Empson was 'very noticeably deaf and has a big white mustache and the florid face of a Col. Blimp.' All this was certainly partly from his Edwardian upbringing—an expectation that a gentleman would be old after the age of sixty. However, plenty of his contemporaries successfully resisted the ravages of age (most notably, Stephen Spender). For William, who had such ambitions to begin with, it seemed to be part of an abdication from youthful conjugal endeavour, although by now his marriage was safe. His ambitions for sexual innovation within the marriage had been completely sincere, but he never had the energy, the single-mindedness, to press it through consistently—he would probably disengage, even if only in his head, to go back to his books. Now it was evident that things were all right, on that front, even if not what he might have hoped for in the beginning.

The most notable party for many years was to be held at the Round House in Chalk Farm. At the time it was still a derelict train turntable shed, which had been acquired by Arnold Wesker with the idea of developing it into some sort of Arts venue. At any rate,

Elizabeth Smart arranged to hold a book launch party there, with very minimal, makeshift furnishings and lighting. Her eldest son Christopher was responsible for the cleanup and the transformation into a place suitable for a party. The occasion was the re-publication by the Panther Press of her greatest work, *By Grand Central Station I Sat Down and Wept*. Literally hundreds of people were invited to this event, which took place on July 14th, 1966. Of Jake's generation, it seemed that everybody that he knew or was even acquainted with through his parents in London was there. There was a circular mezzanine floor, around which they perambulated, watching the band, and the dancing, on the floor below. Hugo and Roger Davenport, Gregory Harris, Corinna MacNeice, Oriel Glock, Tessa and Dan Topolski, and of course the four Barker children, Georgina, Christopher, Sebastian and Rosie, were all there.

Of the grownups, there were all sorts of literary figures, as one would expect at a book launch, but there was also the Soho crowd, including artists, photographers and media people as well as hangers-on, who Elizabeth knew even better than Ma. Josh did not get cross at this do, where he was amongst a lot of old friends. However, Hetta heard Eddie Linden, a young Irish poet and editor of *Aquarius* magazine, refer to one of her friends as a 'chink', whereupon she slapped his face, knocking him to the ground, and then threw a glass of whisky at him. But, in the order of things, that was a minor incident—the mere disciplining of a mindless fool. There was so much booze on and under the trestle tables that nobody went dry, despite, according to Josh, people putting bottles of Scotch under their coats and stealing out with them the entire night.

As their second year began Brian and Jake again organized the same film show for the CND Society, and, with Brian standing at the back ready to field any tearful absconders, signed up a respectable number of members again. At the same time they had joined the Vietnam Solidarity Campaign, and one of their most notable meetings was one attended by a couple of mining union representatives, and Tariq Ali, the charismatic president of the Oxford Union in his white suit. They produced a monthly news digest of the war in Vietnam during the next couple of terms. In particular, they were focussing on possible war crimes, and on evidence of disaffection in the ranks of U.S. troops—the so-called 'fraggings', when officers were gunned down by their own men. This was a lot of work, in addition to their efforts for CND, and they only produced about three of them, but they were well received.

Janet had decided to transfer to psychology, which meant that she was now back in the first year. She and Jake were now an established couple, sharing their flat in Beech Hill Road, and entertaining friends to meals and parties.

In February 1967 William was admitted to hospital with throat cancer. It was said that it was first noticed by the famous pathologist, Alan Usher, who examined him in the staff club when he had complained of having a lump in his throat. At any rate, he was promptly referred to Guys Hospital in London for an operation to remove the growth on his uvula. To be on the safe side, he was given a course of radiotherapy, which continued until May. There was a second operation to remove the lump in his throat, when the surgeon also removed a considerable amount of what he regarded as unnecessary tissue from his neck, again, 'to be on the safe side', giving him an oddly youthful appearance once he had recovered. His stoicism stood him well during this difficult time—the radiotherapy, for instance, had made it impossible to swallow any solid food, and he was drinking through a straw.

Jake was largely unaware of the seriousness of Pa's illness. He presumably did not want to bother his children with his problems, and was simply getting on with it without any help. Jake was bemused to be summoned, on one occasion, by Harry Kay, who asked if he didn't think he should be taking him in hand, so to speak. (William had got into difficulties on one of his trips to London, getting off the train at the wrong station, probably drunk. Harry had been told of the incident by Roma Gill.) Jake could not conceive of any situation when he should somehow 'take him in hand', or do anything unless he was asked to do. It was an embarrassing interview for both of them.

Pa was back in Sheffield when Mog rang, in June, to tell Jake his results—he had got a Pass degree. Jake couldn't believe it, and he had to repeat himself. It seemed that he had fallen down badly on the Chinese language sections of his joint degree, although he would have achieved a modest honours degree on the Economics side. In terms of university examinations, languages and mathematics are notoriously unforgiving of ignorance: in subjects assessed by essay the examiner is liable to read more into an inane but long answer than is actually there, and complete failure can only be achieved by writing nothing. It was Jake's job to convey this news to Pa in his burrow. He was astonished, and Jake had to repeat it, and confirm that he did not mean that Mog had passed his Finals, but that he had been awarded a Pass degree. There was nothing much to be said after that, and they had a glum cup of Scotch together.

Janet's parents became aware that Janet and Jake were living together, and were most alarmed at this development. They did all they could to persuade them to get married. With the wedding agreed, they were invited to dinner at Studio House, to get to know their daughter's future in-laws. Josh was sent off to Soho with some money for the evening. Ma's account of this event was that they all got on famously, and the Beards were good sports and got quite drunk. The Beards account was that the Empsons were drunk when they arrived, and that Hetta did a hottentot dance (one of her party pieces) claiming to have a black grandmother, and that Janet would more than likely produce a black baby. William discovered that Janet's father was a tax inspector, and launched into a tirade against all tax officials, saying they were responsible for the death of Dylan Thomas, before leaving them to go to his room without another word.

Janet and Jake were secretly rather pleased to be getting married, despite their protestations that they wanted to live together as bohemians, and were disappointed when it had to be delayed until late July, to give time for Dorothy (Janet's mother) to make all the arrangements.

In fact July 1967 turned out to be a very busy month for Jake in Hampstead, although Janet was in Rickmansworth helping her mother with preparations for the wedding. Despite his recent illness, William was to read his poetry at a Poetry International Festival, directed by Ted Hughes and Patrick Garland, and held at the South Bank in the second week of the month. John Haffenden wrote in his biography,

> 'A truly international pageant of poetry, the five-day event included appearances by Yehuda Amichai, W.H. Auden, John Berryman, Allen Ginsberg, Patrick Kavanagh, Hugh MacDiarmid, Pablo Neruda, Charles Olson, and Anne Sexton. Empson appeared at the Queen Elizabeth Hall

on Wednesday, 12 July, when the line-up of poets—along with Empson there were Auden, Berryman, Spender, Neruda, Olson, and Hans Magnus Enzensburger—was introduced by Malcolm Muggeridge; the following day, he appeared at the Purcell Room, introduced by his long-standing admirer A. Alvarez, together with Auden, Spender, Yves Bonnefoy, Neruda, and Enzensburger. (Translations, where required, were read by Ted Hughes and the actor Patrick Wymark.)'[xviii]

This was a family outing. They were about to cross from the Embankment when William pointed at the South Bank buildings, and said, 'If the Germans had won the war, they'd have forced us to build things like that'. However, despite his reservations about the architecture, he was looking forward to the event.

Jake was particularly struck by Neruda, who had a considerable presence, and who was greeted rapturously by the audience. At the end of the festival there was a celebratory party held at the U.S. Ambassador's house in Regents Park. They all went along, including Josh. It was hard to know what to say to the performers, so to speak. Jake sat on the floor next to John Berryman, who asked him who he was, and so on. Jake said that he would sit at his feet, and this level of flattery was enough to complete their conversation. A joint was being passed around. The arrival of Allen Ginsberg was accompanied by his acolytes banging gongs and chanting, and holding candles. Josh was bridling, and, sure enough, he was beginning to weigh in on these love-in peaceniks. Jake's last memory of the evening was of leaving through the garden and climbing over a wall to make his way home through Regents Park and Camden Town, getting away from the inevitable. Predictably, Josh had to be restrained at some point and the remaining Empson party were called a cab.

By a complicated series of events, it was the U.S. Embassy which approached William with a bill for a replacement mattress at the London Hilton. (They claimed the mattress had been soiled with urine.) The American poet responsible for peeing in bed had apparently blamed events at the party at the residence in Regents Park for his discomposure, and had passed the bill on to the British Council, who passed it on to the Embassy. Jake always assumed that it was Allen Ginsberg who was responsible, as he was the obvious target of Josh's fury—and one would naturally assume that it was Josh's behaviour which would have caused such an aberration. However, accounts vary: Kenneth Tynan reported in his column 'Shouts and Murmurs' in *The Observer Review*,

> After an obstreperous party to celebrate a poetry reading in London last year, an American poet fled back to his hotel and wet the bed in terror. Next day the management demanded that he should pay for a new mattress: he successfully charged it to the British Council.

Undoubtedly some American poet wet their bed after the party, and an attempt was made to get somebody else to pay for it, who eventually tried to pass the bill on to William. John Haffenden's biography makes it seem most likely that John Berryman was the culprit (or victim), and that it may even have been a remark about his poetry reading by William which had really upset him, rather than anything that Josh had done.[xix]

At a loose end in London, with his marriage only a couple of weeks away, he took the opportunity to go to some of the opening events at the Round House in Chalk Farm of 'The Dialectics of Liberation'—a series of lectures organized by Gregory Bateson, R.D. Laing and two other psychiatrists. As well as featuring the new developments in 'anti-psychiatry' there were lectures on revolutionary theory by political theorists such as John Gerassi, who he went to listen to, as well as Bateson. It was very much a 'happening', with the events being continually filmed by cameramen with handheld movie cameras. Tina Topolski, (the wife of Felix) was very much in evidence in her dark glasses in the front row. It was *the* place to be.

The marriage took place at Rickmansworth Parish Church on the 22nd July. Following tradition, Jake had not seen Janet during the run-up to the wedding. Preparing him for his fate at the church, Mog handed him a large glass of brandy, and offered to drive him as far away as was necessary if he decided not to go through with it. Untempted, he went and waited at the altar. When she arrived Janet looked absolutely stunning—a Tahitian princess with a flower in her hair—and Jake went through the ceremony in a state of euphoria. Brian Turton was his best man, and at the family reception at her parents' house in the garden he was responsible for moving the guests about and introducing people. Both his uncles Arthur and Charles, Aunt Molly and Aunt Monica, and Janet's uncles and their families were all there. They then left in the ambulance to make their way to Hampstead, where they had a 'proper' party, with people their own age as well as their parents and the usual crowd of Ma's friends.

The bridal couple with their parents

Janet in the back of the ambulance

Janet and Jake could not afford any sort of honeymoon on their own. (Jake had not even been able to buy a diamond engagement ring, settling for a garnet, which Janet gamely said was just as good). So they took the chance to join Ma, Pa, Josh and Simon in the ambulance on a camping trip to the south of France. Pa was taking a break to celebrate the end of a difficult summer, of treatment for his throat cancer, as well as the trial of the Poetry International. Janet learned to smoke, 'to keep the mosquitoes away', and the newly-weds swam naked in the Mediterranean before leaving the others and travelling by train back to Paris for a couple of days on their own. It seemed that their newlywed status was written on their foreheads, as everyone they met seemed to know at once. At a Vietnamese restaurant in Paris the waiter was recommending more and more fish sauce to Jake, which had a reputation as an aphrodisiac. The middle-aged couple at the next table became interested in them, and insisted in taking them back to their apartment for a nightcap. Expecting a nice cognac, Jake was surprised to be served neat London Gin. It was difficult getting away from them but they managed to get back to thei hotel, and, eventually, back to England.

On their return to Sheffield, they found advertisements in the Students Union calling for extras for an Italian film company. They turned up to queue at an unearthly hour of the morning at a hotel in the city centre, and were taken on at £5 per day, to be available every day at 8 am, and staying as long as they were required. Thus began about a week of an alternative existence, mostly of hanging about being bored, but with some exciting moments, and, more importantly, plenty of opportunity to observe the film company at work. There were two British actors, Anthony Booth and Stanley Baker, but the rest were almost all Italians, including the star, Miss Monica Vitti. Their first day at work was 'at a disco' and they were instructed to wear suitable clothes. This scene was to take three days of filming, and on the first day they discovered that two of their fellow extras were Thomas Green and his girlfriend Sara. (Thomas was a psychology research assistant, a very intense intellectual type, and his girlfriend Sara a third year student in the department).

Thomas had chosen to wear his interview suit for the disco, which was pretty baggy on his slim frame, and may have belonged to his father. Sara was very chic. At any rate, when the director announced through his megaphone, 'Please to make the couples on the floor', and the music started again, Thomas and Sara where right in front of the camera. The assistant director came down and said to Thomas, 'You shake offal', and pushed him right to the back, with Sara following behind. He took Janet's arm, saying, 'You shake good', and drew her to the front, with Jake trailing along. The music was monotonously unvarying, and it soon stopped being fun. They would stop for a coffee break (for the crew) and leave the extras to their own devices until they were ready to start again. The four of them discovered that they could all play bridge, brought in some cards, and were able to fill in the time with a few rubbers. On their last day on the dance floor one of the stars became involved. Mr Stanley Baker burst in, and made his way through the dancers, barging into Jake and knocking him over as he went. Jake naturally assumed that this was an accident, but as they went for take after take, it became clear that he had been singled out for Mr Baker to bowl over every time—whether by his own choice as a creative actor, or under the director's orders, they never found out.

They had plenty of time to observe the Italians at play, as they tended to completely ignore the extras, as being a lower form of life. There were two female assistants, who they nicknamed 'Scumdrups' and 'Inkypoops', who wore stripy dresses, and were both in pursuit of the assistant director. They would speculate every morning about which of them had been lucky the previous night. The gossip amongst the extras was that the whole company were being housed in one of Sheffield's most expensive hotels, except Miss Vitti, who had insisted on staying in her caravan. She was tiny, standing very straight, with two grandmotherly Italian ladies fussing over her hair, clothes and makeup. She was radiantly glamorous, and when she moved she was completely controlled and professional. We all admired and adored Miss Vitti.

The technicians were as bored as the extras, most of the time, and would be playing 'scissors, paper, stone' for what for the English onlookers were huge stakes—£10 at a time, for instance. One day there was more for them to do, as they were filming at Chesterfield Rugby Club. The idea was that Anthony Booth was to pick up the ball and run the length of the field. Actual members of the Chesterfield Rugby Club team were to challenge him, but when he touched them on the chest they should fall over, and he would triumphantly score a try. At the same time, the cameraman and camera, mounted on a trolley, were being pushed along a little railway track that had been laid along the length of the pitch by three or four Italians, keeping up with Mr Booth. The extras were in the stands, waving their scarves and cheering Mr Booth on. The weather was not good, and it was a long time before there was a break in the clouds, the sun came out, and the director ordered 'Action!'. Anthony Booth started his run, the technicians were heaving along to keep up with him, and halfway up the field one of the rugby players refused to fall over when touched on the chest, and after that none of the others did either. The director was furious, as of course it all had to be done again.

Jake's moment with Miss Vitti was to take place that day, as, once the events on the pitch had been filmed, the camera was brought to bear on the onlookers in the stands. He was enthusiastically waving his Economics Faculty scarf, and then stood up to do it even better, as the camera was getting closer. He felt a hand on his shoulder, gently pressing him down, and he realised that she was right behind him, and the camera was more interested in Monica Vitti than it was in him. She had quietly taken her place at the back of the stand.

At the end of every day they lined up to be paid. A very large Italian in a suit had a briefcase full of cash, and, on the advice of the assistant director, would hand out money to them as they got to the front of the queue. Janet had been singled out to be part of a separate little project, to take some family pictures on a beach. (Her dark hair, complexion, and suntan from our recent holiday in France were enough to make her passable as an Italian.) She had to bring a swimsuit, and they took the photos on a prepared beach next to a steelworks. As they got to be paid there was the question of how much extra to give her for this, and, for some reason, they became aware that she had just got married. Being a sentimentalist at heart, Mr Moneybags agreed with the assistant director to give Jake an extra fiver as well as Janet, for having tied the knot so recently.

The director seemed to spend much of his time on side-issues, and developing little sub-plots. For instance, they were on a coach with Miss Vitti, getting on and off it, and driving up and down, but the director became completely pre-occupied with an elderly Sheffield lady with two young children, making them get on and off again and again. There was also a car—a large American convertible—which had to be painted in psychedelic floral patterns by the technicians, and then driven up and down with half a dozen young people in flowing clothes, headbands and long hair, shouting and waving. They were the face of the swinging sixties. Naturally the extras were never provided with a script, so they never knew what it was all about. However, Jake found out many years later that *La Ragazza Con Pistola* was nominated for an Oscar, so they must have done very well.

More importantly, they had made friends with Thomas and Sara, and were to spend a lot of their time with them during the next year or two.

In October 1967 Pa was admitted to hospital in Sheffield for an operation to correct a detached retina. This involved him being blindfolded for considerable period—a hellish fate for somebody who normally spent almost every minute of the day in reading. He was only discharged at the beginning of December, and went to stay with Roma Gill for a few days. His experience of sight on removal of the bandages was very dramatic—he reported how vivid the colours seemed. He even asked Roma to get Harry Kay to come to dinner, so as to talk to him about 'the psychology of his half-blind-totally-blind state'. This was the first of a series of operations on his eyes over the next twelve months.

As usual, Brian and Jake organized another screening of films to recruit members for the CND society. That November they hired a coach to take their members to Barrow to protest against the launch of the second of the Polaris class nuclear submarines to be built by Vickers. It was an interminably long trip, and a cold, damp day when they got there. The local MP was Frank Allaun, who boldly stood up and made a speech denouncing the independent deterrent programme, despite the fact that almost all his constituents were dependent on it for their livelihoods. He thought that Vickers could equally well be building oil rigs. A more eventful protest took place the following February, when they went to Birkenhead for another launch, by Cammel Laird. This was a smaller group, having lost some members after the extremely arduous trip to Barrow. They weren't allowed to go to Birkenhead itself, but joined the demonstration on the pier-head in Liverpool, where they could see the proceedings on the other side. They were all booing and waving their banners until the submarine was launched into the water—such an impressive sight that they quietened down considerably. The people on the Birkenhead side were cheering and waving their flags. It became apparent however that all was not well with the launch when the submarine did not reappear—or rather, only the back end did, above the waves. The front was obviously stuck in the mud of the Mersey. At this point the protestors all started cheering and booing and waving their placards, and the opposition on the Birkenhead side all went quiet. A most satisfactory result, and a thorough embarrassment for Cammel Laird, even if it didn't hold up the commissioning of the boat by any significant amount.

During the summer Janet and Jake visited Studio House, where Janet was given the job of taking the ambulance to have it tested for the newly introduced 'MOT' certificate. The mechanic asked, 'Who drives this usually, a gorilla?'—the steering was impossibly heavy, even for a three-ton lorry. It transpired that the problems with the ambulance went further than its steering, and would be too expensive to put right. Rather surprisingly, Ma took the opportunity to buy a luxury car, a second hand Alvis saloon. This was going to be the car that would last for ever. Pa thought it a splendid idea.

Ma with her Alvis parked in Hampstead Hill Gardens

The following summer they were invited to a Buckingham Palace Garden Party. Still under the spell of the car's aristocratic presence, Jake volunteered to act as chauffeur for them. On the day he wore what they imagined approximated to what the chauffeur for a couple of bohemians might wear—a Chinese jacket and a peaked cap. They queued up with the Bentleys and Rolls Royces for Jake to drop them off. (People arriving in taxis were sent to a different entrance). He was then directed to a car park, to wait until it was time to pick his 'employers' up. There, the other chauffeurs ostentatiously turned their backs on him, clustering around one of the older Rolls Royces (presumably, one with a working samovar). They also spent time inspecting under each others' bonnets, and doing quite unnecessary polishing with chamois leathers. Jake regretted having volunteered, spending two or three hours smoking cigarettes and listening to the car radio before finally being called to return. Hetta and William had really enjoyed the day, even though they hardly caught a glimpse of royalty in the throng. What with the number of people there, Ma's intention of getting some cuttings from the royal gardens also went unfulfilled. It was the continuation of Pa's love affair with the idea of monarchy, and the beginning of Ma's, confirmed a few years later when Pa was knighted. It was not a political decision—more that the Queen was adorable, and royalty was therefore a private joke, rather than that the whole royal family were to be approved of.

Janet and Jake had their own transport by now, however, a secondhand Minivan which they eventually discovered had been repaired after an insurance writeoff—it had been crushed and then returned to its proper proportions. (The corrugations in the metal flooring were to give its secret away.) However, at this stage it was their latest acquisition, and freshly sprayed with off-white paint. They drove it at very high speeds up and down the M1 to London. They even made an epic trip across Europe, the Alps, and down into Italy and visiting Florence, taking their small tent. Jake drove most of the way despite only having a provisional license—they'd discovered that you could get an International Driving License through the Automobile Association on production of any sort of license. Fortunately this was never tested in the courts.

Camping in the heights of the Piazza Michangelo, they visited the churches and museums, admired the public statues by Cellini and Michangelo, and bought prints from *Fratelli Allinari*. Despite not speaking Italian, they felt at home in the city in just a few days, as they found their way around its tortuous streets.

During this, their third and final year, their political activities were beginning to wane, as they took the impending exams more and more seriously. In Sheffield, at that time, there were no Final examinations before the end of the final year, when all the work for the previous two years would be assessed in a series of twelve or so three hour examinations. Despite this, Jake managed to get drunk with his landlord, Derek Guyton, on the day after the beginning of the Vietnam Tet offensive in The Nottingham, a tiny pub in Broomhill, and, with socialist resolve, made their way to the post office to send a telegram of congratulation to President Ho Chi Minh, Hanoi, Vietnam, which the cashier duly took down and charged them for. They became aware of the events of May, 1968 in Paris, and the associated actions by students in London and elsewhere. A handful of Sheffield students did abandon their studies and go over to France, but the majority of the politically active did not.

Chapter 9

Post graduate Frolics and Academic Life

As a result of keeping his nose firmly to the grindstone in the final months of the course, Jake achieved a 2:1 in psychology. Brian got a 2:2, but was already accepted onto a training course in clinical psychology in Manchester, so it was not such a disappointment. (Jake had also applied for the clinical course in Leeds, but had been rejected, or, to be precise, put on their reserve list.) There were surprises, such as Tony Routledge, drunk for much of the time during Finals, who wasn't available to be interviewed by the external examiner, and had to be flushed out from the student union bar. Brilliant but very nervous, he impressed Professor Ian Hunter to the extent that he was given a 2:1 after all. Al Little, who had hoped for a third, but expected to fail, got a First. Peter McKellar had arranged a postgraduate studentship in the Department of Psychiatry in the event of Jake getting a 'good' degree. There he was to be supervised by Professor Alec Jenner, the head of department and the MRC Unit in Metabolic Studies, and Peter Clarke, a clinical psychologist in the Psychiatry department.

Tony Routledge and Anthea Keller during Finals

That summer Jake and Janet took their bikes on the ferry from Hull to Rotterdam, for a holiday in Holland. They met up with Hetta and Josh, who had taken a tandem, and were making a visit to Peter Duval Smith's sister, Penny, taking Simon with them on his little red Raleigh. Peter had died in Saigon the previous year, in what were unclear if not mysterious circumstances. He had been investigating reports of a CIA-funded army composed of Chinese soldiers, perhaps even remnants of the KMT that had been so thoroughly defeated almost twenty years before by the communists. Penny and her husband were most hospitable, entertaining them all on their yacht, and providing bottle after bottle of *oude Geneva*.

One day on the beach Hetta was tuning her little transistor radio, when she started yelling, 'They're sending in the tanks!' It was very difficult to make sense of what she was going on about—and she wasn't very clear for a while herself, as she listened to broadcasts in German and then Dutch, covering the invasion of Czechoslovakia by the Soviet Red Army. Hetta was experiencing flashbacks to her own war-time experiences, and was panic-stricken. It didn't help that nobody else could understand any of the stations that she was tuning into. Eventually the true picture emerged, and it became clear that the world was not headed for nuclear Armageddon after all.

Rose and Derek had separated over the summer, and she was now living in the house with Geoff Pearson, whom she was to marry. They didn't need the rents, and told Danny, Janet and Jake that they would rather they found somewhere else to live. Janet was now to start her third year of the psychology course, so they were both to be based in Sheffield, and that August they moved from their attic rooms in Broomhall Road to a self-contained flat in Clarkehouse Road, still in walking distance from the university.

William's health had not been good. He had been teaching at a summer school in Buffalo, New York, but on his return was again admitted to hospital, this time for a cataract operation. He was told, he said to Hetta, to take things slowly, and 'to live under proper female supervision.' Hetta came up to Sheffield for a few days to see how things were going, and stayed with Janet and Jake. Alice was keen to come too, and to do what she could for him, but late in September he was writing to put her off until he was going to be 'more lively', telling her that he was walking up the hill every evening to sleep at Janet and Jake's flat (although, as he wrote, not promising to eat Janet's cooking). All very diplomatic.

An interesting development, for him during his periods in hospital when he was blindfolded, was his introduction to pop music via the hospital 'piped radio'. Unable to read, he was forced to listen to this, and found that he liked the Beatles, and was particularly impressed by the lyrics of 'Hello Goodbye'. He would subsequently often recite it, and Hetta was convinced that he had totally rewritten it, making it more poetic, possibly even to conform to a formal structure such as a villanelle. (Unfortunately nobody thought to write his version down.) Fortuitously, he also took on a new graduate student this term who wanted to study the lyrics of Bob Dylan as poetic literature—John Brown, with wild long hair and an intense expression, who would often join the Psychology post-graduates in the pub.

Jake's graduate studies were to be based in the Whitely Wood Clinic, a small psychiatric hospital up the Fulwood Road towards Manchester. Peter Clarke was in charge of his day-to-day supervision, although he was formally under the joint supervision of him and Professor Alec Jenner. Jake was accommodated in a small room at the Clinic, where Peter also had his office, and spent most of his days there although he had also been allocated another, even smaller room at the MRC Unit building in Middlewood Hospital. (Middlewood was one of those huge mental hospitals which were to be phased out over the following ten years.) Pa gave him £30 to buy a little scooter to help get about between these hospitals and their flat. Surprisingly, he found that one of the psychiatrists on the staff was none other than Gerry Silverman, Oriel's friend from Brighton who had been a venereologist the last time they met. Also, there was Dorothy Rowe, who had recently migrated to the UK to start a PhD in clinical psychology. She had been fairly recently divorced, and had brought her young son Edward with her. She had had a mixed career including being an educational psychologist. She was now using techniques devised by an American psychologist, George Kelly, to attempt to map out individual patients' views of the world, in terms of 'personal constructs'. Her focus on what she termed the individual 'microcosm' was an early application of what might later have been called cognitive psychology in therapy. Of course she was to become a best-selling author of books on depression, and much else, and an international psychological guru, described by Fay Weldon, when they were on good terms, as one of the wisest women in the world.

Peter was enthusiastic for Jake to become a clinical psychologist like himself (a graduate of the Institute of Psychiatry, a 'Maudsley man') and was teaching him how to administer the standard intelligence tests—at that time still the mainstay of clinical practice. As part of his projected training as a clinical psychologist Peter encouraged him to attend the weekly case conferences, where patients were discussed by the entire staff, and usually brought in towards the end of the session. Dorothy almost always had something to say at these, and Alec would be acting as mediator between the various factions. They were always interesting: on one occasion a man had been brought in by the police, who claimed to have lost his memory. In fact he had every reason to, as he was on probation and in trouble with the police in Liverpool. They brought his probation officer over from Liverpool to come and to sit in the front row, and observed his response when he was brought in. He said 'hello' to the probation officer, and, when challenged about this, said that he looked familiar. The psychiatrists were acutely concerned to establish whether he was bluffing, or whether he 'really' had lost his memory. Was he mad or bad? (And had they been taken in by him?) Pride was at stake. Alec was in his element, and animated discussions continued on into the canteen afterwards.

Alec Jenner was a polymath. He supervised research ranging from organic chemistry, through biochemistry and physiology to analytic psychology. His research unit employed two or three dozen people. His innovative research had been on bipolar disorder, and the regular variations in mood in some patients which seemed to mimic natural biological rhythms. Historically, these cyclical symptoms had been more common in the days when patients were not treated, but simply held in secure wards with virtually no outside stimulation. The psychiatrist who first described this syndrome was a Scandinavian called Gjessing, who had observed these symptoms during World War 2, when psychiatric treatment was even more perfunctory than in the past, and patients on the back wards were neglected for months on end. Despite the increase in what Alec called 'therapeutic optimism', and the increasing number of interventions and treatments during the years after the war, Alec had discovered one patient who was depressed and manic on alternate days. He could even pinpoint the moment in the man's sleep, in his sleeping EEG, when the transition occurred. Jake's mission was to develop psychological tests which would discriminate mood states, and this patient, 'Chalky' White, was naturally going to be the prime subject of his researches.

Chalky had been given a range of medications during his time as Alec's patient, and had not improved with any of them. As a last resort, during the summer of 1968 he was given lithium bromide. This seemed to have a magical effect, smoothing out his mood changes so that, by the time Jake started at the Unit, he was fit for discharge. From being the prize patient of an MRC Unit, and accompanying 'prof' on trips to international conferences, he was to be discharged and employed as the supervisor of a lavatory in a factory. As for

Jake, he was left without a subject on whom to test out any of his measures of mood.

Peter found him an alternative patient, a long-term epileptic called Charlie with occasional outbursts of rage, to try out his measures of mood. Charlie was very inarticulate, and virtually illiterate, so questionnaires were not feasible. They decided to try out some rather odd measures of decision-making style, for instance using the comparison of weights. Charlie submitted to these strange tests in good heart, regarding Jake as rather an odd sort of cove, but possibly not to be thwarted. Charlie's biggest fear, according to the charge nurse in who had most to do with him, was that the hospital might discharge him back into the outside world. He was one the many completely 'institutionalized' patients at Middlewood, which was a community of its own the size of a small town. All this went on for a while, and it gradually became obvious that it was not going anywhere useful. During October there was a visit to Sheffield by Ardie Lubin, a psychologist from the U.S. Navy Institute in San Diego, California, where they had been doing groundbreaking work on the effects of sleep deprivation. Jake went to his talk, and was so excited by it that he followed him to Hull, where he was to do it again, so that he could hear him once more. (In the U.S., as in the U.K., it was military interest in the effects of sleep deprivation on servicemen that initiated and provided the funding for the research during the 1950s and 1960s which first addressed these issues in a systematic way. The British research was funded by the Ministry of Defence through the Royal Navy, and was conducted at the MRC Unit for Applied Psychology in Cambridge by Bob Wilkinson.)

Dorothy Rowe, Janet and Jake on a walk

During these first months as a post-graduate Jake was continuing to visit Pa in his burrow in the evening about once a week, and of course he was telling him about the problems he was having in finding a suitable patient to act as a guinea pig for the psychological tests of mood. Alec Jenner was famous amongst the medical community for his studies on individual patients, and 'interesting' patients would often be referred to him. One of these was a highly educated young man who suffered from periodic bouts of psychosis (a sort of schizophrenia) but was reasonably coherent in between them. Alec introduced him to Jake because he was also an admirer of William's work, and had in fact written poetry in his style. He gave Jake one of his poems, a villanelle, to show his father to ask him what he thought of it. Jake took the poem down to the burrow, to show Pa. He was deeply respectful of the young man's effort, and confirmed that it was, technically, a villanelle, but not a very good one—lacking an understandable point, as it were. It was during this meeting that Pa confided in Jake that he had frequently suffered from depression—or, as he put it, feelings of guilt which were overwhelming, but without any particular source. He asked if there was someone in the Psychiatry Department who could help him. Jake was incredulous at this revelation, and tried to imagine any of the psychiatrists he had met coping with him in any realistic way. He was very pessimistic about getting any useful help for his father, although he did suggest, that if he liked he would ask Lawton Tonge, the social psycho-analyst on the staff, if he would speak to him. Pa agreed all too quickly that it was unlikely that any of them could help him, and he never mentioned the matter again.

The young patient (Pete) who had written the villanelle told Jake that he had liked to play bridge before he became ill, so Jake arranged for Thomas to join Janet and himself in a game or two, when they all got to know him a bit better. Pete was an excellent player, and knew even more about bidding conventions than Thomas. During play however he was highly distractible, infuriating himself as he lost track of which cards had been played. They seemed to be getting on all right, sharing cigarettes and chatting between rubbers, but, when Jake rang the clinic to arrange another visit, he found that Pete had unexpectedly killed himself, slashing his wrists with broken glass.

As a registered postgraduate student in psychology, Jake was also part of the Psychology Department's new Graduate School, which gave a range of courses in methodology for postgrads in their first year. Jack Clarkson, the statistician in the psychology department, held tutorials, rather than giving lectures, and Jon Baggeley, Jake, and a couple of others were in one of his groups. They didn't take it entirely seriously, and Jack, who was taking them through a statistical text, would routinely ask, 'Which chapter are we on this week?' and Jon would wickedly invariably say 'Chapter four'. After a fairly brief and expert discussion of chapter four they would talk about their research, and Jack was particularly interested in the psychology of sleep. He had heard Ian Oswald recently (the principal British sleep theorist at the time) and met him, and was most impressed by him.

Jack was an interesting loner, discovered and appointed to his lectureship in Sheffield by Peter McKellar, in the days before the department had a professor. He was a very well-read Cambridge graduate, impressed by Wittgenstein, and very much the positivist devoted to hypothetico-deductive method. He lived on his own in a hall of residence, where he had a small suite of rooms in his role as warden. Sometimes he would join the graduate school expeditions to the pub, and, if the conversation became interesting enough for him, would invite them back with him to his rooms, where he would bring out bottle after bottle of rather good Bordeaux from his private cellar.

What with Jack Clarkson's enthusiasm for Oswald's theories about the mental functions of sleep, and Ardie Lubin's explanations of the novel technologies available to measure and quantify sleep states, Jake became drawn to the idea of investigating the effects of sleep on memory. This was a practical plan because there was a fully equipped EEG laboratory in the MRC Unit, which was hardly used, although employing a full-time technician. He started by recording the brainwaves of a fellow student, Tony Egan. He succeeded in identifying his 'alpha rhythms' running at 10 cycles a second, although, curiously, instead of being in a sine wave as usually described, they were U-shaped. Chris, the EEG technician, told him that this meant Tony had epilepsy. Jake took the trouble to look in a text book before telling him the bad news, and discovered that U-shaped alpha rhythms were an uncommon but perfectly normal variation.

The next stage was to record at night, and he enlisted Peter Clarke as a subject. With no specific instruction manual, he did the best he could imagine, with suggestions from Chris the EEG technician, but they didn't seem to get anything like the patterns in the sleep books. Apart from their errors in recording technique, it didn't help that Peter hadn't slept a wink.

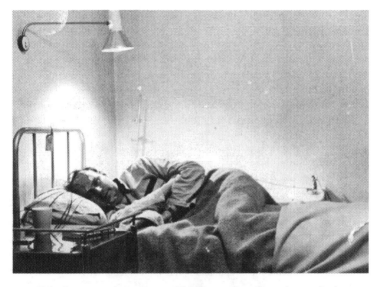

Jake's supervisor, Peter Clarke, acting as guinea pig in
an early trial of sleep EEG

He did some other trials including Mike Fitter, and Janet, and they seemed to work out better—with brainwaves looking more like the ones in the texts. Finally, Alec Jenner suggested that he do a little experiment on the effects of barbiturates on sleep. An advert card in the students union brought him a deserter from the army, a very smelly young man on the run and in need of a bed (and, obviously, a bath), who boasted that he had brained an officer with a tank starting handle before running away. Gary, as he was called, had to spend two nights in the lab before being given the active pill, to compare the effect with the nights before when he'd been given inactive placebos. He confided to Jake, in the morning after the third night, that he'd realized that the pill had 'something in it' and had struggled to stay awake all night, succeeding all too well (despite the fact that prof had prescribed enough amylobarbitone to sedate a horse). So much for his first attempt at a drug trial. He was very relieved to say goodbye to Gary, who had begun to frighten him with his unpredictable rages.

It now seemed a good idea to have some expert advice on the EEG recording of sleep stages, and Peter wrote to Ian Oswald in Edinburgh to ask if Jake could come up and see him. He was most welcoming, inviting him to come and stay for a fortnight in the lab. On arrival at Waverley Station he had his five or so best boxes of EEG recordings, and his suitcase, stacked on the platform while he tried to find a taxi driver who knew where the Royal Edinburgh Hospital was. It was a Sunday evening. He kept explaining that it was in a park (the address was Morningside Park, as he knew well, not only from his correspondence with Oswald, but from the address given on almost every one of his academic papers that he'd read). After half a dozen drivers had denied any knowledge of the hospital (or the park), he found one who knew it, and loaded all the boxes and the bag into his cab. He was very chatty, wanting to know Jake's business, and telling him how his daughter had just finished a degree in psychology at Reading University.

The reason why he knew the Royal Edinburgh Hospital, he confided, was that he was an alcoholic, and he attended a clinic there. It turned out that 'Morningside Park' was the name of a little side road, and there wasn't any park at all. The Psychiatry Department was in a tower block, which was completely in darkness. As Jake took his boxes and bag out of the taxi the driver said to him, 'There's nobody here, what are you going to do?' Jake said, 'It's a sleep lab, there'll be somebody here in an hour or so. I'll go and have a drink somewhere.' This got him really excited. What Jake didn't realize was that as it was a Sunday, Scottish licensing laws required that pubs were all shut, but a 'bona fide traveller' would be allowed to have a drink in a hotel, and the driver could indulge a vicarious pleasure in seeing him served. 'Get back in!' he said, 'I'll make sure you get a drink!'

Jake sat on his boxes for a while, but it wasn't long before somebody turned up and let me in. Hugh Firth was a psychology graduate student, working on the habituation of sleeping EEG responses to regular stimuli. He was one of three or four graduate students at the lab, including Stuart Lewis and one or two others who Jake didn't meet during his stay. While their fees and expenses might be covered by their research council scholarships, the high costs of running a sleep lab were being met by projects funded by pharmaceutical companies, which cross-subsidised the more theoretical work when research council project grants weren't available. His fortnight at Oswald's lab was very busy, for a start because he was himself so driven, arriving at 7 or 8 in the morning, and not leaving until the evening. He was very kind about Jake's recordings, and put him right about how to place electrodes in the Edinburgh manner. To learn how to score sleep stages Jake acted as 'scribe', sitting next to Oswald as he went through a night's recording of three or four subjects on one continuous sheet, noting his decisions about sleep stages, and listening to his explanations for his decisions. During the day he was preparing conference presentations for Oswald, as well as trying to catch up on some sleep in the afternoons. At night they were expected to get a few hours sleep, once the subjects had been put to bed and they had ensured that all was well with the encephalograph, but they had to stay in the room with it so that if anything went wrong they were up and sorting it out.

He had some outings in Edinburgh. One day he went to look out John Scott, an old friend of Hetta's, who was a lecturer now in Edinburgh University's Department of Chinese. He was a linguist fluent in German, Dutch, Japanese and Chinese, and a great mimic. He was usually very good company. Jake found the department in a house in 'the Buccleugh', as a passerby called it, confusingly labelled 'Chinese Computing'—presumably because they shared a building, rather than indicating an oriental system of arithmetic. He wasn't there, but Jake got a phone number from a departmental secretary, and eventually turned up at his flat in Marchmont with a bottle of wine. John's wife Kobe greeted him, and took the bottle immediately to open it and pour out five huge glasses, including two for their children, which surprised him a little. It became apparent that she was mainly preoccupied with getting rid of the stuff. It seemed that she felt John's drinking had developed into a problem, and although he was still his affable self, there was a bit of a frosty atmosphere domestically. Jake didn't stay long, but not before John had arranged to meet him in a pub the following day at lunchtime.

At the pub John had been joined by a couple of his colleagues from Edinburgh University by the time Jake arrived. They were drinking 'heavy'—what they called bitter up there, and also sampling the malt whiskies. John was in full flow, doing his party pieces—impressions of Dickensian speech, his Scottish brogue, and snatches of Afrikaans (remembering Hetta). They were a hilarious little party. It was a busy pub, and the other drinkers were all men, who mainly stood at the bar with their pints of heavy. There was an additional narrow counter running under the main one, on which they put their small glasses of whisky. There was a continuous and bewildering exchange of whiskies and pints between the men, as they kept each other topped up. Jake had never seen such serious drinking, either in bohemian Hampstead or even in Soho. He didn't stay very long, as he'd been working the night before, and needed to get back to the lab to have an afternoon nap in time for the evening recording session.

In the students union at Edinburgh University it was a different matter. There, as in the bars, there were only men, but in the union bar the game was to buy a pint of heavy and take it up onto a mezzanine floor, where you could pour it onto the chaps below. The place was continuously awash with beer.

It was not many years later that female students were allowed into the Union, and were presumably a civilizing influence.

He was now competent, under Ian Oswald's tutelage, to do the recording and scoring of sleep stages, and he committed himself to changing the direction of his PhD research into sleep psychophysiology and memory, rather than the development of psychological tests to measure bipolar mood changes.

He was well into his experimental work in the lab, working up to four nights a week, some of which he had to be up all night, during the summer of 1969. One morning, as he was headed off home for some sleep, Alec accosted him, saying, 'Did you stay up to watch the landings?'—it was the 21st July, and Apollo 11 had arrived on the moon. It was hard to share his enthusiasm. However, sleep research did have an aura of glamour of its own, back then, what with the revelations about dreams being identified with rapid eye movements, and even the idea that depriving people of dreams would drive them mad. As Mick Jagger sang in *Ruby Tuesday*, 'Lose your dreams and you will lose your mind'. The other graduate students would ask if they could come and share the experience, and watch as the subjects progressed from one sleep stage to another. He even had a young American friend of Alice Stewart's, Richard Zeeman, come all the way from Oxford to be in a real sleep lab.

His experimental program completed, he took some time off to go and be a tutor at an Open University summer school at Sussex University, just outside Brighton. It was a very intense experience, like spending a week on a lifeboat with a dozen or so other people. He got to know two of the other tutors, John and Andrew, very well. They all worked hard, and were available well into the evenings. Every lunch-time they had a tutors' meeting, held in their own seminar room which had been equipped with a barrel of Young's bitter—a very refreshing beer for a summer's day. John, Andrew and Jake did their best to spin out the discussions while they topped up their glasses.

Graduate School members Mike Fitter (half visible),
Dave Jerret, Pete Derlien

At the same time, Harry Kay and Neville Moray were hosting a two-week NATO Advanced Study Institute in Sheffield, focusing on the use of laboratory computers in psychology. There were over two dozen invited delegates, some from the United States, including Don Norman and Dominic Massaro, and others from European NATO countries, including Henri Brudzevski from Denmark. Janet and Chris Walker were taken on as hostesses and general helpers, along with Mike Fitter. Jake got back from his summer school in time for an 'encounter group' which was to be held in their flat. It seemed that Henri had decided in advance that there should be an encounter group at the conference, as he'd been to one or two before, and felt that these hard-nosed experimentalists should be given the chance to loosen up a bit. Anticipating the need for dope, but not knowing if he could obtain it easily in England, he had posted a package from Denmark, cunningly addressed, not to himself at the Sheffield Psychology Department, but to a 'Peter Smith'—a name he chose at random, so as not to be associated with him if it were intercepted. Unfortunately there was an actual Peter Smith, a graduate student in the department and actually attending the conference, so he had to break cover, so to speak.

About a dozen of the delegates volunteered for the session, including Don, Dominic and Henri (obviously, as he was in charge). There were various exercises, interspersed with rest periods when they sat and smoked the dope, and listened to Janet and Jake's LP of *The Doors*. There were significant insights exchanged, such as, 'Consciousness is the content of the accumulator'. Towards the end, they had an exercise in touching each other with their eyes closed, moving about at random in the sitting room and serenaded by Jim Morrison and his band. Opening his eyes, Jake noticed that three or four of the lonely North Americans were clustered around Chris, like male frogs around a female in a mating frenzy. Henri called a halt to the proceedings after this, as Chris was finding so much attention a bit excessive, and they all went to the pub.

Janet had done well in finals, getting a 2:1, which Harry Kay told Jake was a bit better than his. She had applied for a place on the graduate school, and was awarded a research council studentship in physiological psychology. She was to start by doing experiments on herself, injecting fine gold threads into her legs to act as electrodes recording the activity of 'single motor units'. A motor unit is a collection of muscle cells which are all under the control of a single neuron, and act together. Her idea was that she would be able to gain conscious control of individual units by monitoring their activity. If this were possible, there would be important implications for patients with disabilities. Janet shared a room with Ann Harrison, who was working on a similar line, although directly with what they still called spastic patients. Janet and Jake's friend Anne Geraghty had also got a research studentship.

From being Secretary of the Psychology Society, Janet was now, albeit informally, the social secretary of the more outgoing psychology postgraduates. They had their own pub, the Fox and Duck in Broomhill, and would go to the same parties. Mike Fitter and Iain Davies, who shared a room in the department full of ripe sports gear, were frequent companions. (They had both come from Bristol, where they had shared a flat). Mike drove a decrepit Hillman, necessary as he'd rented a cottage in a village called Beighton. It was in the grounds of a house belonging to an interesting medical academic, Dr Rowe, an epidemiologist. The distinctive smell of marijuana hung about the cottage all the time.

Alec had not let go of the idea of Jake doing some work on biological rhythms, even if it were not as originally planned. One of these projects was simply to record the sleep of a couple of people over the period of a week each, to look for periodicities in the timing of the sleep stages which might carry on from one night to the next. It would also give him even more experience of sleep recording before he was to embark on his more experimental studies. This was an experiment with interesting outcome, although it was, in the event, pre-empted by Gordon Globus (an American psychiatrist and researcher into biological rhythms) publishing some similar data, with a larger sample size, so that Jake's data were never published beyond his report in the PhD dissertation. Essentially, the periods of REM ('rapid eye movement') sleep in each subject seemed to occur at particular times during the night, rather than at times determined by sleep onset. That is, the sleep process (of a sequence of 90-minute cycles of slow wave sleep and REM sleep) did not proceed as a washing machine might, so that the timing of each event in the cycle was strictly determined by the time that the wash began. Rather, once the machine got started, the next REM phase was determined by the next opportunity given the individual's own time pattern. The logical consequence of this was that the REM/nonREM cycle must be continuing during the day, without being expressed in terms of sleep stage, but in some other way. William was intrigued by the notion of biological rhythms, and their mathematics, and Jake had been writing to him in London about some of his work. In one of his enthusiasms for science, he wrote back,

> Thank you for your letters, which we enjoyed very much.
> I don't believe your laborious German has asked the right
> question, viz: do the brain-waves begin at the same time
> as the belly-waves, or half an hour later, or in any such

relation? That is what you must look for, first in his text
and then in the busy lab.

Very good of you to mend my typewriter.

It was during the autumn of 1969 that Jake did his first serious experiment on forgetting during sleep. Jack Clarkson was closely involved with the design of the experiment, which they discussed at length in his rooms in his hall of residence. There had been a number of papers published suggesting that REM sleep, which seemed to be the phase of sleep during which dreaming occurred, might be the phase of sleep supporting 'special' mental operations. A computer analogy, developed by the journalist and psychologist Christopher Evans, was that too much information was taken in during the day to be processed by the brain, and that during REM sleep there was further, 'off-line' processing, perhaps resulting in improved or consolidated memories. The 'information processing' approach to mental functioning had recently been suggesting a very limited processing capacity in human beings, even less than that achieved by the computers of the day (with laughably limited capacities, by modern standards). It thus made sense that, like some computers which processed information on-line, the brain should also rely on further, off-line, processing to complete its calculations, as it were. John Delius, at Durham University, had asserted that since every mental event involved the production of heat, there was a limit to the amount of processing that could be achieved during wakefulness, with the limited capacity of the vascular system for cooling the brain. Therefore some of the processing left undone during wakefulness would have to be done during sleep, and particularly during REM sleep (when, again, the brain typically produces heat and consumes oxygen as much as during wakefulness). There were others, including Dr Dewan who worked for the U.S. Government in some capacity, and who, when replying to Jake in a letter, had the words 'Research—the key to aerospace superiority!' printed on his stationery. Ian Oswald's persuasive arguments that REM sleep was a time for brain growth and recovery, with an underlying increase in protein synthesis and turnover during REM sleep, provided a physiological underpinning for these ideas.

With Alec Jenner's help he was able to recruit medical students as subjects (with the idea of getting as homogeneous a sample as possible.) All male, as they would have to share a bedroom, they stayed two nights in the lab, in pairs, the first night to acclimatise to the environment, and the second on which they were asked to memorise a series of lists and a story before going to sleep. One of them (chosen by the toss of a coin) was then systematically deprived of REM sleep by being woken up. The other one (the 'control') was woken up at the same time, and kept awake for five minutes in just the same way as the 'experimental' subject. It was hoped that the control subject would fit in a reasonable amount of REM sleep despite the interruptions, while the experimental subject would get as little as possible.

Ten pairs of students went through this procedure, and the results showed an interesting advantage in recall for those who were allowed some REM sleep—about 20% more remembered of the story, a significant amount more of nonsense sentences, while no advantage for recalling completely nonsensical lists of words. It seemed as if the effect of REM sleep was to improve recall of material which made sense—to be precise, as if it were being accommodated into syntactic and semantic structures. Jack Clarkson was most excited by the results, as was Peter Clarke. With Jack, Jake was to try and think through alternative models of how the memory system might work to achieve the results he'd found—for instance, that some sort of 'ink' might be produced during REM sleep which was used in the final recording of daily memories.

After the Christmas break he was to start writing up the results for publication, with Peter's editorial help, and to plan new experiments to further explore the relationship between sleep and memory. These 'control experiments' were intended to assess, and if possible rule out, the effects of selective sleep loss on recall itself, rather than the memory process, as explanation for the results. They were inevitably less exciting than the first experiment which had come up with such exciting results. However, by March 1970 Peter and Jake had completed a draft paper, which they submitted to the journal *Nature*. Alec was keen for it to appear in *The Lancet*, which would add even more prestige for his MRC Unit, but he was persuaded that it would have more chance with *Nature*, under the editorship of John Maddox, who was unusual for a leading science editor in regarding psychology as a proper science. It was returned for some revisions in April before being accepted for publication.

Alec Jenner had been continuing to pursue his ambition for Jake to work on biological rhythms, and had been in correspondence with Ray Meddis, a psychologist at Bedford College, London, who had developed a psychological test for measuring mood states, and was interested in cyclic variations in mood in normal people. Ray had also experimented on himself and his wife Valerie, subjecting themselves to a 48-hour schedule of sleep and wakefulness, to test the hypothesis that, in time, their bodies would adjust to this. Their bodies did not adjust, and they still felt sleepy and exhausted on alternate nights, staying up and decorating their house, or finding other things to do. Poor Valerie was a martyr to Ray's enthusiasms.

Now he was keen to test the idea that the 90-minute sleep cycle persisted during the day by keeping subjects isolated and without clues as to time of day for as long as possible. They recruited two subjects, Mike Fitter and a dental student, Mervyn Pickles, to stay in the lab for a 54 hour stretch each, staying in bed in a lighted room and having their brainwaves continuously monitored. Ray came to Sheffield with a movie camera to record the experiment, and a great deal of enthusiasm. The outcome, in terms of detecting 90-minute cycles, was indecisive. An interesting event did occur, however. Melvyn was awake, in the middle of the afternoon, when his brainwaves suddenly showed him entering REM sleep. (This is unknown in people not suffering from the very rare condition of narcolepsy, as the first REM sleep period normally occurs after at least 40 minutes of slow wave sleep). After about five minutes of intense eye movements he woke up shouting, calling for help. Jake went in, and when he had calmed down he said that he had had the weirdest experience. He had become immobile—paralysed, unable to move his arms—and, with his eyes open, saw in the distance what looked like a small face. This got bigger and bigger, until he could see the mouth was open. Eventually the open mouth, with all its teeth, was all that he could see, and that was when he woke up.

What they had subjected Mike and Mervyn to was what used to be called 'sensory deprivation'. In experiments done in the late 1950s and early 1960s (funded, perhaps apocryphally, by the CIA) it was found that people isolated, sometimes suspended in the dark in tanks of water, would, after a while, experience hallucinations. This is what had happened to our Mervyn, and now they could prove that his hallucination had occurred during an episode of 'sleep paralysis'—something which a large minority of people will have experienced at least once during their lives, but quite commonly reported by sufferers of narcolepsy (which Mervyn definitely was not). So the hallucinations of sensory deprivation could in fact have been caused by sleep paralysis episodes, induced by the isolation.

Their paper in *Nature* (a 'letter', as is the convention for short reports in that journal) came out in September, and there was a paragraph about it in *The Times*. This pleased Pa immensely—he felt it showed that his son had truly arrived as a scientist, and he waved the paper about in the staff bar as a proud father.

The rest of Jake's research at Middlewood was more mundane, involving him in doing sleep laboratory experiments which were intended to rule out various alternative explanations for the interesting results of his first experiment. The only relief was an experiment on school-children, when he was allowed to test three classes of primary school children's memory performance over time. 'Reminiscence'—the improvement in memory over time, typically occurring in children—is a paradoxical phenomenon, known about since the 1920s. It was his hypothesis that this reminiscence effect occurred after an interval including sleep (and of course presumably REM sleep). Comparing recall of a Spike Milligan poem they had been given to learn after periods of wakefulness and sleep, and controlling for time of day effects in time of recall, he showed that this was indeed the case. There was forgetting over the course of the day, and improvement in recall after a night's sleep.

From Easter, 1971, he was on the last lap, writing up his results into a PhD thesis, and doing the library research for the literature review, and so on. He spent much of his time in the little spare room in the flat in Clarkehouse Road, typing away on his office typewriter, smoking incessantly. Once a week or two he would take his efforts along to show Peter Clarke, and to hear what he had to say about the work that had been delivered the previous time. He was an excellent help, more as an editor than as an expert (because he had little detailed knowledge of either sleep or memory research). But his precise mind and friendly encouragement was exactly what was required.

As the summer came along Jake was applying for lectureships at every university which advertised a post, along with many of the others in the graduate school. On one occasion four of them came into the common room brandishing gracious letters from Professor Stuart Sutherland, at Sussex University, sincerely regretting that he was not calling them for interview. When he went to an interview at Leicester University it seemed that the prof had been brought up in South Africa, and, seeing his Afrikaaner name, insisted on addressing him in Afrikaans. He stopped when Jake told him he understood no Afrikaans, but, after the interviews were over and he had been told he was not to be appointed, he put his arm on Jake's shoulder, and gave him what seemed to be avuncular advice, but all in Afrikaans. At Exeter University they asked him if he would be prepared to be in charge of the departmental workshop. At Trinity College Dublin they were very merry during the interview, wanting to know how many miles of paper he could get through in a night, recording sleeping brainwaves. He began to suspect that he was being asked along to provide credibility to the proceedings (with his publication in *Nature*) but that he was obviously unsuited for any particular post, as his research was not in a mainstream undergraduate subject.

Finally, at Surrey University, he was interviewed along with Iain Davies and Mike Fitter from the graduate school. The panel of five interviewers tried to put him at his ease, offering him a cup of tea. Knowing perfectly well that he would not be able to hold it steady, if at all, Jake declined. They insisted. He demurred. They absolutely insisted that he should have a cup of tea, and provided one. As they asked him questions, with the cup and saucer in front of him, he decided that he would have to deal with it before it got completely cold, and swooped on it with both hands, managing to get it to his face and drinking it all in one go without spilling much. They offered the permanent post to Iain, and possibly because of Jake's performance with the cup of tea, they offered him a one-year contract. It was a new department with hardly any staff, and the prof (Terence Lee) had decided to spend the entire budget allocated for part-time teaching on Jake, rather than employ any of the individuals who had been helping out before—'sociologists and dead-beat nuns', as he called them. Although unsuccessful at Surrey, Mike was also to get a one-year appointment, at Birkbeck College in London.

That summer Janet and Jake did another cycle tour in France, this time on a tandem. Instead of youth hostels, they now usually stayed at 2-star hotels in small towns, where they found they almost always provided a table d'hote dinner at a set time. These were almost always really good, and provided an education in French cuisine. The tandem suffered a terminal failure, with spokes breaking and making holes in the inner tube, outside a little town called Richelieu. They pushed it along a railway track, ominously covered with waist-high grass. When they got to the station, it was as they feared, that there was no train service except once year when the grain harvest was transported off to Paris. Even the buses to Tours only ran two or three times a week, so they stayed at the rather nice hotel overlooking the square, eating their table d'hote meals, until eventually the bus came, the tandem was thrown on its roof, and off they went.

At the same time Hetta was embarking on a transformation of the living arrangements in Studio House, in anticipation of Pa's retirement—both in terms of what would be convenient, and also to maximise rents to supplement his pension. Tony and Phillipa Snoaden had been living in the big billiard room for almost ten years. This was the room originally used as a puppet theatre auditorium by John Wright. However, they were now moving on to somewhere more suitable for them and a young baby.

Hetta divided the billiard room into three bedrooms, with a corridor, and to provide extra light each of them now had a 'porthole'—a low circular window facing onto the street, as well as their windows which were up at the ceiling, facing over the 8-foot wall which encircled the house at that point. The 'Christie room', under the studio, was transformed into a kitchen and sitting room, with its own access onto the street. The first bedroom leading off from the Christie room was Simon's, and she had a wooden bed built on high stilts, to give him room for a desk underneath. He did not make much use of the desk. He and his friends would be up on high, smoking their cigarettes and joints and listening to their music, and then abruptly climbing down and trouping out of the house without a word. She kept the studio, of course, but it was now divided from the rest of the ground floor, which was upgraded to become a 'luxury flat'. The ground floor bathroom and kitchen were much improved, and the whole flat was re-decorated to a high standard.

The first tenant of the luxury flat was Holly Bronfman (daughter of Edgar, part of the Seagram's whiskey clan). She was about 18 at the time, and was enjoying a social whirl in London. After 18 months she returned to New York and a reassuringly wealthy extended family of Persians moved in. They were staying in London while the head of the family was being treated at the London Clinic. Ma thought that he had syphilis. While these were just the sort of people she had hoped to attract, subsequent tenants were less satisfactory—inevitably being in a different mould from the traditional Studio House inhabitants, who paid their low rents regularly, and were part of a large friendly tribe. After the Persians there was the engaging Mr Blackman, who had the accomplishment of being able to supply marijuana. It turned out that he was not just a dealer in a small way, but it was his only living. He failed to pay his rent as he had difficulties with the law, and had to be evicted after lengthy court proceedings. After him there was a fashion designer, who, it turned out, wanted the premises as a workshop, and brought in half a dozen industrial sewing machines to turn out illegal copies of designer frocks. Gradually the 'luxury flat' was becoming degraded. Up to then, the house had been a virtual commune of like-minded people, but the ground floor flat was now to remain an anomaly, and a permanent headache for the next ten years or so, despite it being a good source of income.

Barry Carmen with Hetta and his wife Edna, in convivial mood
(Josh in the background)

It was at this time that Josh managed to break his leg again, and was confined to the house in his large cast, moving about painfully on crutches. He was not a good patient, and would become easily frustrated, and, when in drink, violently angry, throwing his crutches about. Hetta had finally had enough of him, and once he was reasonably mobile he was asked to leave Studio House for the last time. Unlike his previous banishments, there were no attempts to return, or to plead his case with William. Josh simply went away.

Surrey University had only recently changed its name from Battersea College of Advanced Technology, and relocated from London to a brand new campus in the centre of Guildford. Psychology had first appeared on its syllabus as part of the general studies courses required for engineering students, which gave them a more rounded education. These developed into a degree course of their own—the Humanities BA, and in the previous couple of years it had become possible to major in Psychology in the Humanities degree, giving a course which was accredited by the British Psychological Society as being a qualification which entitled its graduates become fully fledged psychologists. All this was the work of one man, Russell Wicks, who had managed to achieve it all on the strength of part-timers. With Iain, there were now four members of the embryonic Psychology Department. Harry McGurk was appointed later on in the session to teach developmental psychology. A quick count on their web-site gives a staff of ten times this number today.

Iain, Mike and Jake decided to rent a house together in Guildford. Mike would commute to Birkbeck, which would not be so bad as he wouldn't be going during the rush hours, and Jake would commute on a weekly basis from Sheffield. Iain's girlfriend Christine was to join them later in the term, and to try and get work of some sort in Guildford.

Jake's first lecture at Surrey (and his first ever) was to a large audience of engineering students, as part of their general studies course. He gave an animated lecture, walking up and down in the front of the auditorium and enthusiastically describing the surprising and innovative contributions which the study of psychology had made to science and, indeed, to everyday life. At the end of it, as the students were leaving, he discovered that the floor where he had been walking was littered with paper darts thrown by the bored engineers whenever his back was turned. Fortunately, he was not required to give any more lectures on the general studies course.

His other teaching was in small groups, by 'seminar'. In order to cover a broad syllabus (satisfying the requirements for 'accreditation' with the British Psychological Society) and with only part-timers to rely on, Russell had devised a series of prepared lessons, with supporting material in the form of photocopied articles, since there were few texts and no psychological journals in the library. Students were supposed to prepare for two of these every week, in groups of about six. This meant that Iain and Jake were teaching the same two subjects to three different groups in any one week. The students made little effort to read the background material before the class, so that each session would degenerate into a series of four or five ten minute lectures. It would then become difficult to remember during a class which topics had been dealt with (with that group rather than the one before) and which were still to come, and particularly, which jokes had been told, so one didn't repeat oneself. It was a very demanding introduction to university teaching.

Jake's routine during the first term was to get the train to London on a Sunday, and carry on to Guildford on Monday morning, going the opposite way, during the rush hour, to all the traffic into town. Every Sunday then ended with a rather a boozy evening at Studio House, where he would be sleeping in the middle bedroom, between Simons den of vice and Pa's bedroom and study, which connected through to the other basement rooms. So he normally started the week with a bit of a hangover. During the week Iain and Jake would more often than not go to the pub as soon as classes finished, to be joined by Mike later, so things didn't necessarily improve.

He shared an office with Russell Wicks, who was friendly, genial, and an interesting person to talk to. He'd worked for the military as a psychologist in the past, being involved in the human factors aspects of the 'TSR2'—a low level supersonic bomber project which was eventually dropped. (It was intended to replace the 'V' bombers, which had become obsolescent about a year into their service as Soviet air defence systems had improved. There was then little chance that any one of them would ever 'get through' to their targets.) The major problem that would have been faced by pilots in the new replacement planes was the vibration that was intrinsic to flying so fast and low. Basically their eyeballs would have been bouncing up and down so much that vision would be impossible. Because of this the plane was redesigned to include a pod to contain the pilot which could be kept stable—but of course this added so much to the payload that the whole thing had to be redesigned with a larger propulsion unit, and so on. He had been with Surrey University since it was a technical college. Having established Psychology as a subject 'major' in the Humanities degree course, it was his ambition to develop an occupational psychology degree. With the appointment of Terry as professor Russell remained very much the administrative genius.

Jake's PhD dissertation had been virtually finished by September, and Peter Clarke had given his blessing to every last chapter, but there were still odds and ends to be finished—illustrations, and, in particular, all the references to works cited in the text, which had to appear in alphabetical order at the end. The Surrey University library was completely inadequate, and he could only do this work back in Sheffield, so progress was frustratingly slow. However, he managed to get it all done, bound and submitted by December, so was proud to tell the binders to put '1971' on the spine—even though it was obvious that it would not be examined until the following year.

There had been some debate about who to ask to be external examiner—Jake's first thought had been Ian Oswald, but Alec wanted somebody attached to the MRC, so Donald Broadbent was mentioned. Nobody could object to such an eminent man (and without any reputation for being an asshole). The big day came, and Don was taken out to lunch by Alec and Peter before the viva, to get him into a good mood. This seemed to have worked, as his first words to Jake were, 'I read your thesis on the train, and I really liked it', so he felt pretty confident from the start. In the event, after three hours of quite detailed discussion of the various experiments it was passed with corrections (such as including a graph, which was repeatedly referred to in the text, but had never got actually included).

After the Christmas vacation Jake decided to discontinue the house-sharing arrangement in Guildford. He would stay at Studio House, and perhaps join Iain, Mike and Christine when necessary. With Josh out of the picture Ma had found new friends, probably more easily than when he was about, with his intimidating, hostile manner. At *The Flask*, a pub up the hill in Hampstead Village, she was to meet John Hurt and other regulars.

She was now acting her age in taking up archaeology, and joining a jewellery class. She went on a number of digs, sometimes joined by her grandson Saul. At the jewellery class she started by polishing stones, then graduated to silver, and finally to gold. She met Laureen Sylvestre and Pat Tormay ('Pat the Hat') and acting her age went out of the window. She had never lost the ability to command attention, and when she arrived in a bar, even in her sixties, the men would sit up a little straighter, hoping to be noticed, so her chronological age has always seemed somewhat academic, to her. She had not lost her sexual presence, by any means.

Pat lived up the hill in a flat near the Hampstead tube station, with her boyfriend Andy Black and a little dog. She had a son, Simon, but he was not around during term times as she'd managed to get him sent to board at St Christophers School, on the NHS. That is, she boasted that she'd persuaded a psychiatrist that she was mad, and might murder him if he stayed at home. Who knows how

275

his school fees came to be paid. (An inoffensive boy, he became in time a successful university professor of political theory.) Pat created complicated erotic silver jewellery, as well as making pieces on commission. Andy had been involved in a very successful publishing venture entitled 'Man, Myth and Magic', rather before his time in capitalising on the occult and the off-the-wall, and they were in the process of spending the proceeds of this, as well as an inheritance. They were excellent company. Jake didn't see much of Laureen, although Ma had was involved with her in a couple of catering projects as well as the jewellery—for instance, selling 'pockets' of pitta bread stuffed with various fillings outside football grounds. During this year Ma seemed happier than she had been for a long time. Without Josh, Ma was also able to develop her relationship with Elizabeth Smart, and visited her at her country retreat, swapping cuttings and drinking whisky. Elizabeth frequently stayed in Studio House when she visited London, sleeping with Ma on the k'ang.

Pa had officially retired in the summer of 1971, leaving Sheffield for good. He did not approve of old buffers who haunted the place, as he put it. He had worked in the British university system for only eighteen years, so his pension was limited. He got a substantial lump sum, reflecting the size of his final salary, but the annual pension was very meagre. For the next few years he was to supplement his income with a series of appointments at American universities, which were not always happy experiences. What he did not know was that the scheme that existed then was a 'tontine'. As the other old boys (and girls) in his cohort died off, the remaining pension pot was divided every year between the rest. His small annual payments were to increase, as time went by, so that after ten years or so he was getting as much as Jake did on his lecturer's salary.

The poet W.H. Auden joined the many well-wishers from Sheffield on his retirement, and wrote this poem:

A Toast

As *quid pro quo* for your enchanting verses,
when approached by Sheffield, at first I wondered
if I could manage *Just a Smack at Empson*,
    but nothing occurred.

All I could fault was your conceit that Milton's
God, obtrusive prolix baroque Olympian,
is our Christian one. Who, though, but you has pondered
    so deeply on *Alice*?

Good voices are rare, still rarer singers with
perfect pitch. If Graves was right, if at Cambridge
the tuning's a wee bit sharp, then at Oxford
    it well may be flat.

Our verbal games are separate, thank heaven,
but Time twins us: both learned to person Life in
an open-hearthed, nannied, un-T-V'd world, where
    cars looked peculiar.

To wish you long long years would be heartless (may you
leave when you want to, no earlier): but I gladly,
dear Bill, dear fellow mandarin, smile to your
    future holidays.

Philip Hobsbaum wrote this poem about his PhD supervisor.

William Empson at Sheffield

The students whisper as he shuffles by,
Point to his Chinese beard, intent wild stare.
The traffic veers to get out of his way.
The drivers curse. He contemplates the air.

At Leavygreave the air is dark with cranes
Wheeling preposterous burdens. Shanks and baulks
Jut skeletally skyward. Georgian homes
Crumble to dust, and through the dust he walks,

Staring ahead. Around him falls the night;
The fuel tech labs, glass skyscrapers, rise up.
He'll joke "A clean sweep, but it's quite all right",
Relieved at stumbling on to a friendly pub.

The air is full of voices. Now and again
He listens to them. Then our talk dies down;
We nudge and wait. He recollects, "But then
I'm rather deaf," he says, ignores the sound.

A sage once spent his life in a deep well
Peopled by ghosts, and worse. He tried to joke,
Talk to his friends, teach sometimes. From the hell
Of gathering night insistent voices spoke.

It was quite out of the blue that they heard of the death of dear old Aunt Molly, who had been such a brick when Ma was off in Hong Kong. Her heart had finally given in, as predicted by the medics fifty years before, who had told her she would not have long to live. So they were right in the end. Her funeral began with a service at Blacktoft church (the parish church for Yokefleet), but the burial was at Pickering, where her coffin was to join her husband's, in a Kitching family vault. Jake was standing with Dick Atcherley, Mog, his parents, Uncle Arthur and Janet around the grave when there was an almighty noise, louder than two express trains, as a couple of RAF fighters swooped down and flew at some dangerously low level over the graveyard. Uncle Dick swore it was nothing to do with him, but it was obviously his final salute to Molly that he had organized—a marvellous gesture from a sincere and grateful admirer.

Jake's one-year appointment at Surrey was coming to an end, and there seemed no prospect of another job, when one day there was a telegram from the University of Hull informing him that the interviews were scheduled for the following Monday. Getting out his suit again, he came across, in a jacket pocket, a letter from the University of Hull inviting him to attend for interview, which he had never answered. The last time he'd worn it was at the funeral, and must have been too distracted to pay attention to it when he'd opened it and just put it away in a pocket.

Arriving in Hull on the appointed day, it was now hard to take it seriously, as it seemed such a casual chance that led him to be there. The interview passed in rather a blur, and, afterwards, Don Kendrick told him that he hadn't answered a single question. Don had been there as the departmental administrative academic. However, Jake was offered a post, along with Dave Bartram and Dave Sewell, and Don took them all on a tour of the area in his car, to show them where they should be thinking of purchasing their houses. While the two Daves had specialisms which were obvious matches for undergraduate courses, Jake, as always, did not. It seemed that there had been two posts advertised, and, rather than appoint a senior lecturer and a junior, the committee had calculated they could afford three junior posts with the same budget. A warm reference from Donald Broadbent, and, perhaps, the glamour of a publication in *Nature*, persuaded the committee to take him on, as well as the two more suitable candidates.

Ma had been banned from driving. She had taken off, with her new boyfriend Lee at her side, to go to Simon in hospital after hearing that he'd crashed on his motorbike, breaking his leg. She had of course been driving for many years when drunk. Every trip to the Creek would be broken by at least one stop at a pub, and coming back from the Butt and Oyster in the evenings she would always have been well over the limit, in modern terms. Always a cautious driver when sober, she tended towards even more caution when drinking, driving ever more deliberately. On this occasion she had been called to the telephone late in the evening, and the news about Sye was not good—he had compound fractures and the initial prognosis was very gloomy. When she took off in the Alvis she was hysterical with anxiety, and drove like fury. Its powerful engine took her to speeds that she would not have dreamed of travelling at, in any other circumstances. For some reason she was heading towards Golders Green when she lost control and hit obstacles on both sides of the road before finally coming to a halt. Lee recalled struggling with her to get control of the steering wheel before being stunned in the impact. She was patently drunk, and resisted attempts to prevent her from getting to Simon's hospital at once. The upshot was that, after a humiliating court appearance and a fine, she gave Jake the car to go with his new job. Simon was to stay in hospital for six months, but he and Janet were to arrive in Hull in some style.

The Alvis was a pleasure to drive, with its 6-cylinder 3-litre engine purring along and giving one a sense of lazy power when proceeding within the speed limit. It was however large, heavy and awkward to manoeuvre at low speed—but other drivers seemed to recognize this, and would regularly give way on roundabouts, as if one were driving an ambulance, or were royalty. The front suspension was in fact quite badly damaged by the accident, which was responsible for the heavy steering. It consumed impressive quantities of 5-star leaded petrol, and was constantly in need of being filled up with water and oil, so one had to have both on hand all the time in the boot. However, these prodigious appetites seemed completely appropriate, given the privilege of being transported on leather seats in Park Ward oak and ash coachwork.

During the summer they went house-hunting, with the inheritance from Aunt Molly giving them a sizeable deposit. They stayed at Yokefleet with Uncle Arthur, who was most welcoming and kind, giving advice of an old-world sort. If they were to live in Beverley, it should be 'without the bar', as that was where all the society was. 'Without the bar' was (and still is) about twice as expensive as 'within the bar'. In his mid 70s, he was still living in an Edwardian time warp with Mrs Sellars the housekeeper. One evening Janet was served a special treat at dinner—a woodcock which Uncle Arthur was very proud to have shot. He explained that they have a way of flying close to the ground and at speed, so that they are as hard as to hit as a cricket ball in flight. 'What's this?' asked Janet, pointing with her fork at a lump in the middle of the blackened carcass on her plate. 'That's its heart, my dear,' said Uncle A, with satisfaction.

Uncle Arthur at Yokefleet Hall

They also stayed with the Clarkes' (Ann and Alan, he being the professor and head of department) in their house in Newland Park, just across the road from the university. Ann was an eminent scholar in her own right, but would play the role of professorial wife on demand, and was a source of practical advice about estate agents in the area, and which day of the week on which to buy the *Hull Daily Mail* for the Property section. She did however have some prejudices of her own. She told Janet on no account to buy a house in 'the Avenues'—an area of Hull with large Victorian terraced houses, popular with academics—as everyone who lived there got divorced.

They became very taken with the charms of Beverley. Every week they would pick up piles of estate agent's brochures to take upstairs in the coffee shop opposite St Mary's church to browse through. They looked at a number of period houses before finally instructing an agent to bid for them at an auction for a house in Highgate, a narrow cobbled street between Beverley Minster and Wednesday Market. 17 Highgate, a double fronted Georgian house built in 1756, became theirs for the princely sum of £8,400.

As for his parents, the new arrangement in Studio House turned out, eventually, to suit them very well. William liked his room at the end of the little corridor, with its own access to the other rooms in the basement, and to the street. To begin with, however, he hedged his bets on his return to London by joining the Savile Club, where he could have lunch with like-minded chaps after a morning's work in the British Museum (where the British Library was still sited) or after a visit to the London Library. At a pinch, and if things were disagreeable at home, he could always get a bed there, although he never did, and in fact he allowed his membership to lapse after a couple of years.

The tenant who had taken over the front basement flat (where Barry Carmen had lived for many years) was called David Jones. An academic chemist who had dropped out of university life to become, at one time, a Buddhist monk, he was an erudite man with a deep interest in literature. He and Pa became good friends. David could call in on Pa in the mornings without going through the rest of the flat, bringing the day's *Times*, with its crossword puzzle, which they would do together. William was working on Marlowe's version of *Faust*, which excited David tremendously, and David was to do his own translation of *Faust* from the German, for which Pa wrote an introduction. David could also share William's mathematical preoccupations. One of these was the calculation of the trajectory which might be taken by an actor, perhaps playing Puck in a *Midsummer's Nights Dream*, in their flight across the stage of the Globe Theatre. He had precise ideas of the height from which the trapeze might be suspended, the height from where the actor took off, from the roof of the gentleman's lavatory on one side of the stage, to their arrival at the other. The requirements of the trapeze would perhaps provide clues as to the minimum dimensions of the building of the Globe Theatre, which De Jongh had neglected to include in his painting of London Bridge, now hanging in Kenwood House.

Puck announces himself as having 'girdled the Earth' in forty minutes, from which Pa deduced that Shakespeare was referring to the Law of Fall, or its concomitant 'escape velocity', which meant that a circumnavigation of the Earth would have to be in 90 minutes (and, stretching a point perhaps, that 'girdling' meant going half way around.) This was a coded message from Shakespeare to the *cognoscenti,* particularly those in audiences at private performances, that we all now knew about these mysteries. (There was a complicated theory about sea-farers' chronometers, metronomes, and experiments perhaps funded by the 9th 'Wizard' earl of Northumberland which supported this particular narrative.) With his scientific training David was able to join in these mathematical speculations, as well as the Faustian world of the supernatural.

With the pathologically jealous Josh out of the way (he had never got the hang of being truly bohemian) Hetta was also able to invite Walter to come and visit the family in London, and also in Yorkshire, where he and she stayed with Jake at his cottage in North Yorkshire.

Among other places, they visited the ruins of Whitby Abbey, with the atmospheric graveyard on the clifftop next to it.

Walter and Hetta in the graveyard at Whitby

Back in Hampstead William enjoyed the company in the Christie room, with its large table and the open plan kitchen, but could escape down the corridor to his room when he wanted. It was in some ways a resumption of the arrangement in 11 Dong Gau Fan, where he had had his own back door from his courtyard. Life had come a full circle.

Hetta would come unsteadily down the steep stairs from the Studio in the mornings carrying the plastic bucket she used as a pisspot, to disappear into the bathroom behind the stairs, before eventually taking her station at the head of the kitchen table, seated on her high-backed Shaker chair. From here she ruled the house. With the telephone close at hand, she smoked her cigarettes rolled in liquorice paper, taking a small Scotch with water to start the day. (She had been sent to a neurologist for a consultation about her shakes, who turned out to be the Olympic runner Roger Bannister. He had been most understanding, and had sanctioned a glass of whisky in the mornings to steady herself.) Or so she said. Their migration, over twenty years, from the first floor through the ground floor to the basement had been slow, but at last they had found their true home in Studio House.

Chapter 10

Postscript

B y the early 1970s, Mog and I had both well left the nest, and our parents were living together in Hampstead in retirement. The new arrangements in Studio House were ideally suited to the semi-detached life which William and Hetta had developed over thirty years or more. However, despite the increased rents from the house, with the 'luxury flat' providing a premium rate, their income was still inadequate, as William's pension from Sheffield University was only about £500 per year. (To put this in perspective, a junior university lecturer's salary in 1972 was not much more than £1000 per year). They were now to spend a whole year, from July 1972 to June 1973, in one another's exclusive company in Canada: York University were paying $30,000 Canadian. Ma was to resume the part of 'faculty wife', living with Pa in their university flat with Simon, who was enjoying the novelty of school in Toronto.

With Sye going to school, and William going off to the campus, Hetta was left to her own devices, and had to invent ways of keeping herself occupied. She made friends with people in the neighbourhood, on her trips to get her lunches of 'lox on a bagel', and took bus trips into town to explore Toronto. She developed enjoyable routines over time, but, unusually for her, she was more than ever reliant on William and his network of academic colleagues for a social life. They were invited to departmental parties, and to dinner parties, at which they distinguished themselves with their bohemian challenge of convention and heavy drinking. Their hosts were counting their blessings in having such an academic heavyweight amongst their midst (York University was very much the newer, junior university to the University of Toronto), but baffled by his and his wife's behaviour. In his graduate seminars William was communicating well with the better students (the ones who were to become professors themselves later in their careers) but there were a number who gave up on trying to understand him, whether it was his delivery or his arcane referencing, and his group dwindled as the year went on.

At dinner parties Hetta would target the more attractive young men for their attention, to their confusion. Sometimes William would even join her in this enterprise, to their increasing confusion. They were having a generally enjoyable time, even if there were boring longeurs in between parties. A high-light of the year was the invitation to dinner by Marshal McLuhan, an academic at the University of Toronto largely forgotten today, who was internationally famous at the time for his slogan 'the medium is the message'. He was the ultimate 'media don' who had recognized the importance of the medium in modulating if not defining what the message was going to say to its audience. Pa wrote to me to report on this event, when the Canadian celebrity asked him whether he had been totally serious in his criticism of Christianity as being a religion celebrating human sacrifice if not cannibalism, and with a wicked God, in his recent book *Milton's God*. Pa reported, 'he asked me whether my book on Milton hadn't been all spoof, assuming that it was; so I thought I had to explain to him that he was worshipping the Devil, being a Roman

Catholic. It was at his own dinner-table, but the ladies had gone for their pee, so it wasn't really rude.'

They had a number of outings in the car, for instance taking Simon to Niagara to see the falls, and also going skiing in the country. Simon was a big 16-year-old, but couldn't keep up with Pa, whose skill on skis had not been forgotten since his own teenage years, when he learned to ski with his mother. He had not had many opportunities to keep it up, except for his trips with Michael Roberts and Janet Adam Smith to the Alps during the mid 1930s.

Ma's first grand-daughter, Rachel, was born in April 1973, which was a big event for her, as she had always wanted a daughter, and her miscarriage in 1955 had been a little girl. There was an excited exchange of letters and photographs.

All in all their year in Canada was a resounding success for them, so when a year later there was an opportunity to repeat the performance at Pennsylvania State University William agreed to it without hesitation. The appointment was for a full year, starting in the summer of 1974, at a salary of US$20,000. This time he went on his own, and was accommodated in a furnished apartment which was a twenty minute walk to the campus.

Things were not good from the start. He found the apartment noisy, and it was difficult to work. The university was located in the middle of the state, which was handy for people with cars, who could get anywhere in the North East of the United States. Of course, William could not drive, so renting a car was out of the question, and he was more or less confined to walking distance of his apartment, except for the few occasions when he was to get a taxi to the airport. He had suffered from problems with his teeth before he set off, and they got worse, with two abscesses developing in his lower jaw, which made it impossible for him to wear his dental plate, or in fact to eat solid food. This prompted him to turn down the invitations from colleagues to dinner which would otherwise have given him the odd break from his solitary routine.

William had been entirely self-sufficient for over forty years, spending many of these years alone, abroad in strange countries, so it did not occur to him or to Hetta that being on his own for a year would be any problem. However, he felt isolated, and became lonely. He drank a great deal, and his classes were not a great success, with the undergraduate students failing to understand what he was saying. (His usual, rather idiosyncratic, delivery was being made even less comprehensible by the problems with his teeth.) While ten years before, in Sheffield, he had been quite sly in avoiding the 'female supervision' which the hospital had advocated, either from Alice or Hetta (or, indeed, Janet's cooking) it now seemed that it was completely necessary. At some point there was a telephone call to Hetta, from the university, to say that William was not well, and was in danger of coming to harm—he was walking into cars. Ma and Mog went together to Pennsylvania to see how he was, and Ma stayed on for the rest of the session to continue to support him, and to drive him about, including a trip to see Walter in Michigan.

Back in London, on one of her expeditions to Camden Town, Hetta met a shopkeeper called John Saxby, with whom she was to form a long-term relationship. John had a leather goods shop, inherited from his father. He sold trunks, suitcases, wallets and bags, and had a little workshop in the back of the shop where he could do stitching on leather, and even work on locks and keys, if necessary. He was fond of saying that he had been born in the shop and would never leave. This was an unlikely liaison, but it worked. John became completely devoted to Hetta, although he never gave up his Tory opinions, or his weekly drinking sessions with two or three

life-long companions, starting on a Thursday afternoon. He tended
to repeat himself, and was the butt of Ma's jeering and barracking
whenever he started talking about his shares, about the gypsies who
were encamped close to his garage, or whatever was the main news
in the *Daily Telegraph.*

John never moved in to Studio House, although he often stayed
the night. He would arrive in the evening, after having closed the
shop, with a bottle of scotch whisky ('honourable' as they had
started to call it, supposedly after the Japanese habit of referring
to it as 'honourable whisky') and a copy of the *Daily Telegraph,*
together with whatever else he had been instructed to shop for. The
scotch ensured a warm welcome, and the *Telegraph* always attracted
a hostile comment. Ma called him her 'trunkologist'. John got on
well with Pa, going to the pub with him on occasion for a game
of shove-ha'penny and a pint. Very different from her previous
boy-friends, John was a perfect gentleman, in the best senses of
that, and was always perfectly well-mannered, even when drunk.
His devotion to her outweighed anything she could punish him
with, in terms of jeering. While she recognized his qualities and
was genuinely fond of him, she found him a bit dull as a permanent
companion. She was likely to ring Lee when John was having one
of his Thursdays with the boys, and summon him to Hampstead for
some more exciting partying.

William continued to take an interest in my research, and wrote
to me in April 1976, after reading about a symposium on 'The
functions of sleep' which I'd organized at the British Psychological
Society's Annual Conference.

My dear Jacob,

The Times report of your conference at York makes clear that all the smart psychologists are teasing animals now. You must not lag behind. You should be giving psychedelic drugs to moles and tortoises, and staying up all night pinching their tails to make them dream. Special equipment will have to be designed, of course.

I think the public would be dubious about snakes, but tortoises are sure-fire. I am glad you have thought of moles; they have great charm too. Probably they will enjoy your attentions, but that must remain one of the secrets of the lab.

> Your affectionate father
> William

He could also make demands for scientific answers to literary questions which were pro-occupying him—for instance,

There were one or two things I thought of asking you, but there never seemed to be an occasion, with family life what it is. Have you a History of Science man in Hull, tolerably willing? I am always wanting one. Ask him whether Carlyle had the use of bicarbonate of soda—when did it come in? And, when the Portuguese sailed round the South of Africa or got near it, did anybody say that the Milky Way goes all the way round? I think nobody did—they had been sure it went all round for thousands of years, so finding they had been right wasn't news at all. But surely it must have been mentioned.

I never did find a tolerably willing History of Science man in Hull.

There was another American sabbatical, in September 1976, at Delaware University. Ma went with Pa this time, to keep him company, and John Saxby took some time off to join them. This trip went without incident, and they all returned together on 29th December 1976.

Pa had started to become the recipient of honorary degrees, from the University of East Anglia, and Bristol University, but most significantly in 1977, from Cambridge University. Janet and I wore our academic robes for the occasion. This was an about-turn of huge proportions, from an institution which had actually attempted to erase all record of his time there, and the abortive award of a 'junior bye-fellowship', back in 1928. His mentor, I.A. Richards, was to be given a doctorate on the same day. The oration in Latin, given by the Professor of Classics, made no mention of his disgrace, although I noticed that when it came to the words describing his departure from Cambridge the professor digressed from the printed version, to say that he had been 'expelled'. Mother Theresa of Calcutta was the third (or, rather, perhaps, the first) person to be honoured. For such a tiny person she had an incredible presence, and when she entered the room there was a clearing of space around her by the graduands and their guests. One felt that one was indeed in the presence of a saint. The Duke of Edinburgh awarded the degrees.

William's achievements were also recognized in the award of a knighthood. He, of course, ascribed this entirely to his early blandishments of flattery, in his masque performed for Her Majesty in Sheffield in 1953. Mog and I joined them in the expedition to Buckingham Palace on a cold day in February 1979, where we spent rather a long time in a large ballroom being serenaded by the band of the Royal Marines playing tunes from popular musicals—'elevator music' as Ma called it. The ceiling was decorated with swastikas, put there no doubt long before the Nazis had made the ancient symbol theirs. He told Christopher Ricks in a letter that the Queen had spoken to him when he was about to rise,

'She touched my shoulder, and then, in a rather strangled voice, as though She were telling me my flies were undone, She said, "I'm so glad". It was the nearest She came to pretending we were old friends.'

At Buckingham Palace for the investiture

Pa wearing his Knight Bachelor medal
back home after the investiture

At the time I was oblivious of his attachment to his sovereign, and would not have been surprised if he had turned down a knighthood. In fact nothing could have been further from the truth—his attitude to the Establishment was, in the context of his bohemianism, quite contrary. It was at about this time that he confided in me on one our trips to the pub to play shove ha'penny.

'Dear boy, I've been asked to join in a round-robin letter protesting at the treatment of Anthony Blunt, and I've agreed. I've also been asked to join in a mass resignation from the Society of Literature, by some of the other fellows, as Blunt is going to be expelled'.

Anthony Blunt was an eminent art historian, and the Keeper of the Queen's collection of artworks among other duties. He had been a communist sympathiser in his youth, and, employed in Military Intelligence during the war, had passed on some information about the conclusions that had been reached on likely German offensives to the Russians (who were of course our allies at the time). Exposed in 1964, Blunt had confessed, and implicated some co-conspirators. He was given full immunity from prosecution, and a promise of non-disclosure of his part in these activities for at least fifteen years. Now this time was up, and Margaret Thatcher was betraying the spirit of the deal that had been reached, by baying for his blood in the House of Commons—establishing her credentials as a Commie-basher. His knighthood was withdrawn, and now he was also to be expelled as a Fellow of the Royal Society of Literature.

'Of course he's being treated dreadfully, but, the question is, should I join in this resignation?'

"I really don't know. What have you decided to do?" I said—it was obviously something that had been on his mind for a while, and he must have already decided.

'Resigning from things is bound to be self-defeating. What can one do if one doesn't stay a member? I'm not going to join the resignation—although it would be a fine gesture.'

William was of course a victim of institutional bullying from the beginning of his career, with his expulsion from Cambridge, so he naturally had every sympathy with Blunt. He had though evidently decided a long time ago that he would bear no grudges, and carry on as best he could—which of course was extremely well—working within the system.

William had always had some idiosyncratic if not wacky ideas, and he was, in his retirement, able to indulge them to the full. He had a theory that Andrew Marvell had married his landlady: he had come across some letters suggesting that Marvell had a neice in Hull, called Alice, recently born. The landlady came from Hull, and his acknowledging her neice would suggest more than a landlady/ lodger relationship. Pa had written to the clerics at Hull's Holy Trinity Church to ask permission to inspect the register of births. This was a good excuse for coming to Hull, and staying with me and Janet in Beverley.

I went with him to the church, where three black-cloaked individuals were waiting for him. They had obviously decided that he was up to no good, and wouldn't allow us to see the register: instead we had to supply a name, surname and date, whose presence on the register they were prepared to confirm or deny. This was quite impossible, and we retreated to the university, where we found that there were facsimile copies of all the relevant registers in the Brynmor Jones Library. We were taken to a private room with a large table, and the ledgers were brought out. It was surprisingly easy to flick through searching for an Alice, with a surname of either Popple or Blayde (names still existing in the Hull telephone directory), although the project was not a success. While we were doing this Philip Larkin entered the room on some pretext, and he and William slowly circled the table, each on his own mission, but without speaking to the other.

Another longstanding bee in his bonnet was to do with Puck's flight in *A Midsummer Night's Dream*, when Puck announces that he had 'girdled the earth in forty minutes'. For Pa, this was a clear reference to orbital escape velocity, and a wonderful opportunity to combine his interests in science and mathematics with literature. Now that he had plenty of time on his hands, he felt that some practical experimentation was in order. He wrote to me in November, 1981,

> My dear Jacob,
>
> I hope all is well. Your mother is in the Sahara and Mog has gone to Taiwan again, so I can get on with my typing. I want to ask you a technical question which is up your street.
>
> It seems absurd that no sixteenth-century scientist found the law of fall, though they knew they ought to, and that even when Galileo got round to it in the seventeenth he was counting his pulses for lack of a clock. *Ephemera* were printed every year for seamen, timing the prominent approaches of a planet to a fixed star, so that a ship with a decent clock could tell its longitude. I think Hariot had done the work about 1590 in England, but was muzzled by the censor; that is why Puck claims to go at the actual speed of Major Gagarin, but less by the right amount, as they made the radius of the earth too small by about a seventh. Hariot had been accepted on a voyage to Virginia, with a "spring clock", because he knew how

to use *Ephemera*. On return he was accepted into the household of the Wizard Earl of Northumberland, who would readily let him use the Long Gallery and ten skilled carpenters to make a runway for a small car or frog. The reason why nobody had done it before is merely that it is more expensive and time-consuming and demanding of skilled labour than one easily realises; the momentum of the wheels takes part of the energy of fall, so must be allowed for by running the car empty and then with varying weights of lead, also it must be run with varying sails to allow for air resistance.

Well then, granting that young Hariot, finding himself in clover, would want to do a thing widely recognised to be important, what are the limitations in the reaction times of his artisans? A slope of one in five seems the most convenient, and the new expensive clock must be made to tick every second (apparently they did not tick till Galileo's pendulum came in.) Men holding chalks stand beside the runway, ready to mark the wood just where the back of the frog is, at the tick; better say the back, as there is an inherent delay. The law of acceleration is readily shown by the marks at the first four ticks, but what accuracy can one get for "g"? At the fifth tick the distance is about 40 feet, and the velocity (of the frog) about 16 feet a second, a bit over 10 miles an hour.

The first thing Hariot needs to be sure of is whether he can say "32", meaning nearer that than 31 or 33. If it is 32.5 the frog will have gone 7.5 inches further, which seems easily detectable; but it does that in only 1/25 of a second. Considering the feats that are similar, catching cricket balls and so on, that must be possible, but could he get the next decimal place, which is (in our latitude; it gets bigger towards the pole) 32.2? The skilled men would be acting in 1/125 of a second. I wouldn't be surprised, but I hope you say they couldn't, because there are signs that he resisted the absurd accuracy of the figure for the radius of the earth, regularly copied out to the nearest mile.

Love,

William

I don't know that he had any use for an accurate measurement. But after doing it in such a full-dress way he would to expect to get closer than 32.

The clocks were likely to be 1/4hr hour out in 24 hours, I read somewhere, and this should be good enough to get 32, but also he could correct the clock by the stars—given two clear nights running. But one might easily be 3 mins out in timing on conjunction.

My assistance with this venture involved me in writing to the then Duke of Northumberland—enquiring of colleagues and graduate students in the psychology common room about how one should address a duke, I was told by a research assistant, Pauline Smith, that the correct form was, 'May it please your Grace', which is how I duly began my letter. This was to ask whether the ninth ('Wizard') earl had been involved as a patron. The duke replied in a most friendly manner saying that his forbear had spent most of his adult life in the Tower of London, so it was most unlikely that he would have been helping young Hariot with his experiments.

All the same, we went to Kew to visit Syon House, to measure the height of the ceiling in the long gallery. This was a likely site for the experiments to have been performed, as it was being rented by the ninth earl of Northumberland at the time (and Hariot had in fact been staying there). As Pa said in his letter to me, a substantial ramp would have been required, down which one would slide the 'frogs', while timing their descent. The ceiling height at Syon House was quite inadequate, but we did have an afternoon at Kew Gardens, with the opportunity to seek out the sensitive plant yet again.

Following Pa's suggestion, I re-created the experiments that Hariot may have conducted, using students in the Psychology Department. We found that it was indeed feasible, using only a metronome as timer, to achieve reasonably accurate results. Interestingly, it was when the ball bearing (which is what we used, lacking suitable polished 'frogs') was at its slowest, at the beginning of the descent, when observation was most difficult. The task was to mark with chalk where on the ramp the frog had been when the metronome had ticked. When the ball was moving slowly the observer's eyes followed it, making the judgement of where it had been when the tick came rather a retrospective one—the eye had moved on by the time the hand was to make the mark. When it was moving fast, towards the bottom of the ramp, the eye did not follow the ball as it flew past, and it was much easier to judge where the ball was when the tick came, giving the most accurate results towards the end its fall. We did not attempt the variations, with different weights attached to the frogs, or indeed with frogs with sails. William was unimpressed by our efforts, and wrote from Miami, Florida,

> Very glad to hear that you are getting psychological results from rolling balls, and that the dogsbodies are

enthusiastic. But you seem to be making an elementary mistake; you need to contact some unassuming member of the Physics department. Part of the energy of the fall goes into making the ball spin, and a small one has to spin faster. I forget the "moment of momentum" for a sphere, maybe a third, but with ball-bearings it would be quite enough to reduce your value of g from 32 to 20. I should think larger balls would be steadier anyway.

William's last foreign tour of duty was in 1982, for one semester at the University of Miami, who paid him $19,500. This was hardly necessary in terms of the salary, as his pension had been steadily increasing over the years as the other pensioners in his cohort had started to die off. By now he was receiving more than I did as a lecturer at the University of Hull, rather than only half as much, as he had when he first retired. However, he had been invited to Florida by his old student, O.R. Dathorne, now a senior professor, who had studied for his PhD in Sheffield, and the visit promised to be a congenial one. In the event Pa got on well with his colleagues and the students, teaching a course on modern poetry. He was working hard on his Faust book, wanting to have it ready at the same time as David Jones' translation from the German. However this involved a good deal of drinking, which made him ill, giving him a severe backache. He spent the final weeks of the stay drinking diet Coke, and no vodka. Ma rented a large car, and they made trips to the Everglades, and down to the Keys. John Saxby joined them for some of the time, bringing Laureen Sylvestre from her jewellery class, and Walter came down from Michigan for a week or two, joining them on one of their trips.

That year we had a Christmas get-together at my country cottage in North Yorkshire, with Simon and his girl-friend, Ma, Pa, John, and my cousin Ronelle (Ma's brother Kootie's daughter) and her husband Bryan Smith. What with the children, there were eleven of us crammed into the house, with the children sleeping in a row on the floor downstairs. Mog was spending that Christmas with his Swedish family.

During 1983 Pa's health declined, and he was admitted to hospital in February 1984—the Royal Free, just around the corner from Hampstead Hill Gardens. They diagnosed his problem as being a liver disorder. He was sent home after a week or so, but was never to get completely back on his feet. Mog was closely involved in helping look after him until his departure for China in March, where he was to visit Yunnan, the province where Pa had spent his time with the 'Temporary University' in 1937-1939. Pa insisted that he should go, and was delighted to be able to talk to him about his trip on his return a couple of weeks later. All this time I was unaware of the severity of Pa's condition, which had been getting worse so gradually. He was re-admitted to the Royal Free on 12th April, and encouraged Mog to take Ma off to the Creek, to give her a break—'She will just have to tough it out', he said.

I was summoned from Hull to keep an eye on things, and to visit the patient in hospital. I arrived late morning, and was blithely enjoying my break in London, and didn't get to the hospital until early afternoon. I was shocked to find Pa looking dreadful and in considerable pain, with a urinary catheter. It took some time to get anybody's attention to get him a pain-killer. Later, I went back to find him in a different ward, and more composed, even pretending to take an interest in a *New Scientist* that I had brought with me. Later again, Pa was barely conscious, and I was becoming alarmed.

I found the young doctor in charge of him, and asked him straight out whether I should tell my mother to come back from Suffolk. He started on a 'giving bad news' routine, not answering my question but saying that 'people don't live forever', and so on, and I had to interrupt him and ask him again. He finally said that my mother should come immediately if she wanted to see him before he died.

By the time that Mog and Ma got to the hospital Pa was no longer speaking, and was breathing noisily—he had pneumonia. He was not to recover, and died in the small hours that night without saying any 'final words'. David Jones was to recall in an article he wrote about their relationship, entitled 'Empson soup', 'There had been no famous last words in that day-long fight for breath, but I have little doubt what they might have been, for he had said them on a previous occasion when he thought he was going to die. I was visiting him on the eve of his last operation, which he fancied he would not survive; and maybe he thought he would not see her again. After a brief pause in our conversation, without any display of emotion but with deeply moving sincerity he said: "If I die, tell Hetta I love her very much." Then he squeezed my hand briefly and we parted.'

The Wife is Praised was William's longest poem, which was not published in his lifetime. It is a sort of explanation of, and celebration of, his ideal for sexual relations, and expresses his love for, and gratitude to Hetta. It is completely unlike any of his other verse (except, perhaps the doggerel composed for the Queen's *Masque*). It has a jolly, rollicking rhythm, and, while explicit in what he is talking about, is also self-mocking, with a feeling that the whole subject perhaps ought not to be taken so seriously.

He and Hetta were both concerned about how it might be received if it were published, first of all by Mog and myself, and then the world outside, and any consequences for William's reputation. Once, when I was staying in the middle room on one of my trips from Sheffield to Guildford, I found it on the bedside table. I had no idea of its existence, and was completely puzzled the appearance of this long piece of verse, which had its title but no clue to authorship (although that was obvious enough). I guessed that it must have been mis-placed, and didn't comment on it to Pa (or anyone else). The next time I was in the room it had disappeared. The ideal that he is describing in the poem was hardly ever achieved in his life. However, despite all the trials, no marriage could have been so well founded, by its end, on loyalty and love. What was discovered during its course William took with him to the grave, but its process could perhaps be summarised by Stephen Dedalus, when, in the novel *Ulysses*, he says, 'A man of genius makes no mistakes. His errors are volitional and are the portals of discovery.'

The Wife is Praised

Much astonished to find you were handy
    I proposed when we first go to bed;
This was viewed as too pushing or randy
    And not what was usually said;
I urged you have lovers beside me
    O lots, and I'd just as soon know.
It took time and an angel to guide me
    To make the thing go.

Did I love you as mine for possessing?
    Absurd as it seems, I forget;
For the vision of love that was pressing
    And time has not falsified yet
Was always a love with three corners
    I loved you in bed with young men,
Your arousers and foils and adorners
    Who would yield to me then.

It was true and is why one should be male
    That this makes a viable plan;
Taking turns at a generous female
    Is the best act of love with a man.
But I may not have thought to begin with
    That this would make you such a power;
That so nameless a sin is akin with
    The heart of the flower.

It is chiefly to know you are willing
    And not what I get on the side
That I find at once quieting and thrilling,
    A peace, an insurance, a pride.
And indeed when they care for you only
    And think me a price they must pay
That is proof I should really be lonely
    With Hetta away.

But one likes to have something to offer
    And how vain to assume it is charm;
It is low to fling open the coffer;
    To give wisdom—the thought is a qualm.
There is really no other proposal
    One can make to the ones that will do
But "a stunner, and at my disposal,
    And be nice to me too".

And besides, it is that situation
    Two thirds of the men would prefer;
I make a reclassification
    By which few are left buggers that were.
And the third are the men who see double
    For whom *two* girls in bed would be It;
So the Lesbians are out of their trouble
    And the numbers fit.

Indeed I propose a policemen
    Ought nightly to raid the retired
And demand why a Moral Release man

Is not in this bed as required.
"The State will not stand for a couple;
    It makes all its beds to hold three;
And you are not permitted to tup all
    Alone like I see".

The practice of marriage however
    Outlasts this great change in the law;
There are two whom no time will dissever
    And a third who is quick on the draw.
He comes as a learner or teacher
    Or he comes as a breath of the air;
And O may we happen to reach a
    Ground yet more fair.

And how nice when the man brings the tea-things
    And knows that three cups are required,
And my children so eager to see things
    See nothing that need be admired.
They may all patter in in the morning
    And the bed is no cause for surprise;
And if that isn't heaven—the warning
    Is not to fear eyes.

There is need for a quantum of terror
    In handling this secular theme;
It is hubris and brash and an error
    To present it as strawberries and cream.
The queen of the gods and of mortals
    Insatiate and searching and rich

Who must open for all men her portals—
    They call her a bitch.

She is death and the craving for torture;
    She alone is the Muse, but the price
They all paid—they report her a scorcher;
    They are glad to agree she is Vice.
And for thousands of years on her altar
    Her man was castrated and flayed
Ere he died lest fertility falter
    O mother and maid.

We must all take advice and our bearings
    But what are these tortures to me?
I deduce that the practice of sharing's
    A lust on which all men agree.
An unnameable horror, a monster,
    No torture can blast it enough,
But while it is being well sconced, a
    Thought "That's the stuff".

I shall not assume then there follow
    Desertion, castration, and death
From retracing the source of Apollo
    Resaying the older Thus Saith.
But I dare not be sure it's not tragic
    When all the first sources agree
And (God knows) it is patently magic;
    We must see what we see.

I am rather too readily injured
    And you have no lust to endure;
If I feel the match powerfully cinctured
    It is where one might think it needs cure.
Oh the kindness of each loving two ways
    And one man not tied up at all.
A neurosis? Angelica Lues
    That holds love thrall.

[One might claim this ideal is mere fancy
    Since no man can lust after both,
This presumes a man's either a nancy
    Or not, and thus totally loath.
He is not to reject my affection,
    But how little I have to require;
The mechanics are under direction
    And the central fire.]

The Triangle called the Eternal
    Here asks for a passing surprise;
For the history of love is a journal
    Of fashions in whom to excise.
They would cut out the first or the second
    Or revolt and then cut out the third,
Proving only that Nature had beckoned
    Absurdly unheard.

For the wife was locked up in the kitchen
    When Greeks got ideas in the gym;
And the troubadour's lady was rich in

309

A husband both powerful and dim.
The Reformers then claimed a fantastic
    Reversal of all men adored
And screwed up love parts for domestic
    Bed and board.

And then for three centuries of printing
    We get a great gush every year
About what may the husband be hinting
    And is the young woman sincere;
And there must be one loser however
    They shuffle their sins and their suits.
They could jump into bed all together
    The silly coots.

Not by me are reformers resented;
    I too offer practical norms.
For the marvellous thing was invented
    In two over-specialised forms.
Love is sodomy, love is adultery,
    Say the sources; in pain you must roam.
Nearly true, but I give to each cult a re-
    Vision at home.

It is fair to recall contraception
    (Perhaps about seventy years old)
Was required for the easy reception
    Of truths men went mad to behold.
Granting this, I am surely belated;
    It is time the machine was employed

If three generations have grated
　　Desire on a void.

And the great homosexual story
　　(Well I know) was the message half read;
I have always felt men were the glory
　　And found them quite pointless in bed.
Not that love did not make it a splendour
　　But how acid the things one must do,
And what milk when permitted to send you
　　Own cocks to you.

I revere the Swinburnian Dolores
　　With 28 rhymes upon Pain,
But the lust to spread hurt through this whore is
　　A puritan taint in the grain;
He had got in his bones, before Fraser,
　　The White Goddess of Graves and her power,
And made that great marvel to praise her
　　Both true and too sour.

I want it more homely and jolly—
　　This is coarse and like Leopold Bloom—
But he craves to bed Stephen with Molly
　　On more grounds than the critics assume.
With this Son in his bed he could sire one;
　　Ten years (since the death) he's felt barred;
The theme is a bold and entire one;
　　Joyce hiding it hard.

And the answer comes after the story:
    Jeering Stephen became Mr Joyce
Knowing all of both Blooms to his glory,
    And how he got healed is your choice.
But I would not agree it's refining
    Not to care whether Bloom had a son.
Perhaps Joyce was ashamed he kept whining;
    The book's name says they won.

What I want to say, dragging reviews in,
    Is these things have happened before.
What a bore to be smart with a new sin;
    I trace out a natural law.
But it's true that few women can handle
    What so many men want to do,
Or (the phrase is) can "hold up a candle"
    To rival you.

[The stanza in brackets was omitted on William's typescript].

Endnotes

i   *William Empson, Vols 1 and 2.* John Haffenden, Oxford University Press, 2005, 2008.

ii   William Empson 'Orwell at the BBC' The Listener, 4th Feb., 1971, p 498

iii   J. Haffenden, *William Empson, Volume 2: Against the Christians*, p 37.

iv   Paddy Fraser 'G.S. Fraser: a Memoir', 4: http://jacketmagazine.com/20/fraser.html

v   Victor Purcell *China Evergreen*. London: Michael Joseph, 1938, p 76

vi   Purcell, op cit, p 77

vii   C.P. Fitzgerald, *Revolution in China*. London: The Cresset Press, 1952, page 85.

viii   Chassin, Lionel Max *The Communist Conquest of China*. Translated from the French by Timothy Osato and Louis Gelas. London: Weidenfeld and Nicolson, 1966, page 134.

ix   www.davidcrook.net

x   J. Haffenden, *William Empson, Volume 2: Against the Christians*, p. 104

xi   C.P. Fitzgerald, *The Birth of Communist China*, 113-114.

xii   Correspondence and other papers of Sir Pa Empson and Ma, Lady Empson. DEN 5/46. Sheffield University Library, Hull Archive (photocopies)

xiii   C.P. Fitzgerald, *Revolution In China*. London: The Cresset Press, 1952, page 113.

xiv Milton's God p. 263

xv Personal conversation with John Savile, the eminent social historian at Hull University, who was a junior lecturer at the time, and elected by the other junior lecturers at Hull to sit in on this appointments committee. They had heard that Empson had applied, but found that he was not short-listed - at the specific request of the external assessor.

xvi Robert Lowell, letter to Elizabeth Bishop, 12th August, 1963 (from John Haffenden, *William Empson: Against the Christians.*)

xvii John Betjeman, Extract from: Telegraph and Morning Post, July 3 1961

xviii John Haffenden, *William Empson: Volume 2, Against the Christians*, OUP, 2006, p. 539.

xix John Haffenden, *William Empson: Volume 2, Against the Christians*, OUP, 2006, p. 528.